DON JUAN
and Regency England

DON JUAN
and
Regency England

PETER W. GRAHAM

University Press of Virginia
Charlottesville and London

THE UNIVERSITY PRESS OF VIRGINIA
Copyright © 1990 by the Rector and Visitors
of the University of Virginia

First published 1990

Library of Congress Cataloging-in-Publication Data

Graham, Peter W., 1951–
    Don Juan and Regency England / Peter W. Graham.
      p.   cm.
    Includes bibliographical references (p.   ).
    ISBN 0-8139-1254-7
    1. Byron, George Gordon Byron, Baron, 1788–1824. Don Juan.
2. Byron, George Gordon Byron, Baron, 1788–1824—Contemporary
England. 3. England—Social life and customs—19th century. 4. Don
Juan (Legendary character) 5. England in literature. 6. Regency—
England. I. Title.
PR4359.G7   1990
821'.7—dc20   89-48259
                                                               CIP

Printed in the United States of America

For my sons
Austin and James

Contents

Acknowledgments

It would be impossible for me to acknowledge individually, and equally impossible not to appreciate, all the insights and kindnesses that have made the past months of reading, writing, and revising a better time. Let me mention only a few of many such debts. No one can write on Byron in general and *Don Juan* in particular without being continually obliged to Leslie A. Marchand and Jerome J. McGann for the foundation on which any such case must build. The following essays are sounder than they might otherwise be thanks to that foundation—and to the advice graciously offered by John Clubbe, Malcolm Kelsall, Fritz Oehlschlaeger, and David Radcliffe. I have been fortunate in having the chance to read Byron with fine graduate students whose questions and ideas, in class and out, have been most helpful. Among these former students, special thanks are due to my research assistants, Leigh Campbell Garrison and Susan Gibson Mayhew. It was a pleasure and a privilege to discuss *Don Juan* and other matters with the colleagues who comprised Lilian Furst's 1987 "Reading Ironies" summer seminar at Stanford. I am grateful to my fellow ironists, and to both the National Endowment for the Humanities and the Stanford Humanities Center for making possible that agreeable and inspiring experience. I must also thank Virginia Polytechnic Institute and State University for generous support of my research, particularly for granting a semester's leave, during which time this manuscript was completed. For editorial help of various kinds at Charlottesville, I am in the debt of John McGuigan and Cynthia H. Foote. My deepest debt is to Kathryn Videon Graham.

DON JUAN
and Regency England

Introduction

*How deeply rooted in man lies the desire to generalize
about individual or national characteristics!*

Friedrich Schlegel, *Critical Fragments*

Byron's *Don Juan* is a work between times, places, and cultures. It is
a poem facing backward and ahead. Our present tendency is to
recognize (because we value) the latter orientation—the vision
expressed in the poem's self-consciously reflexive, relativistic, revolutionary, iconoclastic, prophetically modern or postmodern
moments—at the expense of the former. Because *Don Juan* so eloquently addresses our own time, we tend to forget that it spoke
first, and perhaps most richly, to an immediate audience of readers
very different from us.

My first goal in setting out to write the following series of essays
was to move toward a more balanced appreciation of the poem's
dialogues of time, place, and culture by exploring some of its
localities in the manner Marilyn Butler has in mind when she
suggests that "The writings of the past ask for an educated reading,
as far as possible from within their own discourse or code or
cultural system."[1] Such exploration of *Don Juan* showed that this
work, begun in and inspired by the cosmopolitan environment of
Venice in 1818 and ranging widely through the world and its history, is grounded elsewhere—in Regency England. The Serenis-
sima, as seen through Byron's eyes, is but one muse of *Don Juan*—
the other is the Great World of fashionable London, intrigued by
him and intriguing him in turn, cutting him dead and provoking a
response in kind: the ultimate cut, a Continental exile ended only
by death.

Though grounded, *Don Juan* hovers. It is, to borrow one of Byron's own metaphors for his composition, a "paper kite,"[2] connected with but not confined by particular literary and social mi-

lieux. Accordingly, the attempt to replace Don Juan in its Regency context soon became a less straightforward matter than it initially had seemed. One quickly notices that the poem is itself concerned with placing things in contexts, but its characteristic gesture is one of displacement by means of contratexts. The fertility of Byron's poetic imagination in Don Juan results from this displacement, which reveals itself in perpetual tensions between topicality and transcendence—between the sense of a highly specified immediate audience and the eclectic contrast or condensation of times and cultures—between Englishness and cosmopolitanism.

That last tension is uniquely characteristic of the England of Byron's day and after. As the Oxford English Dictionary explains, the word cosmopolite, having become common in English during the seventeenth century, was revived early in the 1800s, to which period such derivatives as cosmopolitan and cosmopolitanism belong. The nineteenth-century usages characteristically contrast cosmopolite with patriot. Thus, ideological endorsement of one term makes the other a reproach—and as the following examples drawn from among those cited in the Oxford English Dictionary suggest, cosmopolite was likelier to be the pejorative during the era when Napoleon held the Continent and throughout its aftermath, the age when Britannia ruled the waves and Victoria held dominion over palm and pine. Consider:

> The false philosophy . . . which would persuade him
> that cosmopolitism is nobler than nationality.
>
> —Samuel Taylor Coleridge, The Friend (1809–10)

> Some had passed a great part of their lives abroad,
> and . . . were mere cosmopolites.
>
> —Thomas Babington Macaulay, History of England (1849)

> A certain attenuated cosmopolitanism had taken
> place of the old home feeling.
>
> —Thomas Carlyle, Miscellanies (1857)

> And he was no cosmopolitan. He was an Englishman
> of the English.
>
> —Edward Edwards, Life of Sir Walter Raleigh (1868)

*That man's the best cosmopolite, / Who loves his na-
tive country best.*

          —Alfred Tennyson, "Hands All Round!" (1852)

You . . . have merged the patriot in the cosmopolite.

          —Thomas Medwin, *The Angler in Wales* (1834)

The antithesis established in most of these quotations clearly
indicates a belief that allegiances to one's homeland and to a larger
cultural entity are mutually exclusive. Divided—or, more precisely,
double—loyalties are no more possible than is living in two places
at once. *Cosmopolitan* and *expatriate* are essentially synonymous. Isolated from their context, the Tennyson verses seem to grant that
cherishing one's homeland can enable wider sympathies; but in
fact "Hands All Round!" is a stout endorsement of British insularity
in the face of Napoleon III. Only the passage written by Thomas
Medwin truly acknowledges that patriotism and cosmopolitanism
can coexist (as they did in Byron), though the very act of recording
the merger of these two loyalties implies that such a union is rare
enough to warrant comment.

None of these quotations entertains the possibility that cosmopolitan breadth might actually strengthen patriotic attachment, a
truth Byron understood as early as his *Childe Harold* days. The first
two cantos backhandedly demonstrate this principle in action
as the purposeless pilgrim Harold, disillusioned with prevailing
conditions in "Albion's isle," finds things no better on his travels through Spain, Portugal, Epirus, Acarnania, and Greece. The
poem's epigraph points out the subconscious or unacknowledged
purpose behind Childe Harold's, or Byron's, steadfast pursuit of
multicultural disappointments—and the consolation prize unwit-
tingly gained from them. Interestingly and appropriately, the work
quoted is *Le* (not *The*) *Cosmopolite* and the words are French, not
English: "L'univers est une espèce de livre, dont on n'a lu que la
première page quand on n'a vu que son pays. J'en ai feuilleté un
assez grand nombre, que j'ai trouvé également mauvaises. Cet
examen ne m'a point été infructueux. Je haïssais ma patrie. Toutes
les impertinences des peuples divers, parmi lesquels j'ai vécu,
m'ont réconcilié avec elle. Quand je n'aurais tiré d'autre bénéfice
de mes voyages que celui-là, je n'en regretterais ni les frais, ni les
fatigues."[3]

The result of worldly experience need not be mere tolerance of home gained through heightened awareness of the deficiencies to be found abroad. It is also possible to understand or love one's native land the better for having seen the workings of other societies. Cosmopolitan experience makes possible an enlightened commitment—selective, perhaps, but nevertheless real—to the cultural values that are one's birthright. Such a possibility is suggested in H.M.S. *Pinafore*, where Gilbert and Sullivan offer the following tunefully patriotic, cheerfully parochial, yet undeniably satiric, tribute to a well-known and enduring trait of the English national character:

> For he might have been a Roosian,
> A French, or Turk, or Proosian,
> Or perhaps Itali-an!
> But in spite of all temptations
> To belong to other nations,
> He remains an Englishman![4]

In spite of all these words, remaining an Englishman is in fact a simple function of instinct with Gilbert and Sullivan's "tar," whose steadfastness of nationality springs from unimaginative John Bull-headedness, and who could not be French or Turk or Prussian even if his inclinations ran that way. The tenacity of Englishness is more complex, a partially acknowledged mixture of feeling, taste, and reasoned commitment, in the aristocratic poet of *Don Juan*, a laughing philosopher whose actual and intellectual pilgrimages have taken him far from where he started.

From this point it is not much of a journey to the central premise to be expanded and developed in the following essays. *Don Juan*, in spite and because of its wide exploration of Europe, its extensive and diverse cast of Europeans, its vast range of European attitudes, artifacts, institutions, and events, is always about England—and never more so than when at its most exotic. The poem never ceases to be concerned with the sort of provinciality commemorated in the Gilbert lyric—that assertively self-contained, sometimes smug and sometimes splendid, island spirit and the need to transcend it. The composing poet, at once an English aristocrat and a man of the world, maintains a keen sense of his immediate audience even as he looks ahead, to that dim "posterity" whose good opinion matters more than he cares to admit—and back, to better times in the history of his class and party (the 1780s and 1790s)—and beyond, to the wider world that makes the Great World and even Great Britain seem very small indeed. Faithfully presenting yet ultimately displacing Don Juan's localities calls for sharp awareness of historical and cultural contrast, one of the rewards of cosmopolitanism. That need for cosmopolitanism is itself a distinctively English quality, and one that persisted in the Byron family, manifesting itself in our century in the gifted writer Robert Byron and the world traveler Richard Byron, who died in West Africa in 1985.

Cosmopolitanism by its very nature involves mixture, which can be seen as a good or a bad thing—the incorporation of that which spoils (an "impurity") or that which improves (an "alloy"). For example, the shifting value of cosmopolitanism is evident in two antithetical and persistent English stereotypes of Venice, a city seen both as the site of exquisite civilization and incomparable beauty and as the corrupt backdrop for events too depraved to transpire elsewhere. Don Juan's portrait of Regency England is similarly ambivalent, or mobile, in the positive and negative values it attaches to a culture whose essence is diversity but whose surface is the uniformity of ice or varnish. Whether for good or for ill or for both, mixture in its various guises—impurity, inconsistency, pragmatism, cosmopolitanism—is the distinguishing characteristic of English culture at all levels explored by the poem. To begin in the beginning with the word. English is a diverse, unregulated, organically evolving language. Rooted in and coalescing other tongues, "pillaging" them to "enrich" itself, English is the language of a seafaring commercial culture, one prone to import things—but also an island culture, one that transforms and domesticates them. This process "corrupts" both the exotic import and the native speech. Strategic mispronunciation and multilingual wordplay, matters to which I shall often return in the ensuing pages, intermittently present this kind of mixture, sometimes indicating a genuine cosmopolitanism and sometimes revealing a spurious or superficial sort, throughout Don Juan.

Of course, the intellectual cargo imported into England consists of ideas as well as mere words. Intertwined with Byron's reflections on English and its corruption of foreign words is his presentation of the legendary figure of Don Juan as modified for British purposes, among those purposes his own. Traditionally a corrupter, Don Juan in Byron's hands is corrupted (and made cosmopolitan), both tarnished and taught by experience as he travels across Europe. Byron distorts the Spanish legend for a number of reasons, one of which is a matter crucial to the essay titled "All Things—But a Show?": the contemporary English culture reflected in Byron's poem had rediscovered the Continental seducer and retailored him for the London stage.

The "corruptions" of language, character, and legend in Don Juan are partly Byron's brilliantly playful yet serious innovations, partly his accurate transcription of changes carried out by the eclectic yet insular English culture in which he had lived and with which, to some extent, he had kept up at long range. Moving to a more conceptual level, we find Byron's corruption of the genre through which the tale is presented characterized by the same blend of precedented debasement and personal improvisation. Don Juan has always been difficult to fit into existing generic categories. Is it an epic whose conventional attributes are sometimes but not always neglected, defied, inverted?—a romance with a difference?—a novel in verse?—a story where the nonnarrative elements are really the most important ones? The surest thing to say is that most boundaries are transgressed in the poem's cosmopolitan ramble through time, cultures, and literary styles. What results is a "satire" in the etymological sense—a generic stew or hotch-potch combining and assimilating diverse elements.

Most broadly, there is the matter of cultural corruption and its philosophical implications. Here, as at many other points, the reader of Don Juan confronts a paradox. In one sense the poem is a denunciation of a morally degenerate nation. Regency England's corruption, however, is presented as rising out of what is, in fact, purity, a by-no-means commendable quality variously embodied in the poetical inbreeding of Southey and the Lakers; the self-serving politics of the Prince Regent; the narrowly ruling-class interests that spur Wellington, having struck Napoleon's new chains from Europe, to reforge the old broken ones. In contrast, Byron "corrupts" his fictive world (and announces that he does so) by his cosmopolitan breadth of vision. Introduction of alien elements may reduce purity, but it can serve to strengthen, as lesser metals do when alloyed with gold, and to beautify, as is exemplified in the poem by Julia and Haidée, each of them tainted and graced by an ancestral infusion of Moorish blood.

In asserting the importance of cosmopolitanism in Don Juan I am following a blazed path. What is new in the following study lies in its contexts. On the one hand, I have chosen to go back to some basic yet easily overlooked matters (such as the comically mispronounced title, which is but the first of many phonetic mutilations of foreign languages in the poem) and read them for thematic and stylistic significance. Besides looking at Don Juan in and of itself, I am examining it as part of a literary discourse and as a picture of the culture that frames it, a consequence of Byron's reading his English world, being read by it, responding with a rereading that provokes its own response. It need not be said that all writings, even the cryptic utterances of reclusive schizophrenics, have some relation to the world beyond the page—but given Byron's complex cosmopolitanism, Don Juan's relations to that world are so rich and multiple that we are in little danger of fully accounting for them all. New readers have hope of seeing and saying new things: as Peter Manning has observed, "the text enfranchises all that infinite series of readings, neither idiosyncratic nor stock, which the common cultural context of author and reader empowers."[5] I have tried to avoid the idiosyncratic and the stock in the essays that follow; but whether or not the attempt has succeeded, those essays have the shape they do partly because I am particularly interested in certain corners of Regency England's cultural history that also interested Byron, corners where we find such theatrical spectacles as the pantomime and such literary works as Robert Southey's Letters from England and Lady Caroline Lamb's Glenarvon.

As the individual essays' epigraphs suggest, another force shaping my study is the philosopher Friedrich Schlegel, whose theory of romantic poetry, brilliantly dispersed and dispensed in fragmentary utterances, goes as far as any system is likely to go in accounting for the self-consciously antisystematic vision of the world presented in Don Juan.[6] Schlegel's idea of the "poetical arabesque" is a useful model for Don Juan in that it reconciles many of the contraries spiraling together in Byron's poem. In the visual form called arabesque, the apparent freedom of the artist to be capricious and intrusive exists beside coherence of design and pleasing propor-

tions: complexity dances with lucidity, and naturalness with artifice. Furthermore, the term *arabesque* laconically demonstrates the
principles of intellectual association, cultural contrast, and witty
condensation that act throughout *Don Juan* to form the poem's
cosmopolitan climate. In its first use by Goethe in 1789, *arabeske*
combined literal allusion to Arab style with immediate reference
to Raphael's Vatican loggia paintings derived from the Pompeian
grotesques[7]—and the three distinct cultures and historical moments themselves exist in dialogue with the superb eighteenth-
century German mind enclosing and combining them. Striving to
suit form to content and, more important, hoping to understand
Byron's digressive mode by reenacting it, I have adopted the associative arabesque as the shape for my investigation. The ensuing
study of cosmopolitanism, insularity, and Regency Englishness in
Don Juan takes the form of six interrelated essays that will comment
on one another and that together constitute an intellectual pattern
centering on, though sometimes wandering away from, Byron's
poem.

The first essay, "Nothing So Difficult," studies the opening signals
of ironic intention found in the earliest portions of *Don Juan* (the
title, epigraphs, Preface, Dedication to Southey, and canto I). These
useful signals alert the reader to what the poem's subjects, themes,
and methods of proceeding will be. With such a map in mind, we
can range fairly far afield. Each of the second, third, and fourth
essays might be seen as a digression, an outward curve of the
associational arabesque. Have faith in the pattern: each wandering
line of discourse will finally lead back toward *Don Juan* by going
away from it. A poem as densely topical as *Don Juan* might spur any
number of arabesque digressions, but the three presented here are
not capriciously chosen. I have elected to assess three elements of
Regency culture in crucial and explicit dialogue with *Don Juan*. Two
of these elements are particular literary works—call them sources,
influences, parallels, analogues—by two of Byron's writer-enemies
who, interestingly enough, can be seen as models for the only
fictive poets whose verses ("The isles of Greece" and "Beware!
beware! of the Black Friar") are inscribed in the narrative. The third
is a popular "subliterary" genre that, offering Byron his hero and
providing a technique for subsuming any and all materials, can be
called both the initial and the ultimate source of *Don Juan*.

The first in this trio of digressive essays, "Two Dons, a Lord, and a

Laureate," focuses on Robert Southey's *Letters from England by Don Manuel Espriella*. It is widely known that Southey, the poet laureate and a man Byron hated for a mixture of personal, political, and poetic reasons, is one of the chief objects of satire in *Don Juan*, which is mockingly dedicated to him, but it is surprising to see that one of Southey's own works, the epistolary account of a Spaniard traveling in early nineteenth-century England, can be "reread" in Byron's comic epic. Like *Don Juan*, *Letters from England* observes many of the follies and features of English life from a Continental perspective—and it is no small irony that the despised Southey anticipated many of the attitudes announced by his self-styled poetical antithesis in *Don Juan*.

"All Things—But a Show?" looks at two insufficiently acknowledged sources of Byron's application of the Don Juan motif: the Italian *commedia dell'arte* and the English pantomime, closely related forms of spectacular theater. In tracing Byron's long-standing interest in the pantomime and his newfound interest in *commedia* (highly popular in Venice, where he was living when he wrote the earlier parts of *Don Juan*), we can learn new things about Byron's source of comic Don Juan material. These closely allied forms of theater also offer a key to some of the stylistic features of the poem: like *commedia* and pantomime, Byron's poem is improvisational, topical, eclectic, characterized by rapid and formulaic inversions and transformations. Transformation, furthermore, is Byron's means of blending heterogeneities into *Don Juan*'s poetic stew. And of course this dual dramatic influence—an English taste modified by Italian experience—is an example of the cosmopolitanism Byron advocates in the poem.

"A Don, Two Lords, and a Lady" explores affinities between *Don Juan* and *Glenarvon*, the widely read but deeply flawed *roman à clef* through which Lady Caroline Lamb revealed her own indiscretions, portrayed Byron's "one virtue and a thousand crimes," and brought about her banishment from fashionable society. *Glenarvon* is worth serious attention on several grounds—not least as a case study in the frustration of upper-class women's talent in the early nineteenth century—but here the central issue is how the story offers an English version of the Don Juan myth told from a woman's viewpoint, a portrayal of relations between men and women that Byron seems to have taken seriously enough to refute. One of the most surprising innovations of Byron's comic epic is his changing the irresistible seducer into an unresisting seduced. This reversal of the convention serves as rebuttal of Lady Caroline's novel; but it also seems that Don Juan's acknowledgment of female power and complexity is in part a lesson learned from Glenarvon. In any case, transcending the boundaries of gender is yet another of the poem's various cosmopolitanisms.

The fifth and sixth essays return to Don Juan in and of itself. "England in Don Juan" looks at how the early cantos (2–9) offer oblique, comparative, and digressive observations on and attitudes toward England. I find Byron's habitual undercutting of the poem's fictive world by injecting English realities best understood in terms of Schlegel's notion of parabasis—the point at which a literary work's plot hangs suspended and the narrator or chorus addresses the reader or audience with the author's own views and concerns. This essentially theatrical device (one employed, in fact, in both pantomime and commedia) plausibly accounts for the frequent digressions, the only sections of the early cantos where English matters and values can be explicitly taken up. The final essay, "Don Juan in England," draws on mythic patterns, Byronic biography, social history of the age, and Bakhtin's idea of the "chronotope" to speculate on how Byron succeeds in making Don Juan's portrait of Regency England both topical and universal, timely and timeless. It offers close readings from the cantos (10–16) where Byron takes his protagonist into English society as the climax of his educational progress through Western civilizations, takes up (without presuming to solve) the problem of Don Juan's non-ending, and considers (without managing to explain) the phenomenon of mobility, a crucial if elusive component of the cosmopolitan spirit in general and Byron's temperament in particular. Byron's mobile, cosmopolitan appreciation of the England he left but could not leave behind is a wonderful blend of elegy and criticism: he was the most eloquent of haters, admittedly, but in his case it is also and equally true that love and mockery can coexist.

I

Nothing So Difficult

Every good poem must be wholly intentional and wholly instinctive. That is how it becomes ideal.

Friedrich Schlegel, *Critical Fragments*

In literature and criticism alike, beginnings are difficult largely because they need to be accurately and efficiently significant. Having adopted as my title one of Byron's openers acknowledging the problem of getting started, I shall continue by taking as my own approach to *Don Juan* his professed method of telling the story, to "begin at the beginning" by giving attention to what Victor Brombert would call "opening signals," the useful and often crucial early hints that alert readers to generic or thematic contexts.[1] In the course of this essay, I shall consider *Don Juan*'s two Horatian epigraphs, the prose Preface, the Dedication, and the first canto. The irony of such an approach is that Byron chose or created a number of these meaningful preliminaries only to suppress them: for reasons to be explained later, the original epigraph, the Preface, and the Dedication did not appear in editions of *Don Juan* published during Byron's lifetime. But before looking at these opening signals, let us examine the two words that precede them all, the poem's title.

"Don Juan." The first thing noticed (and then most likely forgotten) by anyone who does not think in British English is the peculiar pronunciation "Joo-un." Those whose first encounter with the title is a spoken reference, such as a teacher's "Tomorrow we start *Don Juan*" or a friend's "*Don Juan* is the one poem I'd take along to a desert island," will immediately detect the alteration of the expected "Hwan." Readers who have not heard the title pronounced do not have much longer to wait. They might suppose the title pronounced in the Spanish way, but six lines into the first stanza of the first canto, "Juan" appears as the third *b* rhyme in a pattern thus far established as *a b a b a*. If "Juan" were part of the first trio, there would perhaps be a further moment of doubt—is the author rhyming a third *a* or setting up a *c*? But because "want," "cant," and "vaunt" have already appeared, it is clear that "Juan" is to rhyme with the preceding *b* words, "new one" and "true one," though the precedent of the *a* group suggests that this rhyme need not be perfect. So whether readers learn before embarking or after arriving at the sixth line that "Juan" is "Joo-un" instead of "Hwan," the awareness of this phonetic mutation comes quickly.

I have spent this much time explaining a small and largely self-evident matter because the point involves more than just humor. Pronouncing "Juan" to rhyme with "new one" is comical, yes. More important, it exemplifies a distinctively English habit of speech that in turn suggests a human trait Byron particularly deplored in his countrymen—the tendency to appropriate and then alter (that is, "improve" or "correct") another culture's property, whether a word, a practice, or a product: "Juan," waltzing, or tea. Byron's opposition to the habit of reducing the whole world to the vision that appears through one's own spectacles and his desire to transcend all forms of such narrowness can be seen throughout his poetry, from the biting satire on literary coteries and political camps in ENGLISH *Bards* and SCOTCH *Reviewers* (my emphasis) to *Childe Harold's* restless roving through lands and civilizations and its denunciation of the spirit that thinks packing Grecian marbles off to London will save them, to *Manfred, Cain,* and *Heaven and Earth,* where the highest mortals (if not always the happiest ones) are those ambitious to go beyond the boundaries and values of more complacent human bipeds, to *Beppo's* practical and courteous Venetian counterpoint to English prudery and hypocrisy. I would suggest that insularity in all its protean shapes, but particularly those guises it assumes in Great Britain, is one of *Don Juan's* most important topics. Byron shows it to be so in a number of ways, but first in the pronunciation of his poem's title, his title character's name.

How do we know that "Joo-un" is Byron's meaningful choice rather than his using by default the pronunciation current in his day? First, we can be sure that he was aware of the difference—and that he knew his readers would know of his awareness. Byron had journeyed through Spain during his travels of 1809–11; and his Iberian adventures, transparently fictionalized, had appeared in the first cantos of *Childe Harold*. Ever since publishing that poem he had been a poet who could take it for granted that his readers were interested in him—or in the myth fashioned by the public, then polished and projected by the poet himself.[2]

Second, "Joo-un" is far from being the poem's sole example of this particular comic effect. Byron seems to go out of his way to warp Spanish proper nouns. As meter and shifted accent mark show, the name of Juan's father becomes "Jó-se" rather than "Jo-sé." The name of Juan's mother, "Inez," is made to rhyme with "fine as"; "Lope" with "copy"; "Nunez" with "moon is"; "Seville" with "revel"; "Cadiz" with "ladies"; and, in a stanza where the narrator has just shown himself familiar with a Spanish proverb, "Guadalquivir" with "river." That other literary don grotesquely renamed by English readers, "Don Kwik-zut," is mentioned three times, and never could the verse accommodate the Spanish "Kee-ho-tay."

Spanish is not the only foreign language to receive such treatment in *Don Juan*—for instance, "louis" rhymes with "true is" and "Lyons" with "dying"—and the beginning of canto 1 is not the only starting place where linguistic comedy of this sort is highlighted. Byron applies the strategy to an English name at the beginning of canto 9, in the apostrophe to and denunciation of Arthur Welles-ley, created duke of Wellington for his labors at Waterloo but called something else on Napoleon's side of the English Channel:

> Oh, Wellington! (or "Vilainton"—for Fame
>   Sounds the heroic syllables both ways;
> France could not even conquer your great name,
>   But punned it down to this facetious phrase—   (DJ 9.1)

French does to "Wellington" much the same thing that English does to "Don Juan." The joke is funny enough for someone who knows only English, who smiles as Byron looks at a victor and sees a villain, but it becomes yet funnier when taken bilingually. "*Vilain-ton*" imputes vileness and vulgarity to this newly created duke and utterly fashionable hero—and to the entire Ton (as London's Great World called itself) that toasted him.

Just as Byron can do things with English names as well as Spanish ones, he can also use the device for a closing as well as a commencement. *Don Juan* seems by its own nature and by critical consensus a poem that stops rather than ends,[3] but if Byron had wanted to end his poem at sixteen cantos, the last stanza would have been as good a place as he might easily find to leave Don Juan. At this point we see Don Juan, who is presently involved in different ways with four females (Leila, Aurora, Lady Adeline, and the Duchess of Fitz-Fulke), about to distinguish appearance from reality by unfrocking the Black Friar. The scene at once follows and inverts the traditional Don Juan ending. Byron's Juan, like the others, faces a ghostly visitant—but it is a specter most fleshly, a holy being most profane, a man most womanly: "In full, voluptuous, but *not o'ergrown bulk*, / The phantom of her frolic Grace— Fitz-Fulke!" (DJ 16.123). If knowing British English hampers recognition of the humorous significance in "Don Joo-un," it is crucial to the comic effect here. "Fulke" and "bulk" look as if they should rhyme, and in *Don Juan* they do. But in regular British pronunciation, "Fulke" would be said "Fook"—much apter for this high priestess of dalliance. The name is brilliantly chosen in and of itself: "Fitz" and "Fulke" when taken together both aurally and visually suggest the duchess's double nature (her sublime pedigree and her earthy preoccupation) and the two chief sources, Norman and Saxon, of her culture and language. In thus rhyming the couplet and mispronouncing the name, Byron gilds his wit. He concludes the last completed canto as he began his poem, by violating a cultural convention. It is delightfully ironic that here he turns the tables and treats his mother tongue to the phonetic imperialism it inflicts on other languages throughout the poem.

This play on pronunciation is a particular manifestation of Byron's international theme—more precisely, his way of viewing narrowly insular values, practices, beliefs, and happenings (especially English ones) from a wider context. Another form the theme takes is discernible in the pair of Latin epigraphs Byron successively chose for *Don Juan*. Both come from Horace, the poet whose urbane jesting sets a style and tone for Byron to emulate.[4] Both place Don Juan's modern story within an ancient tradition whose origins are not English—and in this way implicitly characterize the poem's readership. Only readers who, like Byron, have enjoyed or endured a classical education (the training typically provided ruling-class British men) will begin—without footnotes, that is—to appreciate the relevance of the epigraphs. Only readers who can add some understanding of Byron the poet and the man to acquaintance with Latin in general and Horace in particular can approach "competence" as they venture to interpret the quotations employed as epigraphs. *Domestica facta*, the epigraph Byron rejected after Hobhouse noted "Do not have this motto" on the proofs, is a particularly witty illustration of this point. In a 26 January 1819 letter to Scrope Davies, Byron proclaims his sense of *domestica facta* to be " 'Common life'—& not one's own adventures" (LJ 11:171), a broadened application of "Roman events as opposed to borrowings from Greek legend and history," as Horace meant the phrase in context, "*vestigia Graeci / Ausi deserere et celebrare domestica facta.*"[5] Byron must have known, however, that English readers—especially his contemporary public, notably inclined as it was to project him into his verse—would first see *domestica facta* as its cognate "domestic facts" in the sense of "Lord Byron's affairs." Even the classically educated Hobhouse took it that way.[6] Reducing *domestica facta* to either private affairs or public events would ignore a dimension of Don Juan, but taken together the contemporary connotation and the classical one do a good job of signaling how wide Don Juan's range of subjects and perspectives will be.

The epigraph replacing *Domestica facta* is *Difficile est proprie communia dicere*, which Byron had earlier translated as " 'Tis no slight task to write on common things" in *Hints from Horace*.[7] Again, the Latin quotation offers a double insight as to what the workings of Don Juan will be and how Byron conceives of his poetic task. Don Juan's subjects may be *communia*, common things, ordinary or shared concerns; and as the poet of *communia*, Byron is quick to strike a modest attitude. In the Dedication he pictures himself "wandering with pedestrian Muses" (stanza 8), and this ironically self-deprecatory stance recurs. But Byron also assumes the contrary position, whose elements are evident in the first two words of Horace's phrase, *difficile est*. "To write on common things" is "no slight task" in that doing so calls for considerable skill and having done so can produce estimable results: a clear, honest view of things as they are, a "moral model," an epic. Not just anyone can write on common things—and, as Byron sees it, two English authors woefully lacking the aptitude are William Wordsworth and Robert Southey, brother Lakers and fellow subjects of the Preface.

The Preface to Don Juan, not published or even printed in proof during Byron's lifetime, made its debut in the Prothero-Coleridge edition of 1901.[8] Some important later twentieth-century editions of Don Juan—the Variorum of Steffan and Pratt, the Penguin of Steffan, Steffan, and Pratt, and the Houghton Mifflin (Riverside) of Marchand—place the Preface where such a piece would be found had its author chosen to use it, before the poem itself. With McGann's 1986 edition, the now-standard text published by Oxford, the Preface no longer stands in conspicuous introductory position but follows canto 1, as does the other unincorporated material, an editorial choice that more accurately reflects the importance accorded the Preface by its author. Byron's decision not to follow through with his Preface seems overall a sound one, whether the omission chiefly serves to avoid the ungentlemanliness of launching personal attack from the safe havens of anonymous publication and residence abroad (as Byron claimed), or to maintain consistently Horatian "plain style" in the work,[9] or to preclude overlap with the Dedication expressing many of the same points and feelings. Though it remains incomplete and, technically speaking, extraneous to Don Juan proper, the rejected Preface repays close attention, as critics recently have recognized. Anne Mellor, for instance, sees the Preface as a brilliantly realized act of romantic irony, a verbal gesture that cancels all it creates, a "hovering" in the Schlegelian sense.[10]

Unlike most such introductory pieces, Don Juan's Preface is not an explanation but rather a répétition, in miniature and in prose, of what is to come. By dint of its "hovering"—its mobility, slipperiness, obliqueness, incompletion—the Preface suggests what Don Juan will be and how it will proceed even more clearly than does the forceful and coherent poetry of the Dedication. Like Don Juan, the Preface enters various states of supposition without settling on a definitive answer, advances claims only to revoke them, starts up and goes along very nicely but does not arrive at an end. Thus, though it contains 125 lines of prose rather than some 16,000 lines of verse, and though it never names either Don Juan or Don Juan, the Preface has in several ways the performative force of the work it introduces.

How so? In the character of its narrator, a highly conspicuous presence always inserting himself into his assertions and altering meaning by his rhetoric, which heavily relies on antithesis. Take the first two sentences: "In a note or preface (I forgot which) by Mr. W. Wordsworth to a poem—the subject of which, as far as it is intelligible, is the remorse of an unnatural mother for the destruction of a natural child—the courteous Reader is desired to extend his usual courtesy so far as to suppose that the narrative is narrated by 'the Captain of a Merchantman or small trading vessel lately retired upon a small annuity to some inland town—&c. &c.' I quote from memory but conceive the above to be the sense—as far [as] there is sense—of the note or preface to the aforesaid poem—as far as it is a poem." (DJ 81). What do we see here? A careful mind, the sort that pays attention not only to poems but to their paratexts—yet a casual or contemptuous mind, one that does not recall and will not bother to check the exact nature of the prose to which it alludes. A paradoxical mind that takes "Mr. W. Wordsworth's" explanations seriously only to mock him, that quotes (and fairly accurately) only to imply by means of "&c. &c." that what is quoted is not worth the quoting. A courteous mind extending the reader's "usual courtesy" the better to be impertinent. An opinionated mind conveying opinion to cast everything asserted, or even merely named, into doubt: "note or preface (I forgot which)," "subject . . . as far as it is intelligible," "sense—as far [as] there is sense," "poem—as far as it is a poem." But however confident we can be of certain attributes of the narrator, we can have no faith (unless we have previously read "The Thorn" and its note and settled on an estimate of their value) in anything concerned with the work under scrutiny.

That lack of faith is just what Byron wants to foster, and he continues to do so in the next paragraph. Our doubts about Wordsworth's verbal artifact intensify as it is turned from something with at least possible literary status, "a poem—as far as it is a poem," to a mere "production." When Byron relates what the Poet "informs all who are willing to be informed" about the thorn, we are ready to believe that few if any readers could possibly be receptive to such information. And now the narrator becomes creative. He takes a work his compliant readers are ready to believe worthless and ascribes to it a cleverly antithetical symbolic significance—the thorn tree "born old" (Byron's emphasis) is ironically suited to stand over the grave of an infant who "died young." Giving a meaning to a purportedly meaningless "production," Byron's ingenious narrator triumphs over the talent—as far as it is meant to be understood as talent—of the Poet. Then, by quoting two of the lines he considers feeblest, the narrator confers prominence on what would otherwise remain obscure. This ironic highlighting prefigures what Byron does yet more brilliantly at the close of canto 1, where four forgettable lines by Southey gain readers, stature, and immortality because Byron takes them up, if only to discredit them in the second half of the stanza, verses of his own production.

Having quite specifically abused "The Thorn" as much as he wants to for the moment, the narrator announces distaste for further dabbling in the tiresome particulars of Wordsworth's poetry, a subject he brought up in the first place: "Let me be excused from being particular in the details of such things" (DJ 81). His attack now becomes more general. As in Don Juan itself, Wordsworth is arraigned not just for bad poetry but for bad poetics and bad politics. In mounting his case, Byron asks much of his reader. To get the point of the attack requires rather specific knowledge of such contemporary British matters as the controversy over Pope, Wordsworth's and Coleridge's ideas on imagination, and Lord Lonsdale's patronage of Wordsworth, but also a wider understanding of past and present European culture. The dense paragraph discredits Wordsworth through allusion—and to follow the indictment a reader must be able to identify(and somehow connect to the case) Joanna Southcote, Emanuel Swedenborg, Richard Brothers, Parson Tozer, Luis de Góngora y Argote, Giovanni Battista Marini, Count Cagliostro, Baroness de Krüdener, Terence's Eunuchus, the Peninsular War, and Ferdinand VII of Spain. Though seldom so dauntingly dense, Don Juan itself will range this far and farther. It will call on its reader to know the intricacies of England's present state and to have sufficient cultural and historical breadth to understand the force of parodies, innuendos, comparisons, and digressions.

Now that he has masterfully insulted the poet and Stamp Distributor who "may be met in print at some booksellers and several trunkmakers, and in person at dinner at Lord Lonsdale's" (DJ 82), the narrator goes on to ask that the reader assist in the construction of a remarkably detailed mise-en-scène for his own work: "The Reader who has acquiesced in Mr. W. Wordsworth's supposition that his 'Misery oh Misery' is related by the 'Captain of a small &c.' is requested to suppose by a like exertion of Imagination that the following epic narrative is told by a Spanish Gentleman in a village in the Sierra Morena on the road between Monasterio and Seville—sitting at the door of a posada with the curate of the hamlet on his right hand" &c. &c (DJ 82–83). This part of the Preface poses some problems of interpretation. Once interpreted, it illuminates certain sides of *Don Juan*. First to name the problems: if evoking Wordsworth's narrator—a superstitious, talkative, indolent sea captain, past his middle years, retired to a residence that is not his birthplace, possessing "slow faculties and deep feelings"—is to be construed as a task beyond the call of readerly courtesy, why does Byron ask a "like exertion of Imagination" on the part of his own reader? If Byron's request differs from Wordsworth's, wherein lies the difference? And if the "exertion of imagination" Byron calls for is a useful and valid undertaking, why does he undercut the effort as he does at the start of the Preface's final phase, with the words "Having supposed as much of this as the utter impossibility of such a supposition will admit" (DJ 83–84)?

The answer to the first two questions is found, I think, in the fact that the "exertion of Imagination" Byron requests is in certain ways quite unlike that Wordsworth demands. Wordsworth's prose note attempts to raise the reader's consciousness. It announces the systematic underpinnings of the poem written (we need to recall that Wordsworth later classified "The Thorn" as one of his "Poems of the Imagination") and attempts at once to replace and to apologize for the absence of a poem not written, an introductory work Wordsworth claims to have been "prevented from writing by never having felt myself in a mood when it was probable that I should write it well."[11] Where Wordsworth offers abstractions to be imagined into life, Byron gives concrete particulars—not imaginings, but recollections from real life—and asks only that the reader grant their reality or suppose their vitality. The resulting tableau vivant, as elaborately specific as the most intricate of Bernard Shaw's stage directions, provides a plausible speaker (whose knowledge of English can be accounted for in two mutually exclusive ways, by his being "either an Englishman settled in Spain—or a Spaniard who had travelled in England"); a richly variegated supporting cast composed of types ("a groupe of black-eyed peasantry," "a knot of French prisoners," "a small elderly audience") mixed with characters on the brink of individuality (such as the "tall peasant girl whose whole soul is in her eyes" and the "two foreign travellers" whom readers familiar with Byron's life are tempted to equate with Byron and Hobhouse[12]); props (amusingly specified down to the "segar" and the "relics of an olla podrida" but not to the point of determining whether the "jug" holds Malaga or Sherry); and a time (it is sunset, the season is one warm enough for being out of doors at such an hour, and the presence of French prisoners implies the Peninsular War era). This exercise in imagination presents to readers several key features of Don Juan: its conversational, improvisational, and dramatic qualities, its location in a real world, and its distribution of "Byron" throughout the poem, just as here we glimpse him in—without identifying him as—a foreign traveler, the storyteller, the English editor who appears in the next paragraph, and the composing voice beyond them all.

Why then is so fruitful an exercise to be deprecated? One response would be to say that Byron is satirizing not just Wordsworth but any readers willing to make imaginative exertions of the sort he and Wordsworth request. This explanation might seem tempting, especially in light of the elastic but overstuffed paragraph packed with "rustic Gongora and vulgar Marini of his country's taste," "this Thraso of poetry has long been a Gnatho in politics," and such phrases. But if Byron held his readers in low esteem, would he waste the power, cogency, and allusive aptness of his invective on them? And if he were not partly serious about his own imaginative or reminiscent act of contextualizing, would he not have made the Spanish tableau ridiculous rather than intriguing, an effect easy enough to attain? Byron's dismissing as "utter impossibility" what he in fact successfully achieves for his reader seems the gesture of a divided mind. He wants to deprecate Wordsworth's experiment in imagination, yet he cannot do so without undermining his own request: Byron's eye is honest enough to see that along with the unlikenesses there are, as he has half-ironically asserted, some likenesses between his subversive Preface and Wordsworth's systematic note—and, more surprisingly, between Don Juan and "The Thorn." "The Thorn" proves in some ways analogous to Don Juan—and to the extent that it is analogous, it is potentially useful, as model or matter, to Byron. Don Juan may be a comic masterpiece and "The Thorn" a less-than-perfect blend of pathos and pedestrianism, but each is an experiment in relating an individualized narrator to a story his attributes shape and shade. The lines (32–33) Byron quotes from "The Thorn" are those that signal the narrator's first explicit entrance into the world of his story.[13] The words are delightfully double-edged, as those of the *Don Juan* narrator so often can be:

> I've measured it from side to side:
> Tis three feet long, and two feet wide.

Viewed literally, the couplet reveals a laughable degree of "matter-of-factness," a Wordsworthian defect scorned by Byron at various points in *Don Juan*, acknowledged by Wordsworth's partisan Coleridge in *Biographia Literaria*. The speaker of those words and calculator of those dimensions was also deplored, on rather different grounds, by Southey. Though a fair-minded reader of "The Thorn" should recognize that the absurdity is a feature of the narrator's mind, not the poet's, Southey had attacked Wordsworth's narrative strategy by charging that "he who personates tiresome loquacity becomes tiresome himself."[14] It is amusing to perceive that this assertion by a poet Byron would come to see as one of Wordsworth's uncritical allies provoked, as a defensive reply, the very Note Byron effectively mocks in his Preface.

But this historical byway has led us away from the puddle under scrutiny a paragraph back. Let us return and reconsider the couplet. With a shift toward figurative reading, the lines become sharp, subtle, self-reflexive, and relevant to *Don Juan*. Imagine this "little muddy pond / Of water, never dry," a stagnant Hippocrene, to be the Captain's partly absurd and partly appropriate image for his poem. As such, it can be "measured," and measured in "feet," and its dimensions can be determined as three (punctuation-stopped units) by two (lines). We can even view this pond as an exaggerated emblem of that Lake District provinciality Byron finds objectionable in the lines where he wishes Southey, Wordsworth, and Coleridge would "change your lakes for ocean" (DJ, Dedication, 5).

There is a further parallel to notice. As we have already seen, Wordsworth's prose appendage to "The Thorn" has a precisely defined relation to the poem; Byron's flippant narrative voice has blurred the issue of its placement. In contrast, Byron never attached his Preface, incomplete as it remained, to *Don Juan*. Byron not having done so, editors have been obliged to make what

connection they can. Thanks to their successive and different decisions since the day of Prothero, it is the prose introduction to Don
Juan that can be justly called, by the great majority of readers who
pay little attention to textual matters, a "preface or note (I forget
which)."

Let us now turn to the Dedication of Don Juan. The Preface at which
we have just been looking swings that way on the hinge of "Having
supposed as much of this . . . ," at which point the reader must
proceed to envision an "English editor" whose work the Dedication is said to be and Byron's attention turns from Wordsworth to
Southey, the principal subject of that Dedication.

Writing to Thomas Moore, Byron described the Dedication as
"good, simple, savage verse upon the [Laureate's] politics, and the
way he got them" (LJ 6:68). This characterization is not entirely
accurate. In his seventeen dedicatory stanzas, Byron does not display Don Juan's full range of moods and subjects, but his target is not
just Southey, his time not only the present, his place not merely
England, and his tone not simply savage indignation.[15] The Dedication's first three stanzas take aim at Southey (with a four-line
potshot at Coleridge in stanza 2), but the fourth draws a bead on
Wordsworth, and the fifth blasts the Lakers as a group. Stanzas 6–8
compare the Lakers with their contemporaries, Byron included; 9
generalizes about the poet who "reserves his laurels for posterity"
to make a transition (stanzas 10–11) to Milton, excellent as the
Lakers are debased. Stanzas 12–15 confront that personage Anne
Mellor perceptively recognizes as the "other Bob" of the Dedication, Robert Stewart, Viscount Castlereagh and foreign secretary of
the Tory government.[16] Stanza 16 offers the narrator's reaction to
Castlereagh's foul foreign policies and turns in its last line back to
Southey, who "lives to sing them very ill," and whose political
apostasy is contrasted with the narrator's faithfulness to the "buff
and blue" of Whiggery in the final stanza.

Byron's choice of Southey to receive the dedicatory honor is
amusing in several ways. At its simplest, the Dedication achieves an
ironic reversal, dispensing a slap in the form of a bow. The feat is
delicately done in that there are credible reasons for Byron to
compliment Southey. Any author might reasonably dedicate his
work to the official poet of his nation. If, as I shall go on to suggest
in the next chapter, Don Juan owes a debt of influence to Robert

Southey's prose narrative of a fictive Spaniard traveling in England, Byron might gratefully acknowledge the begetter (though not the "onlie" one) of his verses. Still, Byron has personal and public reasons, much stronger ones, to turn such a Dedication to satire; and these reasons justify the digressions from Southey himself.

In his Dedication Byron announces what we have seen offered by the Preface in the form of *répétition*, the English subject of his poem. The shape this announcement takes shows the aristocratic Byron as keenly aware as the democratic Orwell would be of the close connection between language and politics. Byron denounces the tuneless, foggy ravings of the Lakers and their turncoat Toryism—the repressive Irish and Continental policies of the "slave-maker" Castlereagh and the "set trash of phrase" that marks his oratory. Against all these stands the historical example of Milton, the antithesis to the Regency Tories, a man and poet sublime in his song, uncompromising in his antimonarchical politics: "He did not loathe the sire to laud the son, / But closed the tyrant-hater he begun" (DJ, Dedication, 10). The vision offered here is a highly stylized one. For now, Byron does not show us mixed cases: good poets with bad politics, bad poets with good politics, principled but tongue-tied statesmen, or corrupt yet eloquent ones.

Instead, Byron presents what he hates and what he admires in their purest forms. He enhances political and poetical incompetence by linking them and by associating both with sexual inadequacy. Each "Bob" of the Dedication (and it is an iconoclastic gesture to address either the laureate or the minister so familiarly) is depicted as sexually deficient. Castlereagh is an "intellectual eunuch," so vile as to warrant no pronoun but "it." Southey, somewhat more virile, is made the butt of the famous "dry Bob" innuendo and along with the other Lakers is obliquely accused of intellectual incest, a charge enriched by knowledge that Southey and Coleridge were married to sisters, Edith and Sarah Fricker, and that the Coleridges for a long time had shared the Southeys' house at Keswick:

> You, Gentlemen! by dint of long seclusion
>   From better company have kept your own
> At Keswick, and through still continued fusion
>   Of one another's minds at last have grown
> To deem as a most logical conclusion
>   That Poesy has wreaths for you alone;

There is a narrowness in such a notion
Which makes me wish you'd change your lakes for ocean.
                                                    (DJ,Dedication, 5)

One way to look at incest is as a particular variety of provinciality, and it is interesting to see Byron so deftly exploit its metaphorical potential to even the score with the man whom he thought had done as much as anyone to spread through England the tale of Byron and Shelley's Diodati "league of incest"—an unjust charge to which Byron may have been sensitive for reasons outside that precise situation.

Byron's grudge against at least one Laker, Southey, is both principled and personal. The brilliance with which he here can blend the two realms, as he does in the application of *domestica facta*, gives an accurate gauge of *Don Juan's* soon-to-be-encountered complexity and economy. Likewise, the Dedication faithfully predicts the cosmopolitan freedom of the *Don Juan* narrator, who takes the long view of one who understands history as well as the present, the broad view of one who knows cultures beyond that into which he was born, the lofty view of one generally inclined to magnanimity but not so priggish as to be above yielding to pettiness when it proves entertaining. In subject, opinion, tone, and method, the Dedication informs us that what follows will be a work where English concerns—poetical, political, and the rest—will be a crucial though not single-minded interest of a composing presence that resists authority, undercuts order, and transcends limits: even that authority called the poet, that order called the poem, and those limits called themes and subjects.

We are now ready to look at the opening signals displayed in *Don Juan's* first canto, though these are not the looming indicators of intent and purpose some works might offer. Byron began *Don Juan*, as his letters say and as McGann rightly stresses, with little forethought and no plans for a poem of length.[17] Thus canto 1 does not shadow forth a coming epic (none being yet envisioned), or trumpet its aspirations (as yet unfelt), or lay out strategy (improvisation being the mode Byron had hit upon). But *Don Juan* is from its first line a felicitous work, and in canto 1 we can see some embryonic features of what will later develop. The poem's habitual reliance on comparison of matters, moods, people, and things and the grounding of these comparisons on English soil are already clear. As we shall see below, the first English readers, who received a sealed manuscript copy Byron had sent from Venice via Lord Lauderdale, reacted to the poem as if the crucial matters in the ostensibly fictive (and Spanish) tale were real (and English) in model and significance.

Those readers were Byron's most intimate Cambridge comrades John Cam Hobhouse and Scrope Davies, his friend and banker Douglas Kinnaird, and John Hookham Frere, author of "Whistlecraft's" *The Monks and the Giants,* the English ottava rima precursor of *Don Juan.* Witty, worldly, well-read, enlightened in their opinions, liberal in their sentiments, familiar with Byron's life, ideas, and manners, these men can be seen as coming as close as any real people could to being the ideal readership for *Don Juan.* Their careful group judgment, relayed by Hobhouse in a long letter of 5 January 1819, is the earliest critique of *Don Juan* and a consistently accurate prediction of the outrage and objections the poem would provoke in some quarters. Despite the Spanish setting of canto 1, Hobhouse and the others immediately saw that its "domestic facts were more English than Spanish."[18] Though Byron took umbrage at their recommendation that he not publish *Don Juan,* there is neither prudery nor detraction in their advice. Fully appreciative of *Don Juan's* merits, they argued against publication on grounds of expediency.

Hobhouse acknowledges that *Don Juan* demonstrates Byron "as superior in the burlesque as in the heroic to all competitors" and sees that "this singular style" may be Byron's "real forte." But, he says, the transparently veiled digs at Lady Byron and the sarcastic hints at the details of their separation (e.g., stanza 28's lines "She kept a journal, where his faults were noted, / And open'd certain trunks of books and letters") would repulse public opinion, which had begun to turn away from Annabella in Byron's favor. The English readership would confuse Byron with his "half-real hero" Juan; and this blend of author and character would confirm the widely held belief in the exaggerated accounts of Byron's Venetian dissipations, rumors whose flames Byron took care to fan and Hobhouse to extinguish. Such coarse or irreverent passages as the discussion of the pox (DJ 1.131) and the parody of the Ten Commandments (DJ 1.205–6) would weaken Byron's position as a champion of liberal causes. The ad hominem attacks would be construed as unseemly—the political ones because Byron could not be at hand to fight Castlereagh, the literary ones because the first poet of the age should not condescend to notice such "wretched antagonists" as Southey, Wordsworth, and Coleridge.

Hobhouse's letter shows that the English focus of Byron's narrative was obvious to his contemporaries. Modern readers have little trouble reaching the same conclusion: the Spanish details are too false and the English ones too real for reading any other way. A suspicion that Don Juan's Spanish scene is a painted backdrop might start at the moment of noticing "Joo-un," and the rapid buildup of other Spanish mispronunciations should only increase doubts of authenticity. So should the line that follows Juan's appearance: "We all have seen him in the pantomime." Don Juan is not "at" but "in" the show, so our "ancient friend" has to be a stage Spaniard rather than a true one watching the spectacle. What of the "we" who "all have seen him"? Common sense says that this is an English audience—and spelling out the reasons why only strengthens the conviction. Presentations of Don Juan in pantomime and other forms of spectacular theater were highly popular in England during the period spanned by Juan's story and Byron's life. Add to this the fact that the poem's language is English and the further fact that the first string of recent "heroes" to be rejected in the next stanza are English soldiers: it is certain that "we" the characterized readers must be English.

And indeed, quite apart from the contorted names, there are many misrepresentations of things Spanish in canto 1 that take the form of communal fallacies prevailing in England (and other Protestant nations). The canto's two betrayed spouses, Inez and Alfonso, do not react as Spanish Catholics would. At the close of the eighteenth century a Spanish lady—even a prodigious one of Inez's sort—would not be divorcing her husband, on grounds of adultery or anything else. If a marriage were to be ended, the alternatives would not be "death or Doctors' Commons" (DJ 1.36) but death or a papal bull, marriage being ultimately a sacrament as well as a legal matter. And should one of the partners in a failing marriage take the former path, a Spanish heir would not be left, as Juan is, with particularly English legal entanglements and rewards, "a chancery suit" and "messuages" (DJ 1.37). Likewise, when Don Alfonso divorces Julia (unlikely), the details would not be featured "in the English newspapers, of course" (unlikely) with the best of the transcripts "ta'en by Gurney" [sic] the Parliamentary shorthand clerk (most unlikely), and once divorced, Julia would not be "sent into a nunnery" (DJ 1.188–91). English Protestant audiences, from Shakespeare's day to Byron's, might suppose convents convenient receptacles for disgraced women; but by the eighteenth century the religious orders typically saw the matter another way.

The *domestica facta* of marriage, inheritance, and separation that seem so wrong for Spain are very like Byron's own English experience, as are some of the principals in these proceedings. Everyone since Hobhouse has noticed many specific similarities between Lady Byron and the "learned lady" who masterminds both separations: the pedantry, mathematical talent, loftiness, cryptic pronouncements, even the choice of dress material. Should a reader miss the specific resemblances to Annabella, Byron sketches Inez with a more general Englishness that can hardly be overlooked. The Prioress of Chaucer's *Canterbury Tales* is evident in the series of accomplishments attributed to Inez and then retracted. When he needs to fashion a comparison to convey something of Inez's "perfection," the narrator always turns to England for his raw materials: to the works of such writers as Maria Edgeworth, Sarah Trimmer, and Hannah More, to the legal career of Sir Samuel Romilly (who had handled Byron affairs and whose 1818 suicide had made recent scandal), to the best English products—such as timepieces by Harrison and Rowlandson's Macassar hair oil.

The associations of these English allusions to high-minded legalism struck down by misfortune and notoriety, female intellectualism and didacticism, the repressive precision of a well-crafted machine, a mundane cosmetic claiming otherworldly powers, can all be seen as relevant to Annabella as Byron might want to present her. But we cannot simply equate the Spanish lady and the English one. Byron denies patterning the former on the latter, though his denial is not without a semiconfessional undertone: "What are you so anxious about Donna Inez for?" he writes to Hobhouse. "She is not meant for Clytemnestra [one of his stock names for Lady Byron]—and if She were—would you protect the fiend?" (LJ 6:131). If we are not inclined to take Byron's word on the matter, then his associative ingenuity will thwart a simplistic "this equals that" reading; for the depiction of Don Juan's family situation offers early evidence of a strategy that recurs throughout the poem—fictionmaking that braids or weaves two or more realities into a whole that resists reduction into any one of its component strands. Relying on this superbly effective means of frustrating the systematizing, oversimplifying impulse in readers, Byron can facetiously exploit material from his marriage without exactly presenting that marriage, for many details of the "ill-assorted pair" who produced Don Juan are also reminiscent of Byron's own parents, Captain John Byron and Catherine Gordon Byron. Donna Inez's circumspection is the reverse of Mrs. Byron's violent frenzies, but she is equally disagreeable to her husband. And that husband has much in common with Captain Byron. He is a gentleman, though not a titled one. His blood is ancient. He is both a cavalier and a womanizer. His wife characterizes him as "*mad*" and "*bad*," words at once recalling Annabella's fears at the time of the separation and Lady Caroline Lamb's famous three-attribute summation of Byron *fils* but also evoking Byron *père*, "Mad Jack," in whose paternal shoes the poet, as estranged husband and absent father, found himself. Having given his wife a miserable time of it and one child, a son, Don Jóse dies as Captain Byron did and leaves to his wife the rearing of that only son, whose boyhood education is puritanical. All these details suggest that Byron was thinking of his parents' marital situation as well as his own when he concocted Jóse, Inez, and Juan; but one further detail seems to make the matter certain. That detail is found in a parenthetical reference to Don Juan's pedigree: "(His sire was of Castile, his dam from Arragon)" (*DJ* 1.38).

These particulars of Don Juan's regional background call up an alliance grander than Don Jóse and Donna Inez's, that of the Spanish monarchs Ferdinand and Isabella. But the allusion is either imperfect or deliberately reversed: Ferdinand was from Aragon and Isabella from Castile. Byron was too good an historian for his confusion on such a matter to be likely; and if we see a certain parallel between Don Juan's and Byron's parents there is indeed a good explanation for the reversal. Like Ferdinand and Isabella, Jóse and Inez, Byron's "sire" and "dam" were from different parts of a united kingdom: Catherine Gordon from Scotland, Captain Byron from England. Byron's twisting the Spanish allusion makes Juan's father, like his own, come from the larger, more populous, prosperous, and powerful region, which is also the one whose language (Castilian Spanish) is the literary one of Spain, as English is of Britain.

Ascribing traits of the British Byrons to a Spanish cast of characters is not Byron's sole means of "domesticating" the Don Juan story in canto 1. Although, as we shall see in the third essay, Byron does follow pantomime convention by starting with the enactment of a well-known legend that is transformed and then followed with an improvisational harlequinade, the ways he bends the tradition and highlights certain aspects or details go far toward making the protagonist of Don Juan Don Juan with a difference. The poem's recurrent strategy will be to remove Don Juan from his customary, legendary contexts and place his character, despite the extraordinary experiences confronting him, in Byron's and the reader's shared frame, which is ordinary reality, an ordinary reality that contains British references to contemporary life (such as the one in stanza 178 to the "modern phrase" *tact* first used in England in the 1790s and the one in stanza 183 to income tax, first levied in England in 1799)[19] and to literature (such as Juan's near suffocation in Julia's bed being compared to Clarence's fate in the malmsey butt in stanza 166, the quotation of Campbell in stanza 88, the burlesque of Wordsworth in stanza 90, the allusion to Moore in stanza 104, and the possible echo of Jane Austen or Lady Caroline Lamb in stanza 194).

Byron could have started Don Juan's story at any point—and even informs us that "Most epic poets plunge in 'medias res'" (DJ 1.6). But his narrative choices in canto 1 present Don Juan not as a full-grown, independent seducer but as a child—a boy whose social background, parents, and education are as plausible as if he were a neighbor instead of an archetype. We have already seen that this Juan's "Spanish" milieu is not particularly Spanish, despite his house being by the Guadalquivir; but it is a densely real and solidly bourgeois realm. Canto 1 unfolds in a world where social connections and personal belongings are more pervasive, tenacious, entangling, and incriminating than are emotional relations—a world filled with people (not just feminine objects of seduction and masculine adversaries but ancestors, family friends, lackeys) and things (erotically illuminated missals, bowdlerized textbooks, doors to stand ajar, shoes for a cuckolded husband to trip over, quills, writing paper, and seals that reveal the letter writer's taste).

It is also a world grounded in time—not historical time at this point, but what we might call practical time, the petty and tyrannical chronology that arranges our days and seasons. The legendary Don Juan's heaven-seeking or heaven-defying ardor is much damped (so it seems to the reader, though not to the lady) when his debut in love is fixed with increasingly laughable precision in this mundane sort of time: "It was upon a day, a summer's day;—" (1.102) and then " 'Twas on a summer's day—the sixth of June:—" (1.103) and finally " 'Twas on the sixth of June, about the hour / Of half past six—perhaps still nearer seven," (DJ 1.104).

Similarly, Byron makes the passion of the first canto's young lovers more ordinary, less a part of the mythic Don Juan realm, by revealing exactly how young each party is and, more important, the extent and nature of the gap existing between their ages. Juan is sixteen and "almost a man" (DJ 1.54). Julia, "married, charming, chaste, and twenty-three" (DJ 1.59), is by both station and age entirely a woman. Knowing her to be Don Juan's senior in years and experience empties the conquest (if such a compound of attraction and self-deception can be called a "conquest" on either side) of masculine rakishness and power. In being older than Juan as well as in taking the initiative in their relationship, Julia sets a pattern to which every woman romantically involved with him conforms in the poem. Only Leila and Aurora, who passively receive Juan's pure and high-minded regard, are explicitly younger than he. Haidée is seventeen (DJ 2.112), as is Dudù (DJ 6.54)—and depending on when Juan's birthday takes place, he must be more or less the same age. Gulbeyaz's years "might make six and twenty springs" (DJ 5.98). Catherine is encountered at that overripe stage when "Her climacteric teased her like her teens" (DJ 10.47), and thus should be in her sixties. When Juan comes into the glittering orbit of Lady Adeline Amundeville, he is twenty-one—and six weeks her junior (DJ 14.51, 54). It might perhaps be indiscreet for the narrator, a habitué of the English world of fashion, to disclose the years of "her frolic Grace—Fitz-Fulke," but her introduction as "a fine and somewhat full-blown blonde, / Desirable, distinguish'd, celebrated / For several winters in the grand, grand Monde" (DJ 14.42) certainly characterizes the duchess as a well-preserved woman "of a certain age." The very fact that three of these unconventionally enterprising women are the same age or only minimally older than Juan stresses that the prosaic distinction of age is an important one—and firmly anchors the grand or grandiose legend of the seducer in domestic or domesticated reality. From Don Hwan comes Don Joo-un—and it is worth remembering that if Byron saw his Continental liaisons in the Don Hwan vein (as his epic epistolary catalogue of Venetian mistresses, a distinct echo of Mozart's *Don Giovanni*, suggests),[20] he retrospectively viewed his amorous career among the predatory ladies of the English Great World, some of them his elders by a few years or a good many, as closer to the experience of Don Joo-un.

We have seen how the presentation in canto 1 of Don Juan's story sometimes is, sometimes is not, and sometimes is and is not drawn from Byron's own experiences, whether these are active or contemplative. The English digressions are likewise close to if not perfectly congruent with Byron's opinions. The burlesque of Wordsworthian romanticism in Don Juan's adolescent mopings, the friendly but not utterly admiring references to lyric love à la "Anacreon Moore," the ironic ambiguity of the narrator's fifth literary commandment, "Thou shalt not steal from Samuel Rogers" (DJ 1.205), all correspond to personal sentiments Byron expressed at one time or another. As for the narrator whose presence is conspicuous from the first line of the canto, he also is like Byron and of Byron without precisely being Byron. The elusiveness of this playful narrator is perhaps the most genuinely Byronic thing about him. Lady Blessington, whose talents and circumstances equipped her to understand Byron as well as most anyone has ever done, sees him as above all loving to mystify, to feign seriousness. He is for her a man of natural mobility who is fully aware of his nature: "Byron is a perfect chameleon, possessing the fabulous qualities attributed to that animal, of taking the color of whatever touches him. He is conscious of this."[21] This shifting color, at once a reflex and an artifice, is equally characteristic of the *Don Juan* narrator; and because there is "Nothing so difficult as a beginning / In poesy, unless perhaps the end" (DJ 4.1), we might do well to end our appraisal of opening signals by seeing how that Byronic narrator ends the opening canto, for the final impression he makes will modify our expectations of canto 2 and all else that follows.

Like the other cantos, 8 and 16 being the sole exceptions, the first one ends with its focus on the narrator, not Don Juan. As the narrator turns from Don Juan's "earliest scrape" in stanza 199, he begins supplying us with professions of his own attitudes and intentions to keep in mind when and if the poem resumes. The claims advanced are wonderfully and deliberately self-contradictory. Their inconsistencies appear in clearest form when we strip away the delicate tissue of poetry and rhetoric from the bones of assertion, as the following series of prose abstracts attempts to do for the canto's last twenty-four stanzas:

—The continuation of Don Juan's adventures is "Dependent on the public altogether" (stanza 199), yet the poem is said to be "epic" (implying continuation with or without popular demand) and then crammed with so many projected "epic" attributes and episodes that its epic nature cannot be taken seriously (200–201).

—Unlike previous epics, this one is "actually true" (202) and proven to be so by reference to such "reliable" sources as history, tradition, facts, newspapers, plays, operas, and, above all, the ever-straightforward narrator's ocular proof (203).

—If the narrator should "condescend to prose," he will write poetical commandments (204), which he then proceeds to do in ottava rima verse (205–6).

—No honest and perceptive reader can assert that this poem is not "a moral tale, though gay" (207–8). But just in case anyone should try, the narrator has assured himself that his public will see the poem as he wishes—he's bribed his "grandmother's review— the British" to guarantee its being understood in these terms (209– 10).

—Like Byron, the narrator is not so prone to quarrel with less malleable reviews, such as the Edinburgh and the Quarterly, as he was back in his "hot youth—when George the Third was King," some six or seven years before he "dreamt of dating from the Brenta" (211–12).

—Now thirty and graying, the narrator is thinking of a wig and (unlike Byron) through with love and wine, left only with that "good old gentlemanly vice," avarice (213–16).

—He's also through with ambition, for fame is futile, as precedent shows (217–19).

—Thus, wisely embracing what consolations are possible for one of such advanced decrepitude, he ingratiatingly bids farewell to the "gentle reader" and "Still gentler purchaser" with many a humble platitude (221), which humility is so unnatural to him that he must now resort to Southey's verse to voice it (222) and then, casting off obsequiousness and Southey, make sure that the reader understands that neither the verses nor the attitude could possibly be his: "The first four rhymes are Southey's every line: / For God's sake, reader! Take them not for mine" (222).

In this resourceful way, the supposedly errant storyteller brings his tale full circle and his reader right back to the Dedication and the laureate. The opening arabesque of *Don Juan*, a bravura performance simultaneously demonstrating the poem's pattern and apparent randomness, sincerity and duplicity, revelation and concealment of "Byron" and his attitudes, is now complete. That much seems clear. What the shifting proportions of this arabesque may be at any one point and in any one detail is less clear and best left unsettled—to please, perplex, and tempt the reader on, as Byron, "Byron," and the narrator seem equally inclined to do.

Two Dons, a Lord,
and a Laureate

*That a prophet isn't heeded in his own country must
be the reason why clever writers so often avoid having
a homeland in the realm of the arts and sciences.
They prefer to concentrate instead on traveling and
on writing travel books.*

Friedrich Schlegel, *Athenaeum Fragments*

A traveling Spaniard, young, wellborn, and obviously some British scribbler's contrivance, arrives on the shores of England. The fabled white cliffs fail to impress him, nor does the port through which he passes or the cow-filled fields and bandit-infested wastes he crosses on his way to London. The metropolis, with its long thoroughfares, gaslights, and doors with knockers, dazzles his foreign eye. He in turn attracts public notice, which takes the form of being called "Frenchman" in the streets. Established in comfortable lodgings, our Spaniard looks round him and sees a world whose crucial act is calculation. Commercial encroachments obscure the cathedral dome of St. Paul's. Marriages are made in the marketplace. Sweated labor of the many, in mines and manufacturies, enriches the few. Those citizens able to vote are held like so many guineas in the borough-lord's pocket—or, if independent, they sell themselves one by one to the highest-bidding candidate.

This modern Tyre is a society in flux. The ancient distinctions between town and country have blurred; the manners of nobles, gentry, and arrivistes are converging. If George III is king and his son Prince of Pleasure, fashion is tyrant. The West End's gentlemen in stays, strong-minded ladies, agriculturists, quacks, fierce reviewers, and pet pugilists fascinate the young outsider. In like manner, his chronicle's rich blend of contemporary detail and anecdote, liberal sentiments, religious speculation, and facetious banter can still interest twentieth-century readers, who find the portrait of a little world as exotic to them as it is to the Spaniard, though for different reasons. What we view is the vanished world of Carlton House and Drury Lane, Francophobia and Franglais, roast beef and punch vaunted as national sustenance while the masses survive on bread and potatoes—a world of galvanism, magnetic girdles, coal fires, card leaving, Methodists, reformers, fops, fox hunters, and renegadoes—a world compounded of contradictions.

In short, the world of Robert Southey's Don Manuel Alvarez Espriella.

Readers who were misled by the introductory paragraphs, who supposed the traveling Spaniard to be Byron's Don Juan and the literary work the one whose opening signals have just been surveyed, should be willing to entertain the idea here to be asserted and examined—that Don Juan resembles Southey's Letters from England: By Don Manuel Alvarez Espriella, Translated from the Spanish closely enough to warrant suspicion that Byron used it as one of the many models for his comic epic. Every reader of Don Juan knows what we have just seen shadowed forth in its opening signals—that the poem is continually allusive and that Southey, the man and the poetical corpus, provided crucial raw material for Byron's satire. Every reader of The Vision of Judgment knows Byron able and willing to make Southey's work a vehicle, not just an object of mockery. But no one has yet suggested Letters from England as a precursor to Don Juan. Proving originality is one complex task; proving indebtedness another. Given that most if not all of the resemblances between Southey's work and Byron's will be matters of more or less debate, the job of conclusively demonstrating that Byron borrowed through amassed internal evidence would be impossible; and there is no irrefutable external evidence, no "I Byron owe you Southey this and this and this," at hand to serve as unfailing bulwark to an edifice of speculation. But even if nothing is proved with certainty, detecting and assessing similarities between Letters from England and Don Juan illuminates meaning by destroying the critical oversimplification, all too widely held, that places Byron and Southey at opposite poles as liberal satirist and reactionary object of satire. And anyway, as I hope to show, somewhere short of QED there are messily interesting likelihoods to consider.

The general shape of Byron's attitude toward Southey is well known—and so it will be especially important to sketch in the shadings that make the actual attitude more complicated than its outline. Everyone is aware that what crystallized was hatred—hatred on personal, political, and poetical grounds—hatred that burns with a threefold flame in the Dedication to *Don Juan* and in *The Vision of Judgment*. But Byron took some time in reaching white-hot indignation, and it is worth following his steps to the fiery furnace.

Byron's first poetic notice of Southey is, like his last one, satirical. A few lines on "ballad-monger Southey" appear in *English Bards and Scotch Reviewers*; but the passage is not personal, and Southey is just mentioned in passing, as are most of the literary figures on whom Byron flings mockery in this diffusely indignant poem. When better acquainted with Southey, Byron was able to recognize the man's merits as well as his flaws. In the letters and journals of 1813, when Byron's round of calls at Holland House, Melbourne House, the publisher John Murray's salon in Albemarle Street, and other fashionable gathering places was well established, we find a number of prose references to Southey. None of these portraits is purely unfavorable. Yet none ascribes unqualified merit to Southey's poetry, the genre that gained his reputation if not his income, so we should perhaps see Byron's willingness to admire the other poet's appearance and prose as backhanded compliments. They are true compliments nonetheless; and the most famous of these assessments, in a 22 November 1813 journal entry, where Byron need not strike a pose for a correspondent, shows him willing to be fair and generous as well as witty when speaking of the man we remember as his arch-enemy: "Southey, I have not seen much of. His appearance is *Epic*; and he is the only existing entire man of letters. All the others have some pursuits annexed to their authorship. His manners are mild, but not those of a man of the world, and his talents of the first order. His prose is perfect. Of his poetry there are various opinions: there is, perhaps, too much of it for the present generation; posterity will probably select. He has *passages* equal to any thing. At present, he has a *party*, but no *public*—except for his prose writings. The life of Nelson is beautiful" (LJ 3:214).

"His prose is perfect." Byron could no longer feel the same when a few years had passed and a few of Southey's offenses, prose and verse, had stung him in exile. But hostility coexisted with this limited admiration even in 1813. One source of the hostility seems to have been Southey's gaining the laureateship after Pye's death and Scott's refusal of the dubious honor, for an occasional poem Byron wrote toward the end of 1813, when Southey accepted the appointment, begins the political and poetical faultfinding we now think of as Byron's characteristic view. The poem's lines, particularly its four alternate conclusions, embody several of the images and phrases later to be associated with the Laureate and his fellow Lakers in *Don Juan*. "And up to Pye's Parnassus he may climb," Byron wryly observes,

> George gives him what—God knows he wanted—laurels,
> And spares him what—he never spared us—rhyme.

Then come the four alternate endings:

> Blest day that shall a double joy insure—
> For us his silence, him his sinecure.
>
> . . .
>
> 'Tis wise, for Herculian were his task, my Guelph
> To please his readers or to praise thyself.
>
> . . .
>
> How like our Monarch and his Bard elect—
> Prince of a party, poet of a sect.
>
> . . .
>
> Impartial Liege! whose equal judgment takes
> Favourites from dirt—and minstrels from the Lakes—
> Oh since so far thy tender mercy reaches,
> With Southey's songs abolish Jenky's speeches.[1]

A reader might be tempted to see the phrase "Pye's Parnassus" as sarcastically referring to a dunghill, dustheap, or other such vile elevation. But during the latter part of 1813 Byron's mind was seriously taken by the poetical mountain and his, Scott's, and Southey's particular places on it. On 17 November Byron's journal alludes to reviews comparing him with Scott, and with Scott and Southey (LJ 3:208–9). The entry for 24 November contains a triangular diagram of the "Gradus ad Parnassum" with Scott at the pinnacle, Rogers next, Moore and Campbell in the stratum just below, and "Southey.—Wordsworth.—Coleridge." filling the layer just above the base, which is reserved for "The Many." (LJ 3:220) As

Byron presents it, Southey's position on the mountain is lowly, but he is on the slope—and the danger seems to be that his political exaltation (to the laureateship) might be misread as a poetic apotheosis.

Byron takes pains to correct any such error of perception in an 1814 letter to James Hogg, the poet called "the Ettrick Shepherd":

"Stick you to Walter Scott, my good friend, and do not talk any more stuff about his not being willing to give you real advice, if you really will ask for real advice. You love Southey, forsooth—I am sure Southey loves nobody but himself, however. I hate these talkers one and all, body and soul. They are a set of the most despicable impostors—that is my opinion of them. They know nothing of the world; and what is poetry, but the reflection of the world? What sympathy have this people with the spirit of this stirring age? . . . Look at their beastly vulgarity, when they wish to be homely; and their exquisite stuff, when they clap on sail, and aim at fancy. Coleridge is the best of the trio—but bad is the best. Southey should have been a parish-clerk, and Wordsworth a man-midwife—both in darkness. I doubt if either of them ever got drunk, and I am of the old creed of Homer the wine-bibber. (LJ 4:85).

In going on at such length, Byron shows how seriously he takes the threat of poets he affects to despise: partly, perhaps, because he sees some of the merit in some of their works, but mostly because his worldly experience has shown him that forms of recognition are easily confused. Byron himself would not stoop to be state poet to the Georges—but he understands that the man who takes up that job will gain some (if not much) literary deference, and he is not sublimely detached enough to suffer in silence while a writer whose poetry he does not esteem reaps the rewards of laureateship, however tawdry those honors may be.

Byron also had compelling political reasons for disapproving of any laureate named by that prince who, after favoring the Whigs in earlier years, had on assuming full powers of Regency in 1812 disappointed the members of the loyal opposition by forming a government that kept them just where they had been under George III—out of place. As Malcolm Kelsall points out, this bitter betrayal of the Whig party just when it thought its long "wilderness years" coming to an end coincided with Byron's decision to involve himself in the politics of the upper house.[2] Byron's chosen party had hoped to take the helm under the Prince Regent's patronage but instead found itself facing the prospect of things as usual—a Tory ministry headed by Perceval and, after his assassination in May 1812, by Liverpool. Indignant at such rejection, the leading Whigs turned on the regent with virulence. For his part, Byron assumed (first anonymously in the *Morning Chronicle*, later avowedly in the second edition of *Lara*) a kind of antilaureate status with his "Lines to a Lady Weeping," occasional verse expressing solidarity with the reversionary interest, as was the Whig custom— the novelty being that this interest centered no longer on the Prince of Wales but instead on his daughter, Princess Charlotte.

For all these political and personal reasons, Byron would perhaps have felt hostility towards any poet who took the laureateship offered by the Prince Regent, that betrayer of Whig hopes. Wronged by such a laureate, Byron would trade mere hostility for hatred, which is just what happened in the final, most famous phase of his literary relationship with Southey—a phase whose commemorative documents include *Don Juan*. The report that Southey had been passing gossip and judgment on him, Shelley, Mary Godwin, and Claire Clairmont (the so-called "League of Incest") and the misconception that Southey had been author of a *Quarterly Review* essay hostile to Hunt but obliquely attacking Shelley engendered the blistering Dedication to *Don Juan*, a masterful piece of invective that was not published during Byron's lifetime. Byron, acting on the advice of Hobhouse and others, honorably held the passage back from publication because he was not within reach to fight the man his lines so effectively impugned. Southey's alluding, in his preface to *A Vision of Judgment*, to a "Satanic School" of poetry led by Lord Byron provoked a harsh published reply, a note in the appendix to *The Two Foscari*. Southey's response took the form of a letter to the editor of the *Courier*. Byron wrote a long and angry refutation to the same paper; but, no doubt recognizing that the prose tirade had served better as private catharsis than it would as public revenge, he did not send or publish his fulmination (LJ 9:95–100). Instead, and far more effectively, he trumped Southey's *Vision* with his own.[3] Thus the war was won by Lord Byron: *The* supplanted *A*, sharp-eyed satire undid cloudy apotheosis, and poetry beat out prose as the weapon of choice. These exchanges of paper bullets were years ahead, though, when Southey published

Letters from England, and Byron may or may not have read it. So let us return to 1804, where we find Southey sitting down to write his fictionalized travelogue.

In setting himself such a task, Southey was mining a vein he hoped to find profitable. A letter dated 15 October 1804 announces the scheme to his friend Rickman: "I have a plan for making a saleable book in the shape of translated Letters from a Spaniard in England, meaning thereby to transmute certain of my opinions and some of my knowledge into chairs tables etc., hoping I should have said, for this is the philosophers stone in the pursuit of which some damned thing or other has always baffled me."[4] This pragmatically conceived enterprise suited both the public's tastes and Southey's talents. Unlike the world of the 1980s, where travelers outnumber readers, Southey's England was a society with more readers than travelers. Going about was more difficult, dangerous, and slow than it would be a few years later—in fact, the substantial parts of the world under Napoleonic sway were downright inaccessible for English people. The resulting hearty English appetite for travel literature can be clearly seen in any early nineteenth-century periodical's list of new books.[5]

Prior to *Letters from England*, Southey had already played some part in the production and criticism of travel writing. In 1797, two years after his first trip to the Iberian peninsula, he had published *Letters Written during a Short Residence in Spain and Portugal*, a volume that, unlike his epic poems of the period, was popular enough to warrant a second edition in 1799 and eventually a third edition in 1808, the year after *Letters from England* first appeared. Besides writing travel impressions himself, Southey read those of others, both for pleasure and for profit. The year before he came up with his traveling Spaniard idea, Southey was reviewing other journeyers' accounts, as he comments in a letter to his friend and patron Charles Watkin Williams Wynn: "I have a heavy job in hand—almost all the last years Voyages and Travels to review!"[6]

Given the popularity of directly reported travels and Southey's previous success in that field, why did he suppress the fact of his authorship and concoct a Spanish persona to voice his observations and opinions? Several reasons are evident.[7] Because he was writing with an eye toward profit, Southey would do well to work in a mode that had proven marketable; and the eighteenth-century success of such itinerant aliens as Goldsmith's Citizen of the World showed English readers to be interested in seeing how their nation and its ways might appear to an outsider, a being privileged to record details of their life and culture too minute or ordinary for a native traveler to mention without looking simpleminded. Contemporary reviewers noted and sometimes deplored this particularity in *Espriella*, whose compulsive fascination even leads him to describe, one by one, the utensils of the English hearth. As a Continental Catholic, Don Manuel comments naturally, fully, and freely on English religion's heretical ways and through his dogmatism obliquely permits Southey to grind his own anti-Papist axe; as a humane but disinterested outsider, the Spaniard pays close attention to, and sharply protests against, the human abuses of British manufacturing and industry, thus allowing Southey to voice his views without being held strictly accountable for them.

Southey's invention of a pseudo-Spaniard and concealment of himself could have wider uses as well. The mystery of an anonymous author can stimulate public curiosity and thereby increase purchases. In an age of fiercely partisan periodicals and reviewers, a work may be more fairly appraised if its author's identity is unknown; and Southey's personal awareness of how unjustly an acknowledged work could be judged appears in a letter he wrote to Miss Barker in October 1807, a few months after the debut of *Letters from England*: "Pretty work, this reviewing, Senhora! I am abused because one reviewer hates Coleridge and now am to be praised because another is a friend of Miss Seward's."[8] Finally, Southey may have relished the joke of concealment: however pompous he seemed to Byron, his letters (especially those of the prelaureate period) sometimes reveal a sensibility that would have savored the prospect of a joke at the expense of his contemporary readers.

Would Byron have been among those contemporary readers, either when *Letters from England* first came out or later, during the time when he first thought of *Don Juan*? Intuition and internal evidence lead to a yes, but external evidence does not offer certainty. Byron does not mention reading the work in his letters or in the "Memorandum of Reading" he composed in November 1807. His friends and memorialists do not, so far as I can tell, report his familiarity with the book. There is no evidence that Byron's personal library contained a copy of *Letters from England* in 1813, 1816, or 1827, the three times his books were sold: but though the title does not appear among the individual items in any of the sale catalogues, each list mentions "various others" or "odd lots," which might or might not have included the book. Nonetheless, even lacking proof positive, one can base an argument that Byron did read *Letters from England*, and that he made use of *Letters from England* in Don Juan, on evidence external to the two texts themselves. Let me begin by addressing the first of these problems.

It is universally acknowledged that Byron was a prodigious reader of things in general—poetry and prose, fiction and nonfiction, classics and the latest sensation—but why does it seem likely that he would have read *Letters from England* in particular? Because he was, over years and even after personal hostility might have made other men overlook an enemy's accomplishments, a reader of Southey in particular—again, poetry and prose. A man of the world, Byron read not only matter of his own choosing but also works recommended by friends or mentioned in the reviews. And the reviews did take note of *Letters from England*. The most sustained and serious critique of the travel letters comes in the eleventh volume of the influential *Edinburgh Review*, a source we know Byron—whose *Hours of Idleness* had, like *Letters from England*, been published in the summer of 1807—did not ignore in January 1808. The same January issue of the *Edinburgh Review* that gives *Letters from England* a twenty-page assessment notices and then dismisses Byron's *Hours of Idleness* in five famously condescending pages that goaded Byron into writing *English Bards and Scotch Reviewers* and also reviews a book that Byron would despise and attack for the rest of his life, the Rev. Samuel Lisle Bowles's edition of Pope.[9] Byron was a faithful member of the *Edinburgh*'s audience, so one might advance a case for his seeing most anything appearing in the periodical during his day; but the issue reviewing *Letters from England* is, for more than one reason, a volume he surely read.

The *Edinburgh*'s reviewer for *Letters from England* was none other than its editor, Francis Jeffrey. His comments single out for particular notice a number of the passages and elements suggesting parallels with Don Juan: substantial descriptions of the port town of Falmouth, St. Paul's cathedral, and Drury Lane Theatre (where Espriella sees a production of Don Juan) are quoted, as are passages expressing Espriella's sentiments on the English manufacturing system and on the widespread belief in scientific fads and quackery. Jeffrey, like most of the other reviewers, acknowledges the transparency of the Spanish mask. He further suggests that this device leads to some of Espriella's weaknesses—the lengthy quasi-Catholic laments over "heresy" that fit ill with the "philosophical liberality and intrepid reasoning" otherwise prevailing and the distinctively English quality of the wordplay. "We have seldom seen a character, indeed, worse dressed or supported," says Jeffrey, "and no one is in any danger of being imposed on by the Spanish title, who would not believe in the reality of ghosts at the playhouse, or vestal virgins at the masquerade. . . . The whole strain of the sentiment and diction is manifestly English; and the author cannot even refrain from indulging himself in a variety of puns and verbal pleasantries, to which it would not be easy to find an equivalent in 'the original Spanish.' "[10] The tenor of this passage is such that I cannot help thinking it, as well as *Letters from England*, stored in Byron's mind for retrieval in the early days of *Don Juan*. At the very least, Jeffrey's review is forceful enough to have compelled any reader's attention, however momentarily, to consider Southey's book. A wide-reading young collegian with his own travels yet before him would be most unlikely, I conjecture, to forget the assessment or forego a fuller acquaintance with Don Manuel. But if Byron did not read *Letters from England* when it came out, in his Cambridge days, a firsthand acquaintance with Spain, Spaniards, and Southey's "perfect" prose would make it likely for him to do so later—perhaps after the third and last of the contemporary English editions appeared in 1814.

If Byron read *Letters from England*, what makes it likely that he would have recalled its details and used them in *Don Juan*? Taken generally, this question is easily answered. Reading and then forgetting would be most uncharacteristic of a man whose amazing verbal memory struck many people—Medwin, Trelawney, Lady Blessington, Byron himself—as worth comment. Elizabeth Boyd builds upon widely held belief and voices what has come to be general opinion when she says that "The combination of an astonishing verbal memory and the rapid association of ideas is probably at the bottom of the reminiscences and echoes in all of Byron's poetry."[11] What Byron remembered, he used, and especially in *Don Juan*, which is nothing if not his recollections of and reflections on literary and personal experiences—a miscellany sufficiently wide and deep that it represents and recreates the history and culture of his society as well. Critic after critic has demonstrated how extensively Byron applied his reading in the creation or enrichment of Don Juan—indeed, it would be more surprising for Byron to have passed up a potentially fruitful source such as Letters from England than to have exploited it.

If Byron read and borrowed from Letters from England, why did he not acknowledge the fact? Why not even call attention to it, as he does elsewhere in naming his satire of Southey's A Vision of Judgment after its subject or, more subtly, in alluding to the perplexing "system" spun out by Coleridge in Biographia Literaria in the Dedication to Don Juan—anti-Laker invective Coleridge's Biographia partially provoked? Byron is not alone among authors in this sin of omission. Such silences seem to rise out of two difficulties: it is hard to be original, and it is hard to be generous. Human nature makes an artist, like anyone else, willing enough to admit using another's effort when that use has involved belittling or refuting the precursor's work and thereby demonstrating one's superiority. Making constructive use of another work is not so easy to acknowledge. Doing so, one admits to achieving a vantage point by standing on someone else's shoulders rather than by looming up in magnificent isolation. And as we shall see, Letters from England is a work more often worth admiration and emulation than mockery.

Let us now turn to the parallels within. A comparison of Letters from England and Don Juan might well start with the acts of jocular masquerade that begin both works. Southey's travelogue begins with a preface by the "translator," who informs his reader that "The remarks of Foreign Travellers upon our own country have always been so well received by the Public, that no apology can be necessary for offering to it the present Translation."[12] The translator goes on to distance himself from the so-called author by appraising him, by telling us that Espriella has been diligent and generally impartial but sometimes misled by the "deplorable superstitions" of his country and his faith. The better to distinguish English translator from Spanish author, Southey then supplies a preface by the supposed don, who notes the passion of the English for publishing their travels and the rarity of both travel and travel writing among Spaniards, announces the extent and circumstances of his visit (some eighteen months, mostly spent domesticated with a London family), acknowledges the aid of his father confessor, whose efforts have enriched the sections on religion, and sets up truth as his goal—a goal shared, much of the time, by the narrator of *Don Juan*. Having contrived an English translator as well as a Spanish narrator, Southey takes pains to keep readers aware of both personae. The means of recalling Don Manuel's Spanishness are varied and fairly continual. A single, simple device, the editorial "I beg to differ," underlines the presence of Espriella's English interpreter, who briefly comments when he judges the don to have misread a detail and even claims to have cut material inappropriate for an English edition. For instance, when Espriella misinterprets the name of an English cut of beef—"The loin of beef is always called Sir, which is the same as Senor"—a note explains, "*D. Manuel has mistaken the word which is Surloin, quasi Super-loin, the upper part of it*" (LE 89). When Don Manuel has explained to his Spanish audience a joke on Carlton House and the duke of York's house at Whitehall, the translator intrudes to excise, giving as his reason, "*There is an explanation of the jest in the text which the translator has thought proper to omit, as, however necessary to foreign readers, it must needs seem impertinent to an English one*" (LE 52).

Setting up personae is not the same thing as making them believable, and from the first Southey does not seem to have intended credibility for either Don Manuel or the translator. There are too many inconsistencies for suspension of disbelief. The ingenuous outsider amazed by hearthside accessories becomes, a few pages later, an ingenious analyst of popular sentiment and political change in the era of Pitt and Addington. Southey's personal preferences and prejudices appear throughout the work—in the political, social, and religious opinions, in the detailed admiration of the Lake District (where Southey lived), in the disparagement of Oxford (from which Southey was sent down). The well-read portion of the public would be aware that Southey had traveled in Portugal and Spain and that he had set up as an expert in things Iberian. Readers with particular talent for induction might recall that he had previously attempted anonymous publication on a Spanish subject, though, as Southey writes to Wynn, "The booksellers have blabbed my name as the translator of *Amadis*, and I have been obliged to make new terms and avow it."[13] Noticing that Longman, the bookseller of *Amadis*, *Letters Written during a Short Residence in Spain and Portugal*, and most of Southey's other works, had published *Letters from England* might have turned suspicions to near certainties.

Though Southey's two prefaces are meant to be less than opaque, Byron's preface to *Don Juan* is, as we have already begun to see, downright and designedly transparent. Like Southey's two prefaces, it ostensibly distances but covertly connects the author and his work. The precise identity of the storyteller is undisclosed, but Byron intends for his own audience to speculate actively on the nature of this narrator, as the following remarks make clear: "The reader is further requested to suppose him (to account for his knowledge of English) either an Englishman settled in Spain—or a Spaniard who had travelled in England—perhaps one of the Liberals who have subsequently been so liberally rewarded by Ferdinand of grateful memory—for his restoration" (DJ 83). The Dedication's previous mentions of Wordsworth (a Laker), added to these allusions to Spanish travels and political opportunism, conjure up the image of that other Laker Robert Southey in the mind of any reader familiar with the workings of Byron's mind. And sure enough, the Laureate's name follows directly: "Having supposed as much of this as the utter impossibility of such a supposition will admit, the reader is requested to extend his supposed power of supposing so far as to conceive that the Dedication to Mr. Southey, and several stanzas of the poem itself, are interpolated by the English editor" (DJ 83–84). The reader is then urged to imagine reasons for the editorial venom. Presume the "English editor" envious of the turncoat success of the author of *Wat Tyler*—disgusted by the applause Southey borrows in "post-obits" payable by audiences from future ages—personally infuriated, it may be, by some "gross calumny invented or circulated by this Pantisocratic apostle of apostasy, who is sometimes as unguarded in his assertions as atrocious in his conjectures." (DJ 84–85) Like Southey, Byron has taken pains to create false machinery for his work. The remarks quoted above present themselves as signs meant to mislead, but no intelligent reader of the day could for a moment have supposed them to do anything but point directly to Byron as author of the piece. The disparagement of Wordsworth, the political, poetical, and personal reasons to hate Southey, and even the details of the Spanish setting, that vividly specific memory from

Byron's Iberian excursion with Hobhouse, afford no other interpretation.

The prefaces to *Letters from England* and *Don Juan* present similar
signals to readers; but there are other affinities, sometimes striking
and sometimes diffuse, other echoes of Southey's work in Byron's.
Early on, Southey's Don Manuel, who is traveling as Juan does in
cantos 5–8 in the company of an Englishman named Johnson, sets
out a literary challenge that might be the one Byron picks up in the
English cantos: "But if ever some new Cervantes should arise to
write a mock heroic, let him make his hero pass through a custom
house on his descent to the infernal regions" (LE 18). Don Miguel's
port of entry is Falmouth and Don Juan's is Dover, but the dirty,
greedy, tiresome introduction to the island is the same. So is the
world encountered, the early nineteenth-century England described some pages back. The details presented in *Letters from England* echo in the ears of someone who knows the English cantos.
As Don Manuel approaches London over that highwayman's haven the Surrey heath, such a reader might think of Juan, assailed
and victorious, on Bagshot Common. Espriella's metropolis is everywhere reminiscent of Juan's: each Spaniard's account contains
reference to the long, well-lit streets filled with vast throngs in
which one feels truly solitary. Both Southey and Byron anticipate
Disraeli in alluding to the two nations, "the Solar and the Lunar
races" as Espriella calls them, the respective denizens of the East
and the West End.

The Lunar race's West End in Espriella's account is much the
same as the "microcosm on stilts" explored by Don Juan. All the
world is ransacked for the aristocratic table, then the French dictionary is pillaged to name the exotic dishes. In *Letters from England*
the exquisites migrate according to that second sense called fashion; and their fads, preoccupations, and varying types receive the
careful attention paid them in the English cantos. This world is one
where, as in *Don Juan*, "Society is smooth'd to that excess, / That
manners hardly differ more than dress" (13.94). Southey's verdict
on the leveling of manners in a mobile society is close to Byron's,
so close that Juan's adventures among the inhabitants of Blank-
Blank Square and Norman Abbey could be taken as an expansion
on Don Manuel's following observation: "The great alteration in

society which has taken place during the present reign, tends to make men more like one another. The agriculturist has caught the spirit of commerce; the merchant is educated like the nobleman; the sea-officer has the polish of high life; and London is now so often visited, that the manners of the metropolis are to be found in every country gentleman's house" (LE 140).

These and other such similarities are striking but not worth belaboring here—readers interested in pursuing specifics can turn to the appended list of selected parallels.[14] Most of the details Southey notices merely recall analogues presented in Don Juan, but sometimes the earlier work gives a sort of gloss on the later. For example, Byron mentions doors with knockers and alludes to "double knockings" (DJ 12.67), but Southey explains why the phenomenon is worth a Spaniard's notice: "The English doors have knockers instead of bells, and there is an advantage in this which you would not immediately perceive. The bell, by whomsoever it be pulled, must always give the same sound, but the knocker may be so handled as to explain who plays upon it, and accordingly it has its systematic set of signals" (LE 76). Similarly, readers of Letters from England learn (LE 290) that "the sigh supprest," a phrase Byron employs in his memorable anatomy of ennui (DJ 15.3), also names a color that was as fashionable as was the affectation of boredom in Regency society.

The chief difference in London as experienced by the two dons is not what is shown but what is meant. Small and prosaic matters described by Southey gain poetic and ethical value in Byron's presentation, as if the narrator of the English cantos, now mounted on Pegasus and out to make his poem "a moral model," had taken it upon himself to refute the inferiority of modern subjects asserted in another of Espriella's allusions to Cervantes: "The histories of chivalry were useful, because they carried the imagination into a world of different manners; and many a man imbibed from them Don Quixote's high-mindedness and emulation, without catching his insanity. But these books [modern chronicles] represent ordinary and contemporary manners, and make love the main business of life, which both sexes at a certain age are sufficiently disposed to believe" (LE 349). In Don Juan this high-minded emulation Espriella admires is a danger to be overcome by looking at things as they really are, and to do that one must confront civilization's present realities as well as its past achievements. The moralist's clear-eyed vision sees that love is the main business of life—and, at least in England's marriage market, "business" in a way richer than Espriella intends to suggest.

It is perhaps not surprising that two comparably educated gentle-men, one talented and one gifted with genius but both poets, should notice many of the same things when looking at more or less the same subject at about the same time. This we have seen to be true of the author of *Letters from England* and the author of *Don Juan*, both observing English society in the early years of the nineteenth century. The literary uses to which Southey and Byron put particu-lars may vary—such variation may be what reveals the difference between Southey's talent and Byron's genius—but the two men's opinions on what they see are not far apart. That similarity is surprising, for Byron's readers have come to expect him to oppose whatever Southey affirms. But the Southey of *Letters from England* is not the Tory laureate he would become. Nor is he the naive Pan-tisocrates he had been. Beneath the Iberian traveling cloak that covers him, the Southey of *Letters from England* is a humane English-man whose reading and Continental experience are potentially broad enough to save him from insularity.

Robert Southey in 1807 was not unlike Byron in possessing these attributes and not unlike him in cherishing the social and moral values such advantages promote. The England of Don Manuel's *Letters* is, like Don Juan's, a nation of shopkeepers. Commerce per-vades both works, just as *usura* does Pound's *Cantos*. London, for Southey and Byron alike, is the great market where all things can be had for a price. The symbolic shape of the capital is clear to Don Manuel, who notices how buildings of the City, London's financial district, shut off St. Paul's Cathedral, thus suggesting the society's true faith and first priority: "The value of ground in this capital is too great to be sacrificed to beauty by a commercial nation: unless, therefore, another conflagration should lay London in ashes, the Londoners will never fairly see their own cathedral" (*LE* 50). It is interesting that Don Juan's first sight of London, from the Kentish vantage point of Shooter's Hill, also includes St. Paul's—though the edifice is accorded more prominence than dignity: "A huge, dun cupola, like a foolscap crown / On a fool's head—and there is London town!" (*DJ* 10.82)

In the passage just quoted, Don Juan looks down from an elevation associated with highwaymen. Don Manuel has an opportunity to gaze from high in the dome of St. Paul's, and what he sees is the City, London's financial district. Viewing London from above, the two protagonists physically approximate the superiority Byron's narrator and Southey's English editor both display; and a mental montage of the two Spaniards' vantage points shows the essence of the metropolis—the connection between thievery and commerce. Espriella voices this insight in language both Southey and Byron would endorse: "I was looking down upon the inhabitants [habitations?] of a million of human beings; upon the single spot whereon were crowded together more wealth, more splendour, more ingenuity, more worldly wisdom, and, alas! more worldly blindness, poverty, depravity, dishonesty and wretchedness, than upon any other spot in the whole habitable earth" (LE 153–54).

Giving Espriella solid objections to the source of this profusion, Southey is no defender of the status quo. Like Byron and his liberal colleagues, Southey shows himself indignant about the country's poor laws (LE 142–43). "Woe to that country where the peasantry and the poor are the same!" he generalizes about rural indigence (LE 146). The miserable condition of the urban poor in Birmingham and Manchester arouses Espriella's compassion as he travels in the Midlands: "When we look at gold, we do not think of the poor slaves who dug it from the caverns of the earth; but I shall never think of the wealth of England, without remembering that I have been in the mines" (LE 197). As Don Manuel continues in this vein, Southey diverges in a small way from Byron, who but a few years hence would be defending the frame-breakers in the House of Lords. Though both writers oppose child labor and the unfair distribution of manufacturing profits, Southey sees mechanization as perhaps the most promising solution to the problems of inhumane industrialization.

Turning to political commodities, as he does in letter 48, Southey addresses the bribed voter, the bought borough, and the placeman, all to be sharply pricked by Byron's satire in the English cantos. What Espriella observes on British politics sounds not unlike what one would predict and get from such Radicals as Sir Francis Burdett or, a few years later, Byron's faithful friend John Cam Hobhouse. "Any thing like election in the plain sense of the word is unknown in England" (LE 283)—even inserted in a Spanish traveler's narrative, these are not words to expect from the pen of a man who, as *Don Juan* tells us, "turn'd out a Tory at / Last" (*DJ* Dedication, 1). Southey would become a defender of the established system, but in *Espriella* he recognizes it as a series of antagonisms and a web of contradictions. The contradictions woven together in the following paragraph of Espriella's observations are not unlike the Byronic narrator's good-humored but judgmental remarks on England's inconsistencies and follies:

> They love to be at war, but do not love to pay for their amusement; and now, that they are at peace, they begin to complain that the newspapers are not worth reading, and rail at the French as if they really wished to begin again. There is not a people upon the earth who have a truer love for their Royal family than the English, yet they caricature them in the most open and insolent manner. They boast of the freedom of the press, yet as surely and systematically punish the author who publishes any thing obnoxious, and the bookseller who sells it, as we in our country should prevent the publication. They cry out against intolerance, and burn down the houses of those whom they regard as heretics. They love liberty; go to war with their neighbours, because they chose to become republicans, and insist upon the right of enslaving the negroes. They hate the French and ape all their fashions, ridicule their neologisms and then naturalize them, laugh at their inventions and then adopt them, cry out against their political measures and then imitate them; the levy in mass, the telegraph, and the income-tax are all from France. And the common people, not to be behind-hand with their betters in absurdity, boast as heartily of the roast beef of Old England, as if they were not obliged to be content themselves with bread and potatoes. Well may punch be the favourite liquor of the English,—it is a truly emblematic compound of contrarieties. (*LE* 92–93)

Granted that *Don Juan* and *Letters from England* both take obviously artificial itinerant Spaniards through England. Granted that both works filter their respective outsiders' adventures and observations through intermediaries (*Don Juan*'s narrator and *Letters from England*'s "translator") less obviously distinct from their authors. Granted that the two works correspond in many particulars of detail and description, matters at which we have briefly looked. Granted that many of the positions advanced and opinions expressed are far more similar than one would expect Byron's and Southey's to be. Even granting all these things, where is truly convincing internal evidence of more than literary coincidence? Why believe that Byron had in mind Southey's model when he set out to be that "new Cervantes" for whom Espriella calls, that sadly smiling philosopher the Byronic narrator more or less admits to being at the start of canto 13 as he vows "I now mean to be serious"?

The most obvious answer to such questions is that Southey mentions Don Juan and the form he took in turn-of-the-nine-teenth-century England in letter 18, where Espriella accompanies his English friend Johnson on a theatrical outing. This episode is one of those discussed and extracted by Jeffrey, though the *Edinburgh* does not quote the particular passage we shall examine below. The theater Espriella and Johnson patronize is Drury Lane, with Byronic connections of its own; the principal attraction is *The Winter's Tale*, with Kemble and Mrs. Siddons; the pantomime is *Don Juan*; and the circumstances surrounding the theatrical evening are a complicated blend of fact and fiction worthy of Byron at his most mystifying. Espriella's letters are sporadically dated, but the fact that letter 13 is from Tuesday, 4 May 1802, and letter 31 from 1 July of the same year makes it seem that the Drury Lane performance described would take place between the two dates, and significantly closer to the earlier one. Sure enough, the *London Times* announces *A Winter's Tale* with Kemble and Mrs. Siddons, to be followed by *Don Juan*, for a single 1802 performance—on Tuesday, 11 May. The promised program was not, however, staged. Instead, on 11 May *A Winter's Tale* was followed by *Adelmorn: The Outlaw*. This change of plan seems to have taken place only a few days before the performance. The playbill for Friday, 7 May, announces *Don Juan*, while the next day's listing gives *Adelmorn*—and the *Times* continues advertising *Don Juan* throughout the period.

Discussion of how the English theater interprets Don Juan is a natural, perhaps almost inevitable, topic for a pseudo-Spanish work of the kind Southey was concocting; but there is no certain accounting for the curious appearance of this particular "half-real" stage production in *Letters from England*. Perhaps Southey simply made a mistake and described the announced performance without verifying his facts. Perhaps Southey knew of the Drury Lane change of plans and selected this particular evening of theater because it was actually scheduled but never really staged—thus blending, and suggesting to the observant insider by its very nature, the hybrid of fact and fiction that is *Letters from England*. Or perhaps the advertisement of *A Winter's Tale* and *Don Juan* stuck in Southey's mind because of the felicitous pairing. The play may be a classic and the pantomime a popular spectacle, but both are based on equally exotic tales; and it is especially interesting that their radically different outcomes are precipitated by a living "statue" (Hermione) in the one case, a "living" statue (the Commandant) in the other.

Whatever Southey's motivation, his mouthpiece Don Manuel has this to say of the production, the character, and the legend:

The afterpiece this evening was *Don Juan*, our old story of the reprobate cavalier and the statue, here represented wholly in pantomime. Nothing could be more insipid than all the former part of this drama, nothing more dreadful, and indeed unfit for scenic representation than the catastrophe: but either the furies of Aeschylus were more terrible than European devils, or our Christian ladies are less easily frightened than the women of Greece, for this is a favourite spectacle everywhere. I know not whether the invention be ours or the Italians'; be it whose it may, the story of the Statue is in a high style of fancy, truly fine and terrific. The sound of his marble footsteps upon the stage struck a dead silence through the house. It is to this machinery that the popularity of the piece is owing; and in spite of the dulness which precedes this incident, and the horror which follows it, I do not wonder it is popular. Still it would be decorous in English writers to speak with a little less disrespect of the Spanish stage, and of the taste of a Spanish audience, while their own countrymen continue to represent and to delight in one of the most monstrous of all our dramas. (LE 101)

Espriella's ascription of monstrosity to the stage versions of the Don Juan legend is an opinion Byron certainly encountered elsewhere. Coleridge's assertions in *Biographia Literaria* about the Don Juan dramas—that they are grotesque, extravagant, and purely imaginative, peopled with mere impersonated abstractions and demonstrating obedience to nature as the sole human virtue—seem to have given Byron positions to reverse, disprove, and explore in his poem.[15] In *Don Juan*, one Laker reminds Byron of another; and thinking of Coleridge's attack on *Bertram* and discussion of the Don Juan plays would surely have led him, had he read *Letters from England* or even heard much of it, to recall Southey's remarks on the "reprobate cavalier." If those remarks came to

mind, Byron must have taken them as material for metamorphosis
or rebuttal. Espriella asserts that "nothing could be more insipid
than all the former part of this drama"—the very portion of the tale
Byron makes piquant in canto 1. If Don Juan's story has hitherto
proven a "favourite spectacle" with Christian ladies, Byron's improvisational epic seems set out from the first to offend contemporary feminine sensibilities. The Statue and his attendant effects may
be a "high style of fancy, truly fine and terrific," but Byron will have
nothing to do with marble footsteps or the high style: neither the
"truly fine" nor the "terrific" has a place in his first canto. Instead it
will be his task to take what Espriella terms "dulness" and make it
the stuff of epic, an accomplishment that can be seen to invert
Southey's customary achievement, the transformation of epic stuff
to dulness.

A reader alert for correspondences will see that many of the
ordinary matters or realities (to use terms less damning than *dulness*) that become epic stuff in *Don Juan* could be taken from *Letters
from England*. The details and opinions already presented could be
such borrowings; but there are also certain passages from Don
Manuel's letters that can be seen as yet richer ore, passages that
may have offered Byron stories, themes, and details to adopt,
assertions to revise, ponder, discredit, or burlesque. Let us look at
two such extracts, the first of which shows Espriella contrasting the
northern and southern races, a recurring intellectual occupation of
Don Juan's cosmopolitan narrator—and also of that Continent-born
cosmopolite Madame de Staël:[16]

One of the great philosophers here has advanced a theory that
the nervous and electric fluids are the same, both being condensed
light. If this be true, sun-shine is the food of the brain; and it is thus
explained why the southern nations are so much more spiritual
than the English, and why they in their turn rank higher in the scale
of intellect than their northern neighbours.

Spanish gravity is the jest of this people. Whenever they introduce a Spaniard upon the stage, it is to ridicule him for his pride,
his jealousy, and his mustachios. According to their notions, all our
women who are not locked up in convents, are locked up at
home; guarded by duennas as vigilant as dragons, and husbands,
every one of whom is as fierce as the Grand Turk. They believe,
also, that a Spaniard thinks it beneath his dignity ever to laugh,
except when he is reading Don Quixotte; [*sic*] then, indeed, his
muscles are permitted to relax." (LE 411)

Don Manuel then goes on to say how jolly a Sunday evening at home in grave Catholic Spain, where he might attend the theater or a bullfight, would be in comparison to the dreary Protestant Sabbath prevailing in London—a contrast remarkably similar to one Byron would set down in *Childe Harold* (canto 1, stanzas 68–81) a few years later.

Sunny south and moral north—British hypocrisy and Mediterranean gaiety—Don Quixote and a Grand Turk whose mustachios, like those of Espriella's stage Spaniard, are ridiculous—all these appear in *Don Juan*. So does the dreariness of an English Sunday. *Don Juan* laughs at Spanish gravity in Donna Inez, Spanish pride in Don Jóse, Spanish jealousy in Don Alfonso. Donna Julia is guarded by a female companion whose dragonlike vigilance serves the cause of adultery, not fidelity. Julia's liaison with Juan sends her to the conventional convent, but Byron's mention of the other part of the notion, securing women with locks, comes later in *Don Juan*, where the cultural contrast being set up is a matter of longitude rather than latitude and the jailer-husband is none other than the Grand Turk: "Thus in the East they are extremely strict, / And *Wedlock* and a *Padlock* mean the same" (DJ 5.158).

As for the "great philosopher" with his theory of nervous and electric fluids, even he is to be found in *Don Juan*. The sage is Newton, whose discussion of the "most subtle spirit which pervades and lies hid in all gross bodies" appears in the General Scholium written for the second edition of the *Principia*.[17] Allusions to Newton appear at several points in *Don Juan*, but he is mentioned most directly and extensively at the start of canto 10, as the Byronic narrator begins a meditation on human knowledge and its fruits with a witty juxtaposition of Sir Isaac, Adam, and the two apples that led, in different ways, to fortunate falls. If Adam's apple-initiated fall opened the way for humanity's ascent to heaven through Christ, the apple whose fall demonstrated gravity to Newton will lead man through technology to the stars: "For ever since immortal man hath glowed / With all kinds of mechanics, and full soon / Steam-engines will conduct him to the Moon" (DJ 10.2). The idea of human "glowing" suggests the conjunction between nervous energy and light mentioned by Espriella. This suggestion grows still stronger in the next stanza, as *Don Juan's* narrator, sparked by his own electrical impulse, speaks of the poet's creative quest for truth in similarly Newtonian terms:

And wherefore this exordium?—Why, just now,
　　In taking up this paltry sheet of paper,
My bosom underwent a glorious glow,
　　And my internal Spirit cut a caper:
And though so much inferior, as I know,
　　To those who, by the dint of glass and vapour,
Discover stars, and sail in the wind's eye,
I wish to do as much by Poesy.　　　　　　(DJ 10.3)

Unable to read the stars, the Byronic narrator aspires at least to shun "the common shore" and to skim "The Ocean of Eternity" (DJ 10.4), an image and phrase reminiscent of Don Juan's earlier allusions to Newton (DJ 7.5 and 9.18), both of which present Newton's picture of himself as but a boy playing on the shore of the great, undiscovered ocean of truth. For all his modesty about the powers of poetry, the Byronic narrator implicitly relies on it to let him outdistance the greatest of English natural philosophers.

As we have observed, Byron's mind may have returned to the Southey passage quoted above at various points during the writing of Don Juan. In contrast, the tale of the "Newbury renegado" can be seen as a possible source for many of the details that build one character, the Englishman called Johnson who is Juan's comrade in slavery and in arms. "Perhaps no place ever sent out so deliberate a renegado as this," observes Espriella during his stay in Newbury. "The man to whom I allude was married and settled here; affairs went on unfavourably, and, at length, he said deliberately to his wife, 'There can be no good in my remaining here; we are going on from bad to worse, and I shall be thrown into jail at last. Do you return to your friends, and I will go to Constantinople and turn Turk.' Accordingly, to Constantinople he went; and it is not very long since his widow, if so I may call her, received a friendly letter from him, saying, that the speculation had succeeded admirably, he was becoming a great man, had already three wives, and was not without hopes of attaining to the dignity of three tails" (LE 464).

Johnson, like the Newbury renegado, is nothing if not deliberate. His calculating prudence restrains and educates the impetuous and idealistic Juan: whenever we see them together, the Englishman plays Experience to Juan's Innocence. Unlike the Newbury renegado, Johnson has not planned to be in Constantinople, but being there he makes the most of his circumstances. Offered the chance to "turn Turk" via circumcision and disguise in Eastern dress, Johnson diplomatically accepts the change of costume and promises to think about the proffered operation. Like the Newbury renegado, Johnson is linked with three wives, though these alliances are serial rather than simultaneous and it better suits *Don Juan*'s themes for him not to acquire but to lose them, and in diverse ways: "I cried upon my first wife's dying day, / And also when my second ran away" (DJ 5.19). Juan, amazed that a man scarce thirty can have had three wives, asks about the third:

> "what did she?
> She did not run away, too, did she, sir?"
> "No, faith."—"What then?"—"I ran away from her." (DJ 15.20)

Tempting though it may be to think that Byron encountered the original of his Johnson on the pages of *Letters from England*, it is impossible to rule out other vectors of transmission. Southey had used the tale before in print, and it was very likely in general circulation for some time. Southey's 21 December 1807 letter to Rickman suggests this to have been so: "I am requested to omit the history of the Newbury Renegado, because it hurts his friends. This fellow, whose name is Baily, was in England about two years ago,—saw this same story told in my review of 'Wittmans' Travels,' and called upon A. Aikin, in his Turkish dress, and with his scymetar, to take vengeance upon him. Luckily, King Arthur was out of the way, or there had been a loss to the Round Table. Here's a Turk for you! He thinks no more of cutting off a man's head than he did of being circumcised."[18] The last sentence quoted, with its several echoes of *Don Juan*'s fifth canto, suggests that Byron may have been familiar with this postscript as well as the published anecdote; and the renegado's common English name may have reinforced, or even suggested Byron's choice of "Johnson" as well as his means of counterpoising the torturous rhymed catalogue of Russian heroes' names at Ismail: " 'Mongst them were several Englishmen of pith, / Sixteen called Thomson, and nineteen named Smith" (DJ 7.18).

Weighing the absurd complexity and variety of Slavic names against the comic monotony of British ones is not a simple exercise of balancing. It involves a nicely calculated blend of truth telling and falsification. Byron's resourceful epic catalogue of Russian heroes mingles real names (Meknop, for instance), travestied ones

(Tschitshakoff for Chicagov), and ridiculous fictions (such as Cho-kenoff). Making those English soldiers dignified by name mere multiples of Thomson and Smith shows that reduction can be as funny as proliferation. The two cultures represented by these sur-names are thus equally mocked. One nation appears bombastic, the other dull. It is the Byronic narrator, the word maker transmut-ing such apparently intractable and intrinsically tedious material to dazzling ottava rima, who emerges victorious from the bilingual skirmish, as is often the case in Don Juan, where, as we have already seen and shall see again, play on words—words imported or indigenous, well used or malappropriated, understood or miscon-strued—deepens into play on cultures.

The double perspective on language so characteristic of Don Juan is also evident in Letters from England. Earlier we observed how competence in English, and the comic mistakes brought on by in-competence, are Southey's means of distinguishing the translator from Espriella, with his explanations unneeded by English readers, his false etymology of "Sirloin," his naive half-understanding of English oaths (a distinctive partial ignorance he shares with Don Juan's mother, Inez). But Espriella devotes one full letter, his seventy-third, to remarks on the English language; and much of what he observes has direct bearing on Don Juan.

Espriella's letter begins with a warning that those who criticize foreign languages run certain risks: "He who ventures to criticize a foreign language, should bear in mind that he is in danger of exposing his own ignorance. 'What a vile language is yours!' said a Frenchman to an Englishman;—'you have the same word for three different things! There is ship, un vaisseau; ship (sheep) mouton; and ship (cheap) bon marché' " (LE 459). Because language is the essence of a culture, those who pretend to more linguistic knowl-edge than they possess are barbarians as well as impostors. Early in canto 1, we saw Donna Inez given a reputation for extraordinary learning "In every christian language ever named" (DJ 1.10), then stripped of the specific accomplishments attributed to her, and very often within the space of a line:

> She knew the Latin—that is, "the Lord's prayer,"
>   And Greek—the alphabet—I'm nearly sure;
> She read some French romances here and there,
>   Although her mode of speaking was not pure.   (DJ 1.13)

Inez's explicitly satirized linguistic hypocrisy swells to a national sin, as we have seen, when Byron marshals rhyme and meter to draw attention to how the English language arrogantly appropriates and then perverts foreign words, Juan and Quixote among many.

Stealing and importing another nation's vocabulary is for the most part a ruling-class crime. In the English cantos this piracy appears most prominently during the banquet scenes, where every food, however plain and homegrown, has a French sauce or style to make it fashionable. Here again Byron could be following the lead of Espriella, who makes this observation on the naming of animal foods in England: "They have one name for an animal in English, and another for its flesh;—for instance, cow-flesh is called beef; that of the sheep, mutton; that of the pig, pork. The first is of Saxon, the latter of French origin; and this seems to prove that meat can not have been the food of the poor in former times" (LE 461).

A more widely occurring Byronic trick also anticipated by Espriella's discourse on the English language involves the vagaries of pronunciation. Espriella writes, "Neither is the pronunciation of the same word alike at all times, for it sometimes becomes the fashion to change the accent" (LE 460). Byron's deft changes in accent or pronunciation create the humor in such lines as "But— Oh! ye lords of ladies intellectual, / Inform us truly, have they not hen-peck'd you all?" (DJ 1.22). These contortions, obviously and immediately comic as they would seem in any context to any fluent speaker of English, are especially funny in Don Juan because in Byron's hands they, like the poem's title, mock the English language by treating it as it treats other tongues in the course of the poem.

In the three cases just examined, what Espriella asserts in his letter on English can also be seen in Don Juan. The last passage I shall quote would seem to offer Byron a challenge instead of an insight: "It [English] is a concise language, though the grievous want of inflections necessitates a perpetual use of auxiliaries. It would be difficult to fill eight lines of English, adhering closely to the sense, with the translation of an octave stanza" (LE 460). Scholars have pointed out and carefully assessed Byron's possible sources of ottava rima. It is amusing, and not altogether implausible, to think of adding Southey (as influence if not model) to the list containing Casti, Pulci, and Frere. Certainly Espriella's comments point to some of the problems inherent in adopting this Italian rhyme scheme to English, problems painfully evident in less skillful English ottava rima poems, for example, in the weaker portions of Keats's *Isabella.*

Filling the octave and adhering to sense, those two verbal tasks Espriella asserts to be "difficult," can be seen as Byron's simultaneous challenges in *Don Juan*—the two unchanging goals amid many and variable aims. Nothing so mechanical as putting expressions cast in one language into another, what Byron takes on in *Don Juan* is translation of a special sort. Diverse materials—prose accounts of shipwreck, a prescription in medical Latin, the Franglicized bill of fare at a West End dinner, a list of Cossack heroes, the clunky envoi of a Southey epic—are carried over into Byron's ottava rima. What results from this portage both is and is not "translation" of the source materials. They never cease to be what they are, and because they never cease to be so, they become *Don Juan.* If, as I have suggested, these materials include allusion to Southey at his best along with Southey at his worst, then *Don Juan* is so much the richer.

Books are not men, and I would not wish for this comparative assessment of *Letters from England* and *Don Juan* to blur the real differences between their authors, a situation that would be as false in its way as is the popular stereotype of Southey and Byron as literary and political antitheses. Here at the end it seems best to turn away from Southey and Byron as authors of cultural critiques with considerable affinities and back to the two men of letters who notably failed to get along. Special circumstances, as we have seen, played no small part in their feud. So, I think, did certain matters of principle and temperament—matters that return us to that Regency contrast between insularity and cosmopolitanism.

Apart from such particularities as the laureateship and the "League of Incest" quarrel, what was the barrier between Byron and Southey? Party divided them—but party also divided Byron and Scott without detracting from mutual regard.[19] Class lay between them—but to much the same extent as it lay between Byron and his good friend Thomas Moore. So the distinctions between aristocrat and middle-class man of letters, Whig and Tory, are surely not the crucial ones. Furthermore, in some basic ways, Southey and Byron can be seen as a good bit alike—both combining literary and political interests, but neither possessing that sys-tematizing bent characteristic of political theorists, and neither having cultivated the patience, thick skin, and other more myste-rious talents that constitute the practical politician. Southey could not be a Coleridge or Byron a Bertrand Russell—nor could either be a Disraeli (though Byron as much as anyone was the inspiration of that Tory prime minister). During the Regency, however, these two men with certain penchants in common moved in opposite directions. Southey withdrew from politics and the wide world to Lake District poetry and domesticity, from which sanctuary he fired off the occasional Tory polemic. After his brief engagement with Whig parliamentary politics and his somewhat longer tenure as London's "grand Napoleon of the realms of rhyme" (DJ 11.55) came to an end, Byron increasingly concerned himself with prin-cipled and practical politics in the great world beyond the Great World, an interest he shared with Hobhouse and other British liberals. Having traveled in their youth and observed nations and cultures beyond England's shores, Southey and Byron noticed identical or comparable phenomena but drew opposite conclu-sions. "And of what advantage has this journey been to me?" wrote a twenty-one-year-old Southey from Lisbon in 1796. "Why, I have learnt to thank God that I am an Englishman: for though things are not quite so well there as in El Dorado they are better than any where else."[20] Byron's firsthand view of things in "fair Lisboa" was no brighter thirteen years later, when he was twenty-one—as witness *Childe Harold*—but his growing awareness of corruption abroad never reconciled him to corruption at home. Nor did the mixed nature of what he encountered impair his lively apprecia-tion for difference. His unsated taste for new cultural experiences is as English in one way as is Southey's progressive approximation of John Bull in another.

III

All Things—
But a Show?

The pantomimes of the ancients no longer exist. But in compensation, all modern poetry resembles pantomimes.

Friedrich Schlegel, *Athenaeum Fragments*

In *England and the English*, that insightful study of culture and character in the last years before Reform, Bulwer-Lytton observes that Byron would never have put a coronet above his bed had he not written poems.[1] This statement tells something about the Regency Ton, an aristocratic and determinedly amateur set of people; but it also shows some important things about Byron: his insistence on being recognized, wherever he was, for what he was (an "English milord") and his coexistent ability or need to be seen as more than just that, as the citizen of many worlds. In *Don Juan* this cosmopolitan ability or need reveals itself in literary matters as well as social and political ones.

As we have already seen in the first two essays, the densely allusive poem seriously and playfully draws not only upon "real life"—Byron's and everyone else's, in a broad sweep from history to gossip—but also upon the widest possible range of literary genres, authors, and periods. Byron's models for *Don Juan* are classical works and modern ones, poems, novels, and plays, masterpieces and less exalted productions (such as *Letters from England*). All of these he manages to bend and blend to suit his own purposes. The many literary realms toured by the composing presence of *Don Juan*, the motley coat he wears on his pilgrimage, and the hybrid nature of his utterances make it impossible to point out *a* source for a passage in *Don Juan*, though many critics from Elizabeth Boyd on have accurately indicated the multiplicity of source materials and usefully characterized the nature and extent of particular sources.[2] But how are these many sources—utterly diverse in sense, subject, style, and period, variably successful in achieving what they set out to do, some of them admired and some wickedly mocked by their borrower—subsumed into one work: and a work with a consistent, effective, strongly individual tone at that? My intent here is to answer that question by looking at how the conventions, subjects, and attitudes of a particular generic micro-cosm, that of popular spectacular theater—the little world from which the "motley coat" mentioned just above is borrowed—influence and parallel Don Juan. I am not suggesting that this influ-ence excludes others. In the case of Byron at least, one is closer to the truth in approaching the study of literary influence as an enter-prise of gathering rather than ruling out—and many of the features I shall present as coming from spectacular theater can also be discerned in conversational or "middle style" poetry or in the art of the Italian improvvisatore. This essay's intent, then, is to examine one particular source among the many—but that one, I suggest, offered Byron a precedent and way to be inclusive, to assimilate all and any sources in his melting pot of a poem.

The extent of Don Juan's relationship to spectacular theater is inadequately acknowledged despite the explicit connection Byron himself makes in canto 1 and despite Frederick L. Beaty's excellent short study "Harlequin Don Juan," an essay convincingly arguing that Byron's poem draws usefully upon the various comic Don Juan plays that, riding the wake of Mozart's Don Giovanni, swept over London in 1817 and the years following—just when Byron took "our ancient friend" as nominal subject.[3] The comparative neglect of this influence is understandable, partly because spectacular the-ater is like Don Juan a shifty and heterogeneous phenomenon, partly because until fairly recent times the works contained in "subliterary" genres have not been widely seen as worth serious examination. My goal in this essay is to look at how two closely allied national variants of spectacular theater, England's panto-mime, burletta, and extravaganza, and Italy's commedia dell'arte, resemble, and may have influenced, Don Juan. Byron's interest in English theater, high and low, was long-standing; and the com-media was a form of entertainment popular and ever-visible at Venice, where he was living when he wrote the earlier parts of Don Juan. It seems likely that the commedia of the world in which he moved and British journals' accounts of what was being staged in that world he had left behind would evoke by association Byron's memory of plays and pantomimes he had formerly enjoyed. Memory, present experience, and the secondhand knowledge offered by reading could well combine, as in fact they often do in Don Juan, to show Byron the rich and happy comic potential of Don Juan, that epic hero and poetical subject he makes great show of choosing arbitrarily, and only after many other possibilities have been raised and dismissed.

Examining the character of Don Juan as he appears in the various forms of spectacular theater can show that Byron's comic don is not quite the unprecedented and idiosyncratic production Leo Weinstein describes in The Metamorphoses of Don Juan, where he states that "By taking the utmost liberty with hero and subject, Byron opened the way to what amounts to license. Henceforth Don Juan becomes a name that an author may freely bestow on any hero, just so long as he has some adventures with women." But surveys of the archetype have been made and well made.[4] Accordingly, I shall say comparatively little about theatrical Don Juans and Giovannis previous to the time when Byron and his readers "all have seen him in the pantomime." Instead, most of my efforts will go toward showing Byron's familiarity with spectacular theater and exploring his poem's affinities with the genre.

Whether we read the resemblances as sources or parallels, we can find in them a key to some of Don Juan's distinctive structures, features, and propensities. Like spectacular theater, Byron's poem is improvisational, topical, eclectic, accumulative, volatile, characterized by rapid and formulaic inversions and transformations, and dominated by the resourceful and potent being (shall we say actor?) who serves as transformer and who constructs what order there is. In offering Byron a precedent and method for assimilating diverse materials (among them the poem's many and varied other influences) through transformation and construction, spectacular theater might even be seen as the poem's ultimate influence. And this double dramatic influence, an imported and domesticated but quintessentially English taste subsequently modified by Italian experience, vividly expresses and embodies the sort of cosmopolitanism Byron advocates in his poem.

If one interesting topic not to be treated at length in this essay is the history of Don Juan's various incarnations, theatrical and otherwise, another equally interesting matter calling for concise rather than exhaustive discussion here is the nature and conventions of English spectacular theater, particularly pantomime, and the Italian commedia dell'arte from which pantomime derived and diverged. Readers interested in detailed consideration of these fascinating theatrical enterprises are encouraged to refer to some of the books indicated in the list of cited works. For now, let me just sketch the basic lines of spectacular theater as it existed in Byron's day.[5] After doing that, I shall go on to examine Byron's involvement with the several forms of spectacular theater, discuss the resemblances between them and *Don Juan,* and analyze in some detail the most richly pantomimic interlude in the poem. First, some background on pantomime and commedia.

The Greek components of the word *pantomime,* joining as they do the notion of universality with that of acting or imitating, suggest a comprehensiveness of range, an ability to perform all parts high or low, tragic, comic, or parodic, that one might claim as the essence of *Don Juan.* But in Byron's day and our own the word *pantomime* meant and means something rather different. As Byron uses it in *Don Juan, pantomime* refers to an increasingly conventionalized form of popular entertainment centered on the pursuits of the Italian commedia dell'arte characters—Harlequin, Columbine, Pantaloon, and Clown, among others. In commedia, which developed sometime during the sixteenth century, these characters, distinctively costumed and masked and based on Italian regional types, act out improvisational, acrobatic farces in which the theme is always romantic intrigue. The particulars of plot and scene vary widely, being specified by a *corago,* or stage manager, in the form of a brief narrative or "argument" to which the actors spontaneously add their personal understandings of the traditional characters as they devise the actual lines, jokes, and comic business of the play.

English pantomime, a more thoroughly scripted form of spectacular theater, differs from commedia most notably in the conventions of plot and scene. Romantic intrigue may lie at the heart of commedia, but the breadth of this topic and the large number of commedia characters allow for almost infinite variations on the theme. Whatever the details of the plot may be, the setting is generally the same: an all-purpose street scene containing several houses equipped with plenty of doorways, windows, trapdoors, and concealed entries and exits for farcical involvements, exchanges, deceptions, and pursuits. In contrast to the simple commedia scene, early nineteenth-century pantomimes provided a wide variation of elaborately contrived settings. Thus a pair of reversals: Visual and mechanical intricacy of scene gives pantomime the variety that commedia achieves through twists and turns of plot; and like the predictable yet serviceable commedia street scene, the bones of pantomime plot remain the same, however the surface may be garnished.

Let us now see just what those bones are and how they are arranged. In Byron's day a pantomime typically was a one-act play divided into some twelve to twenty-two scenes and consisting of two parts, the opening and the harlequinade. The opening, which was the shorter part and the one that generally provided the title of the play, might draw its specifics from classical myth (Vulcan and Venus), popular legend (Friar Bacon and the Brazen Head), a nursery tale (Dick Whittington), a literary production, whether masterpiece or minor work (Swift's *Gulliver's Travels* or Combe's *Doctor Syntax in Search of the Picturesque*), or a well-known play or opera (Mozart's *Don Giovanni*). Whatever the source of the details, though, the plot is unvarying. A pair of young lovers wish to marry but are opposed by a despotic older man who wields paternal authority over the girl, whether or not he is her actual father. His grounds of opposition are the young man's inferior social or financial status, and that opposition expresses itself in an unsuccessful campaign to change the maiden's mind followed by an attempt to have her suitor killed or kidnapped, which proves equally unsuccessful because a benevolent agent (generally female and always equipped with supernatural powers rather than social and economic ones— thus a fit counterbalance to the hostile father figure) intervenes, chiefly on behalf of the lovers but sometimes secondarily to punish a minor indiscretion of which they are guilty. The supernatural intervention constitutes the "transformation scene," a spectacular effect that divides opening from harlequinade. Here the benevolent agent, typically speaking in rhymed couplets, turns the young man into Harlequin and the girl into Columbine, the petty tyrant into Pantaloon, the comic servant or duenna into Clown, the socially and economically preferable suitor (if there is one in the opening tale) into Dandy Lover or Lover pure and simple. Harlequin is assigned a quest or task, the completion of which will demonstrate his worthiness, and provided with a magic bat to help him in his labors.

From this point, all is harlequinade. Harlequin pursues his quest (and thereby Columbine) while eluding Pantaloon and his allies. Speechless during the harlequinade, Harlequin performs feats that are largely gymnastic, acrobatic, and visual. He leaps and soars, vanishes or suddenly appears through trapdoors, rises to great heights and swoops down from them courtesy of stage machinery. His preeminent weapon against Pantaloon and his attendants is the magic bat, which gives him, like the guiding presence who provided it, powers of transformation. He animates the furnishings of a scene, freezes his foes or sets them in hapless movement, makes food appear or disappear, heals wounds, raises the dead. His tricks, or "visual similes," are a principal means of satire in pantomime: the slap of a bat enacts transformation and thereby alters the audience's understanding of an object, character, or setting by disclosing its previously undetected resemblance to something else.

The slapstick comedy dominated by Harlequin's antics (and increasingly Clown's, for reasons we shall see) holds the stage until the harlequinade's penultimate scene, called the "dark scene" because it always occurs in some gloomy place—a grotto, cave, tomb, ruin, or desolate landscape. Here Harlequin, having accomplished his task, embraces Columbine, whom he has won. But in so doing he relinquishes the bat with which he has won her. It is a Freudian field day: Pantaloon recovers the means of potency, reasserts his dominance over Columbine, and threatens to punish Harlequin. Now the benevolent agent intervenes yet again. She reconciles the characters and transports them to an exotic and elaborate final scene, which offers the apotheosis of love and, sometimes, the return of original identities.[6]

The outline above might describe more or less accurately English pantomime from the age of John Rich to the present. The conventional features that distinguished early nineteenth-century pantomime from what preceded and followed it are responses to several constraints, first among them the restrictions established by the theatrical licensing laws enacted in 1737. These regulations limited the use of dialogue to certain "patent houses," Drury Lane and Covent Garden, but permitted a wider range of theaters to stage loosely defined entertainments consisting of rhymed musical comedy with songs, recitative, slapstick stage business, and spectacular effects. Among the dramatic forms that circumvented the Licensing Act were burletta, extravaganza, and pantomime—which like burletta and extravaganza was not an utterly speechless form of theater, though its audience's understanding of what goes on certainly does not hinge on the words.[7]

Early nineteenth-century pantomime was also shaped by forces less abstract than the licensing laws. Until the present day of film and television, theater had always been the artistic genre most directly responsive to public tastes and values; and pantomime was—as it remains—a particularly accurate and collaborative theatrical reflection of what the masses, as opposed to a cultural elite, demanded. What the early nineteenth-century paying public called for was provided by such resourceful and responsive arrangers of spectacle as Thomas Dibdin of Drury Lane and Charles Farley of Covent Garden. But perhaps the most crucial determinant of what pleased the public in Byron's day was the comic brilliance of the actor Joseph Grimaldi, in tribute to whom clowns are now called "Joey." Grimaldi's tastes, talents, and preferences in roles combined with the licensing restrictions, the abilities of the theatrical arrangers, and the demands of the public to make pantomime what it was in the years between 1806, when the great success of *Harlequin and Mother Goose* (in which Grimaldi first acted the role of Clown) stabilized its conventions, and 1823, when Grimaldi retired. During these years, Mayer claims, the form was at its best: "pantomime in this period, by the very nature of its wide scope and satiric tone, was an unofficial and informal chronicle of the age."[8] It is a striking coincidence that the dates bracketing the age of Grimaldi are equally useful for indicating the start and close of Byron's poetic career.

The son of Giuseppe Grimaldi, ballet master at Drury Lane and Sadler's Wells, "Joey" or "Joe" Grimaldi possessed a genius as cosmopolitan as was the art in which he excelled, or as I am arguing *Don Juan* to be. George Augustus Sala characterizes Grimaldi's peculiar powers as the product of two cultures: "He seems to have possessed a talent for pantomimic expression so eminently the gift of the Italian race allied to a strong sense of popular English humour. The happy combination of the fine perception and high colouring which suits John Bull's blunter sense of humor has vanished with him."[9] Grimaldi's preference for playing the role of Clown, the figure who generally emerges from a servant or duenna in the transformation scene, greatly altered the character of the harlequinade. Clown as Grimaldi presented him was no mere comic henchman in the service of absurd patriarchal authority, and thus a butt for Harlequin's bat-induced humor, but instead a free and potent mocker himself. As Mayer describes him, the Clown portrayed by Grimaldi and his son J.S. Grimaldi as an incarnate spirit of satiric buffoonery: "Clown had a buoyancy, a barely suppressed impudence and irreverence that encouraged pantomime audiences to share vicariously and willingly condone his seeming impatience with manners, his mockery of class distinctions, his disregard for property, and his absolute disrespect for authority. If Clown had fixed traits, they were all ones that mocked convention and exposed social habits pretending to morality or self-conscious graciousness. He rebelled against stuffiness and tradition and did what others wished to do but never dared."[10]

The Grimaldi Clown brings all Harlequin's physical agility to his role, but also demonstrates a supple, creative wit that rivals and ultimately surpasses the trick work Harlequin achieves with his bat and its invisible ally the stage machinery. Comparing the younger Grimaldi with his father, the Times reviewer of 27 December 1823 pays elegaic tribute to "Joey" in these telling words: "Apart from all twisting and tumbling there was so much intelligence about everything he did."[11] Grimaldi's Clown deployed this intelligence in acts of "construction," figurative presentations based on the same assumption underlying Harlequin's transformations—namely that objects share unperceived relationships that can be disclosed through artful juxtaposition. Clown begins with a seemingly random collection of articles, things united only by the fact that none of them belongs to him. He proceeds, much in the fashion of a Regency cartoonist or of the composing presence in Don Juan, to marshal these diverse objects into a bizarre order—a human shape, vehicle, or monster, a laughable still life that can become still funnier when Harlequin's bat animates it to its creator's utter befuddlement.

Clown's new prominence and independence were delightful in themselves, but they tended to diminish the harlequinade by rivaling or eclipsing the antics of Harlequin and to weaken the comic pursuit by making Clown, as a subversive persecutor of Pantaloon, an implicit ally to the young lovers. Another device that compromised the classical commedia shape of the harlequinade was the "diorama," the elaborate scenic effect introduced into pantomime during the Grimaldi era and retained to this day as a key ingredient of English spectacular theater. The diorama entertained but also edified as it carried audiences not just to the world of Gothic, Oriental, or mythic fantasy but to real places (English, Continental, Eastern) they might otherwise experience only by traveling—a luxury denied to the general populace at most times, and particularly during the Napoleonic period. Also introduced as an occasional novelty into Regency pantomime was the cross-dressing that, in Victorian times, became an obligatory feature of the entertainment.

Though "dame" and "principal boy" were not yet pantomime conventions in the early years of the century, Grimaldi acted "Queen Rondabellyana" in *Harlequin and the Red Dwarf*, played the duenna who becomes Clown in *Harlequin and Asmodeus*, and in *Harlequin Whittington* represented Dame Cecily Suet while "a very clever little dog" acted the part of her cat.[12] There were other instances of men acting the female benevolent agent or wearing women's dress for disguise in the harlequinade;[13] and "breeches roles" for actresses, though not the defining feature they would later become, were not unknown. Interestingly for our purposes, Don Giovanni was probably the most celebrated of these transsexual impersonations. Moncrieff's extravaganza *Don Giovanni* (1817) first featured in the title role Mrs. Gould, "whose masculine habits won her the name of 'Joe' Gould";[14] but the role came to be particularly associated with Mrs. Gould's successor, the "English Adonis" Madame Vestris. Writing in the high noon of Victorian pantomime, George Vandenhoff paid retrospective tribute to her memorable achievement: "Vestris was admirably gifted, cut out, and framed to shine *en petit maître*. . . . Believe it, reader, no actress that we now have (1860) can ever give an idea of her attractions, the fascinations, the witcheries of Mme Vestris in the hey-day of her charms."[15] We can well imagine that Byron would have heard of such "witcheries" even in Venice.

Although Byron's knowledge of Madame Vestris's bravura performance and the other interesting English burlesques and transformations inflicted upon Don Juan's character after the great London success of *Don Giovanni* would have to be secondhand, in the years prior to his self-exile he had direct experience of English spectacular theater and considerable admiration for its practitioners. Byron's letters and Dickens's *Memoirs of Joseph Grimaldi* both attest to Byron's interest in Grimaldi's performances from 1808 on.[16] If we could seat Byron in the Covent Garden audience watching "Joey" reenacting his role of Scaramouch in the "tragic pantomimic ballet" of *Don Juan* that opened on 20 November 1809, there would be straightforward and convincing evidence of a causal link between pantomime and epic poem. But that evening must be seen as a different sort of anticipation in Byron's life: 20 November 1809 found him not in London but pausing on his travels through Greece to stop at Missolonghi, where he would die some fifteen years later. Although there is no solid proof that Byron knew and admired Grimaldi's performance in *Don Juan*, Dickens speaks of the relationship that evolved between the men as friendship, though their acquaintance started awkwardly due to some facetious hostility on Byron's part when the two met at Berkeley Castle in October 1812. The actor and the poet seem to have met both at private parties and at Covent Garden, where Byron would sometimes wait in the wings to resume a conversation interrupted by a performance. There is palpable evidence of Byron's continued esteem for the comic actor and his talents. On his departure from England in 1816, Byron presented Grimaldi with "a valuable silver snuff-box, around which was the inscription, 'The gift of Lord Byron to Joseph Grimaldi,'"[17] a courteous memento of the sort one sovereign offers to another. Byron, fond of seeing himself as the Napoleon of poets, habitually admired preeminence in others; and his gracious valedictory gesture here strikes a note of sincere regard rather than mere formality.

There is a still more interesting connection between Byron and Thomas John Dibdin, the prolific writer of musical comedies who along with Alexander Rae succeeded Whitbread as manager of Drury Lane Theatre during the years when Byron was officially and informally active in that theater's affairs. As a member of the sub-committee for management, Byron gave more than a noble name to the Drury Lane committee, much to Lady Byron's regret. His involvement with the actors and management was both personal and businesslike. He read manuscripts, even served as go-between for writers of plays, notably Coleridge and Maturin. Once, at least, a brief note to Dibdin shows Byron closely attentive to the smallest details of a Drury Lane offering. The subject of Byron's criticism—a matter of diction and decency—and the tone he takes on that subject are amusingly identical to what he would chafe under some years later when Hobhouse voiced a collective concern about *Don Juan*'s morality: "Dear Sir,—Is not part of the dialogue in the new piece a little too double, if not too broad, now and then? for instance, the word 'ravish' occurs in the way of question, as well as a remark, some half dozen times in the course of one scene, thereby meaning, not raptures, but rape" (LJ 4:304).

As the salutation quoted above suggests, Byron's relationship with Dibdin does not appear to have been a close one; but the comic playwright's lyrics stayed in Byron's mind long after the period of association at Drury Lane had ended. It is from Dibdin's play *The British Raft* that Byron drew the phrase "tight little island," an epithet he was famously fond of applying to his native land, and especially when he was resident of a much smaller and yet much less constrictive island society, Venice (see, for instance, LJ 5:136). Similarly, when Byron chose to mock Henry Gally Knight in one of the doggerel ballads he enjoyed including in his letters to John Murray, the original he travestied was a Dibdin song, "The Grinders" (LJ 6:28 n. 4). During his Italian exile Byron did not encounter Dibdin's plays only in memory or the London papers, though. One night at Venice's Benedetto theater he saw a French farce Dibdin and Kinnaird had translated for Drury Lane. "It turns upon a Usurer personating a father—" recalls Byron as he writes to Kinnaird, "and did not succeed at D[rury] L[ane]. I think it was better acted here than there.————What were the odds at that time—against my seeing the same farce at Venice?" (LJ 5:140; see also LJ 5:143).

What odds indeed? Perhaps not such long ones. Though theater began as a communal ceremony, it has also proved a highly portable commodity. Itinerant actors, alone or in troupes, have traveled far and wide, taking their native dramas with them; and if Byron could watch at Venice a French play he had formerly seen in London, he also could and did reacquaint himself with Italian works, most notably the comedies of Goldoni, plays he had once viewed on the English stage and now could appreciate in their proper cultural frame. If Venice set Goldoni in context, Goldoni also seemed to set Venice in context for Byron. His letters show that he sometimes conceived of the cosmopolitan life he was enjoying as one of those plays brought to life: "I am at present on the Brenta—opposite is a Spanish Marquis—ninety years old—next his Casino is a Frenchman's besides the natives—so as Somebody said the other day—we are exactly one of Goldoni's comedies (La

Vedova Scaltra) where a Spaniard—English—& Frenchman are introduced;—but we are all very good neighbours, Venetians, &c. &c. &c." (LJ 5:238).

Perhaps it is worth recalling that the dramatist whose works Byron's life here imitates was a master of the commedia dell'arte— and produced a Don Juan play (*Don Giovanni Tenorio ossia il dissoluto*) that despite its mediocrity has certain things in common with Byron's masterpiece. One can detect the similarities by looking at the reasons why historians of the Don Juan motif deprecate Goldoni's version. Mandel sees the Goldoni don as lacking "his folk vigor, his humor, and his intelligence"; and Weinstein character-izes Goldoni's play as an unhappy "modernization" that "reduces the grandiose Burlador to an ordinary, vulgar seducer" and dimin-ishes the mythic catastrophe to a naturalistic one.[18] Of course, the story of Don Juan is more pretext than text for Byron, and his poem aims to demonstrate its narrator's vigor, humor, and intel-ligence rather than the protagonist's. Thus what constitutes a weak-ness in Goldoni's work can be a strength or a neutral feature in Byron's—yet the attributes themselves may be more or less the same. Perhaps the most striking common quality the two works share is a teasingly confessional air. Theater historians generally agree that public interest in the play rose less out of any literary or theatrical merits than out of the general knowledge that material from Goldoni's life found its way into the play. In the discussion of canto 1 we have already seen how Byron's disapproving but fascinated readers detected the poet's personal affairs scattered throughout Juan's story; and as Elizabeth Boyd points out, Byron would have known about the dramatist's mixing autobiography with the story of Don Juan from "an amusing and notorious pas-sage" in the Goldoni memoirs, a book Byron valued highly enough that, having sold his first copy in the 1816 auction of his library, he three years later traded Thomas Moore a copy of Ariosto for a replacement.[19]

My chief reason for mentioning Goldoni at this point is not to compare his treatment of Don Juan with Byron's but to stress the connection between real life and theatrical illusion, a point made explicit in Byron's letter quoted above. Fresh ways of looking at relations between acting and being, play and reality, England and Italy, past and present, converged on Byron in various ways, some of which we have already seen, as he was writing *Don Juan*. But

nowhere in Byron's prose does this question of identity's boundaries and the means of getting beyond them present itself more
richly than in the following passage, where yet again we find
ourselves at a pantomime. Here, however, the masked thespian is
none other than Byron, and what he is enacting both is and is not
his own life. "In the Pantomime of 1815–16—there was a Representation of the Masquerade of 1814—given by 'us Youth' of
Watier's Club to Wellington & Co.—Douglas Kinniard—& one or
two others with myself—put on Masques—and went on the Stage
amongst the οι πολλοι—to see the effect of a theatre from the
Stage.—It is very grand.—Douglas danced amongst the figuranti
too—& they were puzzled to find out who we were—as being
more than their number.—It was odd enough that D.K. & I should
have been both at the *real* Masquerade—& afterwards in the Mimic
one of the same—on the stage of D.L. Theatre" (LJ 9:36–37).

This passage appears in "Detached Thoughts," the remarkable
journal Byron maintained between 15 October 1821 and 18 May
1822, a period that found him living chiefly at Pisa and refraining, as
he had promised the Contessa Guiccioli, from continuation of *Don
Juan*. He would resume the poem some two months after abandoning these prose "Thoughts"—or, more precisely, he would
assimilate their gossipy and elegaic particulars into the story of
Juan, whose adventures in English society are the bulk of incident
in the final cantos. The quotation shows that Byron's experience
contained a connection with Regency theater still closer than his
involvement with Drury Lane would generally afford—and it also
hints at certain attitudes and conventions important to the composition and understanding of *Don Juan*. This theatrical escapade
clearly displays Byron's familiarity with and enjoyment of pantomime—his love of mystification—his recurring need to transcend
limitation—to experience everything. For Byron, it is not enough
to know theater as the audience does. He must have the view from
the stage as well, not so much because he needs to feel himself an
actor but because in a mutable world, unstable to its very foundation, the actors in a pantomime are the most blatant players of
parts, but not the only ones. A masked actor is more obviously
role-playing than is an unmasked one—any actor is more clearly
assuming an identity than is any member of the audience—anyone
present at the ritual is more evidently cast in a part than is someone
bustling by outside the theater. Nonetheless, in the world Byron

and the rest of us experience, everyone is both an actor and a spectator. In going masked on stage to see how the collaborative venture of theater looks from there, Byron demonstrates in life and art that in living our lives we are all creating roles, whether we be poets, seducers, slaves, empresses, soldiers, politicians, highwaymen, or poet laureates.

This episode of the perpetually theatrical Byron acting, for once, on a professional stage rather than in the theater of personal relationships has a complexity not yet fully acknowledged. In writing down these words among his "Detached Thoughts," Byron reenacts or relives a past moment of acting and living. Recording the experience, Byron "authorizes" that moment, an anonymous reenactment (Byron and Kinnaird being masked, not known even by the performers) of an earlier enactment, also masked and technically though not completely anonymous in that the spectators familiar with Watier's Club at least could guess who masquers might be. Now what if anything is "real life" in all these embedded roles? What is "acting"? I find it impossible to answer that question except with another one, a query posed in *Don Juan*: "*What after all, are all things—but a Show?*" (*DJ* 7.2). The Byronic self-dramatization through combined self-revelation and self-concealment that we see crystallized in this biographical incident is one of the great puzzles and great pleasures of *Don Juan*.

It is interesting for a reader of *Don Juan* to notice that the Watier's masquerade honored Wellington, whose name appears at the start of canto 9, written a few months after the "Detached Thoughts" were put aside. The subject of the pantomime, which was entitled *Harlequin and Fancy, or the Poet's Last Shilling*, also deserves attention. In this entertainment, Harlequin's bat is associated with the writer's pen. An impoverished poet foreswears Fortune and invokes Fancy, under whose sponsorship he transforms his life—by writing a pantomime. The reflexiveness of *Harlequin and Fancy* is comparable to that of *Don Juan*, widely recognized as being a poem about its own composition. The pantomime's connection between writing and money suggests moments of poetical moneygrubbing (the laureate's, Wordsworth's, and the self-confessedly avaricious narrator's) in *Don Juan's* Dedication and first canto. The mock soliloquy in which the pantomime poet asks himself what to write obviously derives from *Hamlet*, a work alluded to and "colouring the climate" throughout *Don Juan* but especially in canto 9.[20] Here in *Harlequin and*

Fancy we see the starving poet as prince of Denmark, his late last shilling in the role of Ghost:

> To write and what to write, that is the question
> Whether 'tis nobler in the Bard to write
> The Bowl and Dagger of the Tragic Muse
> Or to take arms against a host of critics,
> And make a pantomime—to fly, to run
> To jump and by a jump to say we 'scape
> From Pantaloon, the Clown, and every foe
> That Harlequin is heir to. 'Tis a transformation
> Devoutly to be wished.[21]

"To write and what to write?" That is the poet's perennial question. It would be characteristic of Byron to recognize and exploit the ironical possibilities announced here. Byron, like the pantomime poet, saw himself as ill-used by Fortune—having been once courted (in the days of the Watier's Club masque and the Drury Lane production being recalled), then vilified, by a canting public. Why not embrace Fancy and the fanciful device of transformation? Why not have a joke on the fickle, provincial English public by constructing, as Grimaldi's Clown might, an English epic out of the least promising, most outrageous materials: that collection of odds and ends Byron refers to when he claims "Almost all Don Juan is real life—either my own—or from people I knew" (LJ 8:186). And why not take as the means of reanimating these odds and ends the transforming pen, or wand, or bat, of pantomime?

I have just tried to suggest how English and Italian spectacular theater—especially pantomime, most particularly Harlequin and Fancy—offer subjects, vehicles, roles, and a supply of tricks that could prove useful to Byron in the composition of Don Juan. Now it is time to step into the world of the poem and to see what evidences of spectacular theater we can find there. The second of Leigh Hunt's 1817 Examiner essays on pantomime asserts that "The three general pleasures of a Pantomime are its bustle, its variety, and its sudden changes."[22] All these features distinguish Don Juan with equal validity. Within the poem, bustle, variety, and sudden changes are consequences or companions of transformation, that most important device Don Juan shares with pantomime. All three features characterize both the plot and the intellectual flow of the poem—and here again, comparison with pantomime proves illuminating. As David Mayer understands it, Regency pantomime was not conceived to be systematically and single-mindedly satiric: "Its structure enabled fleeting comedy or satire to be directed at many topics without requiring that they be shown in a logical or plausible sequence. It was more effectual by being random rather than precise. A few laughs on one topic and the action of the pantomime moved on to another subject"[23]—and so it is with *Don Juan*. Those laughs are frequently achieved though the device called construction—and again, so it is with *Don Juan*. For instance, we have already seen in the Southey essay how the Byronic narrator builds a witty and substantial digression on human knowledge out of apples: Adam's and Sir Isaac Newton's. (DJ 10.1–3) Similarly, in the canto we are about to consider at some length, construction operates in the forms of historical resonance and linguistic resemblance, adding three queens (Semiramis, Caroline the wife of George IV, and less importantly for the moment Catherine the Great) and two words (*courser* and *courier*) to make a wonderfully economical yet intricate illustration of the premise that "Love like religion sometimes runs to heresy." (DJ 5.61)

An art that ranges wide, moves fast, and fills the scene to bursting runs the risk of undiscriminating eclecticism or superficiality or both. Mayer recognizes these as the besetting problems that keep Regency pantomime from offering the best chronicle of its age, though he concludes that these flaws are not fatal ones: "Still, the two qualities which are pantomime's weakest, lack of discrimination and lack of profundity, when coupled with its greatest strength, its comprehensiveness, permit seeing this portion of the nineteenth century as Britons of no special perceptiveness were likely to view it."[24] But suppose a similar sort of chronicle offered by a Briton of extraordinary perceptiveness. Suppose that the chronicler is writing a sprawling work over a period of years, and hence is free from the obligation of fitting his vision into the two or so hours an audience will sit without squirming—always able to amplify, change his mind, return to subjects he has presented earlier. Furthermore, suppose this chronicler an expatriate poet, independent of British censorship and consequently free to mock religion, royalty, and politics, three institutions protected from pantomime satire by the lord chamberlain's examiner of plays. What you have supposed is the circumstances that could produce a pantomime with variety and rapidity as well as profundity achieved through recursion, with comprehensiveness and sharp though artfully underplayed discrimination. What you have supposed is *Don Juan.*

For *Don Juan* and spectacular theater alike, one important way of achieving "realism" is through features just discussed—the topical references and details from contemporary existence that so often provide the raw materials of improvisational humor. But truth to life calls for a certain universality along with accurate specificity if an allusive work is to speak to audiences after the fashions, events, and people it presents are gone. In theater exploiting the old commedia types, the timeless element of realism does not come from psychological complexity of the kind exhibited by a Shakespearean character: Caliban, for example, in the course of a single play. Instead, the sense of reality or vitality comes more gradually through a series of theatrical encounters with the character, as the result of what Allardyce Nicoll calls "the dramatic presentation of accumulative personalities."[25] The essence of Harlequin does not vary. It is as formulaic as his obligatory costume. But when we see his character in play after play, pantomime scene after pantomime scene, commedia situation after commedia situation, the very act of endurance over time and through space makes him a real presence to us. Thus also Don Juan, that "variation of the English Harlequin," as Beaty terms him.[26] Byron's chosen protagonist comes alive for us partly because of his having endured as a literary tradition, having sinned his sad or merry way though work after work, and partly because of the many situations and scenes through which Byron insists that we follow him in the course of the full yet unfinished poem.

One great advantage attending on this sort of accumulative character development is that, as is the case with psychological realism, there is room for inconsistency, a real enough quality in life but one fatal to other dramatic methods of comic delineation through type. Jonson's Volpone, his identity compressed into a single play, cannot lapse from foxiness without ceasing to be himself. But Harlequin or Don Juan can vary wildly. Each impression, whether it builds on or contradicts what is already there, is part of a character that is the sum of its particular presentations.

If seeing how spectacular theater creates character can help us understand *Don Juan,* so can knowledge of pantomime's plot. *Don*

Juan may seem an errant epic, but it seems that way largely because of the digressions, those dazzling moments of transformation, topical satire, and verbal construction achieved by a narrator who behaves sometimes as benevolent agent, sometimes as Grimaldi Clown. Digressions aside, the plot is in fact a clear and simple one—and that simplicity emerges most clearly when we consider the narrative sequence in the light shed by our awareness of pantomime conventions. Canto 1, the part of the story set in Don Juan's native country, can be seen as analogous to the opening of English pantomime. Certainly this tale of young though adulterous lovers parted by a cuckolded father-husband (remember Alfonso's fifty years to Julia's twenty-three) has at least as much in common with pantomime as it does with the Don Juan myth. Juan's transformation into Harlequin is oblique but evident, I think:

> Here ends this canto.—Need I sing or say,
> How Juan, naked, favour'd by the night,
> Who favours what she should not, found his way,
> And reach'd his home in an unseemly plight?

So says the narrator in stanza 188, though in fact thirty-four and a half stanzas remain to be sung. The last thing that has happened within the narrative is the struggle between Alfonso and Juan, an encounter that realistically strips away a garment that, in pantomime, would be removed from the young lover by magic. It falls to a supposedly benevolent, certainly female agent, Juan's mother, to provide a new costume, and a new identity (that of Harlequin Traveler), and a quest ("To mend his former morals, or get new")— but those final thirty-four stanzas, increasingly remote from the narrative and progressively closer to the narrator, who progressively comes to resemble the author, remind us who really is enacting the change. It is Byron, the truly benevolent and truly potent transformer, who sends Juan off on his harlequinade in various costumes and through assorted cultures. The order is certainly not random. Juan's travels recapitulate a sort of cultural evolution. He goes from animal existence (shipwreck) to a primitive community (Lambro's island) to an Eastern despotism to Catherine the Great's Europeanizing Russia to what the implied reader of the poem is likely to consider the pinnacle of civilization, which Juan progressively ascends: from Western Europe to England to London, and finally to an aristocratic country house—

Whig emblem, as Malcolm Kelsall has put it, of power's diffusion "away from the centralised autocracy."[27] As the exotic scenes change, Juan's costumes vary from rags to Greek finery to Ottoman drag to a Cossack artilleryman's uniform to Russian court dress and finally Anglo-dandaical impeccability.

We must not push the parallels too far or forget that Byron's comic epic has models other than spectacular theater. A technical or narrative transformation of the sort seen in pantomime does occur between cantos 1 and 2, as the boy is dispatched on his travels like Harlequin sent off on his quest. Still, Juan develops psychologically (as Tom Jones does, for instance) as well as accumulatively, and his personal transformation from naïf to cosmopolite takes place gradually—starting in canto 5 and continuing through canto 8. The chief agent of this transformation may be seen as Byron, or "Byron," or the Byronic narrator with his "supernatural machinery," but his assistant, a character incarnate in the pantomime world of the poem, is the practical philosopher whose name is an Anglicized doubling of Juan's and who plays experience to the Spanish youth's innocence—that is to say, John Johnson. The way in which English values embodied in Johnson preside over Don Juan's transformation is a matter for the fifth essay, "England in *Don Juan*." For now our concern is with the most clearly pantomimic interlude in *Don Juan*, the seraglio episode in canto 5, where our awareness of the story as artifice is heightened by such pantomime devices as sudden and drastic scene changes, exotically artificial settings, recurring personal transformations and gender reversals, blatant manipulation of characters and events by various stage managers, inside, outside, and above the narrative.

As the canto opens Don Juan, whom we have just seen chained in a company of actors, is dramatically situated in the slave market at Constantinople. The crowd scene's contrived quality is stressed: "Like a backgammon board the place was dotted / With whites and blacks, in groups on show for sale" (DJ 5.10). So is the flimsy, backdrop quality of the city itself: "Each villa on the Bosphorus looks a screen / New painted, or a pretty opera-scene" (DJ 5.46). Purchased, Juan is dispatched to the splendor of the seraglio, and it proves a place "Which puzzled nature much to know what art meant" (DJ 5.64), a place where "Wealth had done wonders—taste not much" (DJ 5.94). The stanza last quoted goes on directly to acknowledge that "such things / Occur in orient palaces, and even / In the more chasten'd domes of western kings" (DJ 5.94). Thanks to these words, the gaudy unreality of canto 5's mise-en-scène cannot be seen as a simple slap at Ottoman aesthetics. Even as he evokes an exotic empire through which he once traveled, Byron also calls to mind both the insistently picturesque "Eastern" stage sets of many a West End pantomime and the more sturdily built if not much more authentic or chasten'd dome from which many such sets were imitated: the Prince Regent's Brighton Pavilion. Interestingly and appropriately enough, Byron here draws inspiration from a London fashion he helped promote, through writing his Oriental tales and setting a personal example (his and Hobhouse's Albanian costumes having been the making of more than one fashionable masquerade), and not least through having furnished Dibdin with some two hundred drawings of Turkish costumes. Byron claims to reject inspiration in the act of embracing it, though, for Eastern details offer him a temptation to do what he has done often and profitably in his literary past from *Childe Harold* on, to create a lush verbal diorama for the reader. Thus the narrator grows insistently prominent as Juan, Johnson, and Baba the eunuch are winding "through orange bowers and jasmine, and so forth," eminently describable backdrops

> (Of which I might have a good deal to say,
>   There being no such profusion in the North
> Of oriental plants, "et cetera,"
>   But that of late your scribblers think it worth
> Their while to rear whole hotbeds in their works
> Because one poet travell'd 'mongst the Turks). (DJ 5.42)

This crotchety rejection of easy success in pandering to his audience's love of the picturesque may apply specifically to horticultural description, but it has wider relevance in the canto. Byron seems positively compelled to intrude personal or cross-cultural references that pull out the Turkey carpet from under readers' feet whenever there is the faintest chance that the narrative and its setting will prove absorbing or engrossing enough to offer an illusion of reality rather than just an illusion. This wonderfully perverse parenthesis and other similar references, which constitute a sort of chronic parabasis in the comic tale, will be a major topic of the essay (ch. 5) treating English elements in cantos 2–9.

For now, let it be enough to recognize the perfect timing of the pantomimic "bustle and variety" such rhetoric injects. Byron's cultural contrast and autobiographical intrusion make themselves felt just at the dangerous moment when the reader's critical intellect, lulled by pure description, might go to sleep.

Like the backdrop, the characters of canto 5 are perfect specimens for spectacular theater. The assorted slaves and enslavers from the pirate ship offer a striking crowd scene to start. Juan and Johnson, physically attractive in their different national ways, are perfect "stage gentlemen." Indeed, as Johnson immediately notices (DJ 5.13), they are the "only gentlemen" among the "motley crew"—and that adjective "motley" is crucial—of the canto. Johnson applies the phrase to the various folk for sale at the slave market, but it refers equally well to the people of the palace, all those singled out for particular description being freakish or incomplete, physically and spiritually "ungentlemanly" in different ways. Baba the eunuch, the matched set of mute dwarves who open doors (and close lives) on command, Gulbeyaz the favored bride, and the sultan himself are all flattened out, spectacular figures—people diminished to roles. They are that way partly, I think, because of generic constraints and partly because of thematic ones. The two pressures work together superbly: Byron has chosen a self-evidently "unnatural" form for this episode to show that a palace (Oriental or Occidental, it matters not) is not a hospitable environment for what is natural or what is best in humanity. The headquarters of a despotism is an uncongenial backdrop for that improvisational play we call the human comedy.

Instead, Byron plays out against the imperial stage set an amorous farce of forcible disguise and crude stereotyping, a situation that might prove merely ridiculous but when skillfully handled can allow for crossed purposes, surprises, and rapid role reversals—the sort of situation that has been a staple of pantomime, especially from Victorian days to the present. The sultana Gulbeyaz, having seen Juan and Johnson at the slave market, has commanded Baba to purchase the promising lad for her personal use, the mature man for some unknown end. To be smuggled to the lady's apartments, Juan must submit to a transformation: he must dress, and play, the part of a harem girl, a prospect the highborn Spaniard finds outrageous. Casting Juan in this role is an act of transformation beyond the powers of a slave and eunuch like Baba. Only the voice of independent, sensible, securely masculine experience could convince Juan here—and just how the change comes about is a matter for later discussion when we go into John Johnson's role in Juan's education.

But come about it does, and Byron's use of pantomime cross-dressing enriches, and thereby transforms, the stock humorous device. Dressing a man as a woman may be a comic turn that never fails to amuse a British audience, but the joke does not in itself make any point about traditional gender roles and their underpinnings. Byron, however, is interested in exploring such roles, along with their political, philosophical, and psychological implications.[28] In the scene with Gulbeyaz, Byron obliges Juan not merely to wear the trappings of femininity, but to take upon himself less tangible yet more cumbersome attributes conventionally ascribed to women, while the sultana, operating from her position of power, acts with prerogatives conventionally reserved for men. But the situation is no simple reversal. As we shall see, Juan(na) and the sultan(a) are potential and essential mirrors of one another. Each seems equally well characterized by the mixture of qualities said to be projected (or reflected) by Gulbeyaz's eyes: "half-voluptuousness and half command" (DJ 5.108). Each is in a certain sense a man in women's clothes—Don Juan by dint of nature, Gulbeyaz thanks to the social accident that gives her prestige and permits her to be dominant, imperious, and aggressive. As their comic encounter begins, social masculinity takes precedence over the biological sort. Gulbeyaz is the amorous predator; Juan, the reluctant quarry.

Byron's inversion of conventional roles is brilliantly, somewhat blasphemously highlighted as the sultana issues a command in interrogative form—"'Christian, cans't thou love?'" (DJ 5.116)—and Juan bursts into tears. Weeping, he enacts and embodies the stock spiritual qualities generally ascribed to the woman in such amorous skirmishes. He loves another and intends fidelity to her memory. He disdains a physical liaison with someone else whom he does not love. He resents being objectified, reduced to a desirable thing by that powerful stranger's lust. But what troubles him most deeply is the forcible violation implicit in his circumstances and in Gulbeyaz's command. All the components of Don Juan's deepest being are for the moment denied. He is a noble Spanish Christian male in love with a woman not at hand—yet he is forced,

in rapid succession, to adjust to being a slave, entertaining the possibility of Islamic circumcision, dressing as a Turk and a woman,
and serving as the romantic toy of a woman who is his mistress in
just the way that Haidée was not. Stripped of all his accustomed
privilege, subjugated in every possible sense, our hero in heroine's
costume is forced to feel feminine and reduced to behaving (or
freed to behave, depending on how one chooses to look at it) in
accordance with his disguise—but his crying is a womanly act with
a difference, as both the narrator and Gulbeyaz note:

> She was a good deal shock'd; not shock'd at tears,
>   For women shed and use them at their liking;
> But there is something when man's eye appears
>   Wet, still more disagreeable and striking:
> A woman's tear-drop melts, a man's half sears. (DJ 5.118)

Paradoxically enough, Juan's expression of his feminine side is
precisely what stresses his essential masculinity and evokes Gulbeyaz's innate but undeveloped womanliness. Wishing to console
but not really knowing how, she finds herself for the first time able
and inclined to nurture and sympathize: the "odd glistening mois-
ture in her eye" mirrors and answers Juan's tears and demonstrates
that "nature teaches more than power can spoil" (DJ 5.120). But
while still unshed, the "woman's tear-drop" mentioned above
cannot "melt" opposition; and in fact the sultana's incipient soften-
ing is perhaps what permits Juan to harden his heart and call "back
the stoic to his eyes" (DJ 5.121). His reassertion of self-control is
reflected in Gulbeyaz's resumption of her regal station. She now
draws on both her masculine and her feminine powers to court
Juan with a gesture superbly blended but nonetheless unsuccessful:

> At length, in an imperial way, she laid
>   Her hand on his, and bending on him eyes,
> Which needed not an empire to persuade,
>   Look'd into his for love, where none replies.   (DJ 5.125)

When her suit still does not prosper, Gulbeyaz instinctively
makes an act of submission. She throws herself on Juan's breast
and, playing the simple woman, enables Juan's simple manliness
to reassert itself—as it does first with a proud look, then with a
melodramatic speech beginning " 'The prison'd eagle will not

pair'" (DJ 5.126) and grandiosely terminating "Heads bow, knees bend, eyes watch around a throne, / And hands obey—our hearts are still our own" (DJ 5.127).

I have recapitulated the details of the love duel this fully to demonstrate its great potential for presentation in pantomime. Most of the time, the two characters mutely express themselves through formulaic glances and gestures. When they speak, the words are blatantly theatrical. Juan's heroic resolves are only a little less incredible than is his feminine disguise; and anyone who entertains the notion that the Turkish sultana understands Juan's Spanish eloquence is making a suspension of disbelief tantamount to that required for entry into the international never-never land of Harlequin and Columbine. But however fully pantomime might present the situation, its nature precludes analyzing the implications of what has been enacted. Here then the Byronic narrator— the stage manager, if you will, he who would tack up the "argument" in a commedia performance—inserts himself by means of digression. When the encounter he has set in motion resumes, it is indirectly reported. We return to the exchange of significant glances, but now these looks are relayed and explained by the narrator, whose mediating presence is thereby felt if not literally seen: "If I said fire flash'd from Gulbeyaz' eyes, / 'Twere nothing— for her eyes flash'd always fire" (DJ 5.134).

We do not see but are informed of the sultana's rage and the exact sequence of thoughts it sends sweeping through her mind: to "cut off Juan's head," "to cut only his—acquaintance," "to rally him into repentance," "to call her maids and go to bed," "to stab herself," "to sentence / The lash to Baba." And then the climax: "but her grand resource / Was to sit down again, and cry of course" (DJ 5.139). By explaining the situation as he presents it, the narrator enriches the pantomimic scene. We come to know how Gulbeyaz feels—and a skilled actress could convey the range of feelings described—but also what she thinks. We infer from that prominently placed "of course" that the womanly tears now falling from her imperial eyes were inevitable after all. Just as inevitable, by implication, is Juan's reaction: "But all his great preparatives for dying / Dissolved like snow before a woman crying" (DJ 5.141).

To shed those tears that melt opposition is both the most artful and the most natural thing that Gulbeyaz could do. Juan's tears seared her; now hers soften him. "Juan's virtue ebb'd," the narrator reports (DJ 5.142). This change of heart is conventionally feminine, in that it indicates the willingness to be wooed out of shyness or reluctance associated with coquettes from the golden age of nymphs and satyrs on. Here, though, the reversal signals Don Juan's return to manly form. He is ready to comfort a lovely woman in need of his attentions and in so doing to enjoy rather than resist the erotic adventure put in his path.

Gulbeyaz and Juan's awkwardly achieved Turko-Spanish détente seems well on the way to becoming true concord when the arrival of the sultan delays (forever, as it turns out) the kiss of peace. The sultan as Byron renders him is a stage Ottoman of the first order. Theatrically "Shawl'd to the nose, and bearded to the eyes" (DJ 5.147), he could as easily be played by a woman as by a man; and his stagily masculine appearance enhances the canto's air of androgyny. Though he has come to confer on Gulbeyaz the honor of a night in his bed, the sultan pauses to admire the newly arrived Juanna. His attention brings the disguise plot full circle, and with a piquant twist of the sort especially popular in pantomime, burletta, and the other forms of spectacular theater. By suggesting that both sultan and sultana are attracted to the stranger in disguise, Byron not only reflects, as pantomime is wont to do, a well-known situation (namely the king and queen falling in love with Pyrocles/Zelmane in Sidney's *Arcadia*). He also places the "boy-bride" of farcical convention within the plot generally associated with the "female page"—and the theatrical effect thereby achieved is more or less what would result were the central deception of *Epicoene* to replace Viola's act of impersonation in *Twelfth Night*. The mixture or reversal of dramatic conventions brings about on the metalevel a cross-dressing comparable to Juan's presentation as Juanna, or to that amusing moment in *Harlequin Whittington* where Grimaldi and the "clever little dog" present themselves as Cecily Suet and her cat.

Disguise and exchange of roles, surefire prescriptions for laughter though they may be in pantomime, can serve higher comic purposes—and Byron is quick to exploit them accordingly. Calling into question Juan's and Gulbeyaz's gender roles exposes the inadequacy of all externally imposed or superficially delineated identities. Such definitions, rapidly reversible and largely interchangeable, are not merely shallow but downright false—not identities at all but roles in the most literal sense. Tears, as we have seen, are the crucial determinant of the feminine role in canto 5's amorous face-off. Weeping, a natural human act conventionally deemed appropriate to one sex only, initiates Juan's assumption of the woman's part and Gulbeyaz's resumption of it. Tears thus serve as both catalyst and evidence of the canto's shifting balance of masculinity and femininity—or, as Susan J. Wolfson puts it, as "synechdoche for the demarcations of gender."[29] The ease and swiftness with which that balance shifts or those demarcations are erased and redrawn demonstrates both the power of a surface matter (such as having drops of water spill out of one's eyes) to define a role and the essential absurdity of any such definition.

From start to finish, *Don Juan* stresses that "identity" as we tend to envision it consists of little more than the is-and-is-not of pantomime or masquerade. The poem's Dedication begins by presenting the difference in a man, the mask that is his vocation, and the super-mask that is his title: "Bob Southey! You're a poet—poet Laureate." The last completed canto's final image is a tableau of cross-dressing that reverses neatly Don Juan's nocturnal impersonation of Juanna in the seraglio: as canto 16 ends, the spectral Black Friar's robe falls back to reveal a living and most fleshly woman: "The phantom of her frolic Grace—Fitz-Fulke!" (DJ 16.123). Between the poem's first and last moments, we find Juan always being himself by always acting the part that falls to him, always staying true to himself by keeping faith with the changing demands of time, place, company, and circumstance.

Even as it exposes the deficiencies of roles, *Don Juan's* pattern of disguise and reversal shows, in the very way that pantomime does, how those roles are to be transcended. The key is that all roles are roles—that like the transformations imposed by the benevolent agent of pantomime or the genial narrator of *Don Juan*, the parts humans play conceal as much as they reveal and reveal as much as they conceal. This point is perhaps most perfectly realized at Catherine's court in canto 9, where as "Love turned a Lieutenant of Artillery" Juan is charming youth transformed to conquering hero transformed to charming youth. The arrows and quiver of love turn into the sword and scabbard of war, then resume their former identities; Cupid's blindfold becomes a cravat and his wings a soldier's epaulets, then regain their romantic character. Each appearance is part of Juan's identity, but neither is his whole self.

Similarly, the psychosexual *pas de deux* Juan and Gulbeyaz enact forces each to experience the stock roles of man and of woman—

thus to be for a time in touch with both the masculine and feminine sides of their natures. The serious effect of their farcical encounter is temporary wholeness and balance—momentary escape from the provinciality of gender. Both Gulbeyaz and Juan are changed, and in much the same way. She, the prisoner of palace life, for the first time enters into the feelings of another person. He, though less sheltered from the need to sympathize, nonetheless learns a lesson his mentor John Johnson has earlier in the canto pronounced well worth learning: "We know what slavery is, and our disasters / May teach us better to behave when masters" (DJ 5.23). Having lost all his hereditary advantages, even the most basic one of gender, Don Juan, once one of the ruling few, begins to discover how the world feels to the subordinate many. He grudgingly starts to see that attitudes can and should change, that different situations and cultures make different demands, that practicality must sometimes countermand honor and idealism. He commences the life of cosmopolitanism and more or less conscious mobility that notably distinguishes him in the rest of the poem—and makes this beginning because he has experienced the slippery, topsy-turvy, misruled, inconsistent side of life—a state of mundane reality but the special province of pantomime.

IV

A Don, Two Lords, and a Lady

Women are treated unjustly in poetry as in life. If they're feminine, they're not ideal, and if ideal, not feminine.

Friedrich Schlegel, *Athenaeum Fragments*

The last essay concerned itself with the interpenetrations of fact and fiction, life and art—with the artificial pageant that is theater and how its roles are not really that different from the ones people play with great seriousness in daily existence. We left Don Juan, costumed as Juanna and attractive to both sultan and sultana, in the midst of his most extravagant stint of role-playing. Even that interlude of acting seems understated in comparison with the incredible but actual drama that took the stage of Whig society when Lord Byron (Childe Harold) played opposite Lady Caroline Lamb (Ariel, Sprite, Fairy Queen) in a *pièce mal faite* that ran from March 1812, when the two principals met at a waltzing party, until spring 1816, when Byron turned his back on English society only to be replaced a fortnight later by *Glenarvon* (her novel featuring him as title character) and English society, outraged and fascinated by *Glenarvon*'s blend of fact and fiction, turned its back on Lady Caroline.[1] Or perhaps, as I would like to suggest, the play went on a while longer. Perhaps the novel had something to do with *Don Juan*. In any case Lady Caroline, like many another reader and writer of the day, found herself driven to response by the comic epic she had helped inspire—certainly by her example, and possibly by her writing.

The title I have chosen for this essay announces its main concerns (*Don Juan*, *Glenarvon*, Byron, Lady Caroline) and the relationships among these works and people) and indicates its kinship

with the Southey chapter, a kinship based on its similarly comparative way of proceeding. Here again, the texts are Don Juan and a
neglected English literary work preceding it. Here again, the authors are Byron and one of his eloquent, or perhaps verbose,
enemies. Here again, my contention is that the more obscure work
is reread in Byron's more famous one and that what Don Juan stands
to gain is not just a straw man (or woman) but also a potential
source of themes and insights. But whatever the similarities in
these two instances, the chief obstacles to the argument are rather
different. Unlike Letters from England, Glenarvon is a book we know
Byron to have read. His acknowledgment of the fact is well known,
appearing as it does in the last couplet of a versified account of his
reading, a trifle he liked well enough to put in letters to Thomas
Moore, John Murray, and John Cam Hobhouse: "I read 'Glenarvon,' too, by Caro. Lamb— / God damn!" (LJ 5:187, 193, 199). We
even know when he read the damnable production: some time
between 22 July 1816, when he told John Murray, "Of Glenarvon—
Madame de Stael told me (ten days ago at Copet) marvellous &
grievous things—but I have seen nothing of it but the Motto" (LJ
5:85), and 29 July, when he wrote to Samuel Rogers, "I have read
'Glenarvon'"

> "From furious Sappho scarce a milder fate
> —— by her love—or libelled by her hate."[2] (LJ 5:86)

We also know that Glenarvon reentered his thoughts during his Don
Juan days. In a letter to Teresa Guiccioli, whom in fact he had
characterized as "a sort of an Italian Caroline Lamb" (LJ 6:115), he
writes, "Your little head is heated now by that damned novel—the
author of which has been—in every country and at all times—my
evil Genius" (LJ 7:37).

Though Byron certainly read Glenarvon, its connection with Don
Juan is less immediately evident than is the possible influence
discussed in the Southey essay. Glenarvon does not feature a young
Spaniard traveling in England and observing English life from a
Continental perspective, nor does it contain so many attitudes and
opinions so surprisingly similar to those voiced in Don Juan. What
Glenarvon does offer Byron, I would suggest, is an English version of
the Don Juan myth told (almost uniquely in its history) from the
female point of view. This shifted point of view widens the scope
of a legend that in most of its versions centers rather narrowly on

the character of Don Juan. In *Glenarvon*, Lady Caroline shows herself fascinated with the seducer's qualities—but she gives prominence to the nature, feelings, and motivations of the seduced. Doing so results, I think, in a portrayal that Byron took seriously enough to refute, however dismissive his comments on Lady Caroline's production may have been. As a number of readers have noticed in different ways, one of the most surprising differences between Byron's Don Juan and others is the transformation of an irresistible man into an unresisting one—a good-natured and innately obliging fellow made the romantic toy of a parade of powerful women. I see this reversal of convention as Byron's rebuttal of *Glenarvon*, a work where the male title character actively, treacherously, compulsively seduces almost every female crossing his path in the story; but it also seems that *Don Juan*'s recognition of women as potent, complex beings could be a lesson learned from *Glenarvon*, an intermittent empathy across gender lines that is yet another variety of the poem's cosmopolitanism.

From the moment of its publication in 1816, *Glenarvon* has been a work known and read less for its literary merits than for its not-so-thickly veiled portrayal of Lady Caroline, Byron, and their romantic relationship. When after a few months Byron's attention turned to other women, including her confidante Lady Oxford and her husband's cousin Annabella Milbanke, Lady Caroline made numerous private and public efforts to reclaim him through scenes enacted with varying degrees of outrageousness. She turned up at his lodgings in page-boy attire, ran away from home, made an apparent attempt to stab herself at Lady Heathcote's ball. But having "played the devil," as Byron puts it in *Don Juan*, her final gambit was to "write a novel." The work she produced is occasionally dazzling, far from polished, deeply flawed. Despite its defects, though, *Glenarvon* warrants serious consideration, in part because its very flaws and excesses are testimony to how talent can be thwarted, how barriers of personality, gender, class, and education can keep a mind from achieving its full potential, in part because its view of the relations between men and women can be seen as providing Byron crucial ideas to refute and reflect in *Don Juan*. In this essay, I shall be thinking about *Glenarvon* both as a semiadequate expression of one sensibility (Lady Caroline's) and as an entirely effective catalyst for another (Byron's). Besides showing something interesting about the two writers and *Don Juan*, this examination of *Glenarvon* will, I hope, have relevance as a case study of how circumstance can lame talent, how talent can struggle against circumstance, and how literary texts can be a forum for sustained conversation where author-reader replies to reader-author.

Lady Caroline Ponsonby (1785–1828) was the daughter of the third earl of Bessborough and his wife, Lady Henrietta Spencer.[3] After an early childhood spent in Italy, she was raised at Devonshire House and Chatsworth, in the household of her famous aunt, Georgiana duchess of Devonshire. Pronounced "too delicate" for instruction, she received little formal education; but, growing up in Devonshire House's mixed atmosphere of profusion and neglect, she developed into what David Cecil calls "the most dynamic personality that had appeared in London society for a generation."[4] Slight and even boyish, she possessed considerable but unconventional beauty, spoke with a lisp that enhanced her attractiveness, seemed like what she was: a talented, undisciplined, passionate, naive, charming, obnoxious, mercurial, paradoxical girl. In 1805 this distinctive being married a peace-loving, conventional, gifted man: William Lamb, later to be Lord Melbourne, prime minister under Queen Victoria. Theirs was a love match, and their first years together were idyllic; but despite a deep and enduring attachment Lamb, interested in making his mark in the world beyond their personal one, was not the ideal husband for an intense egotist. Feeling bored and neglected, Lady Caroline became more daring in manner if not exactly in fact. In 1812, she began her notorious affair with Byron. Though the age was a permissive one, her flagrant violation of conventions proved too much to overlook. When Byron ended their connection, the unstable Lady Caroline went into a period of emotional turmoil that spawned *Glenarvon*, with its often hysterical but sometimes dead-accurate portraits of herself, her husband, Byron, and the Great World in which their melodrama took place. Excluded by the final, unforgivable indiscretion of publication from the circles into which she had been born, she sank into a sad and dissipated middle age during which she wrote two other, less controversial novels, *Graham Hamilton* (1822) and *Ada Reis* (1823). She died at Melbourne House in 1828.

As is exemplified in "Shakespeare's Sister," that marvelous exercise in historical supposition Virginia Woolf includes in *A Room of One's Own*, women of talent and energy have at different times and in different ways been kept from effectively exerting their powers. Tillie Olsen voices the recognition, which she goes on to amplify and probe in *Silences*, her study of thwarted creativity, this way: "Where the gifted among women (and men) have remained mute, or have never attained full capacity, it is because of circumstances, inner or outer, which oppose the needs of creation."[5]

England under the Prince Regent was not so uncongenial a place for the development of female creativity as England under Elizabeth had been. Women were writing—writing, publishing, and being read, as the careers of Lady Caroline's contemporaries and near-contemporaries Jane Austen, Fanny Burney, Maria Edgworth, Ann Radcliffe, and Mary Shelley attest. Lady Caroline herself was able to write, publish, and be read, for better or worse—witness *Glenarvon* and her other two novels. Nonetheless, a writer can be muted without being reduced to complete and literal wordlessness. It is thus worth asking if and how Lady Caroline's writing was restrained by her gender, class, and education. It is worth considering *Glenarvon* as an upper-class woman's attempt to do what a ruling-class man (her husband the politician or her lover the poet) or a woman who had been brought up differently might do—to achieve personal, even public success rather than merely promote the achievement of others. It is worth asking if chronic frustration of talent might not have given rise to the famous fits of temper and temperament Lady Caroline suffered—for in any case, her mental sufferings take palpable form in *Glenarvon*, whose very defects and inconsistencies bespeak a naturally powerful but undisciplined mind.

But if the questions are worth asking, the answers do not seem simple. Lady Caroline Lamb was both lucky and unlucky—in some ways society's victim, but not just a victim. Growing up without much formal education was a handicap (one she shared with most women and men of her time) but not an insurmountable one, given that she passed her days in houses where books were present and ideas cherished, where the likes of Charles James Fox and Richard Brinsley Sheridan were regular fixtures. Furthermore, her first years of marriage, like Mary Shelley's, were filled with intellectual adventures. William, entertaining, unpedantic, and six years the senior, liked teaching; Caroline, quick and enthusiastic, liked learning; and their days as she describes them resemble an agreeable tutorial: " 'Wm. and I get up about ten or half after

or later (if late at night)—have our breakfast—talk a little—read
Newton on the Prophecies with the Bible, having finished Sher-
lock—then I hear him his part [William was then acting Captain
Absolute in amateur theatricals], he goes to eat and walk—I finish
dressing and take a drive or a little walk—then come upstairs
where Wm. meets me and we read Hume with Shakespeare till the
dressing bell.' "6 William was not eccentric in appreciating and
cultivating his wife's mind. Unlike certain other circles and classes,
the aristocratic Whigs among whom Lady Caroline lived valued
learning and intelligence in women. She even had examples of
female literary achievement in her family—she was a descendant
of Sarah duchess of Marlborough, and in the nearer past her aunt
Devonshire somehow, amid busy days of gaming, love, and friendship, found time to have written better-than-passable poetry and a
novel, The Sylph. Most important of all, with money, leisure, and a
squadron of servants, Lady Caroline had absolutely no need to be
the "angel in the house" Virginia Woolf had to kill in herself or the
"essential angel," that more mundane provider of daily family
necessities that Tillie Olsen sees as impeding or killing many a
woman's talent.

Privileged though she may have been in many ways, Lady Caroline appears to have been hobbled in certain other regards. The
laissez faire of Devonshire House may have gone far toward de-
veloping her individuality, but nothing could have been less likely
to teach her the self-discipline a writer needs; and she had no
reason to feel any of the externally imposed disciplines that sometimes can substitute for the inner sort. Her upbringing and station
provided Lady Caroline with most sorts of confidence but not the
kind necessary for taking on serious work in a major genre—a
confidence that would come more easily to men of her class,
whose early educations centered on memorizing the classics and
composing in imitation of the classical masters. We shall soon go
into the possible reasons why she wrote Glenarvon; but whatever
her reasons, she chose to write the book as a roman à clef, a form
that seldom gains high esteem. Of course, basing a first novel on
direct personal experience is quite ordinary; but Lady Caroline
chose to highlight the personal source of her fiction. In doing so
she may have been taking a small and relatively easy step toward
ultimate success in a greater and more challenging genre. She may
have been condemning herself to a kind of failure, shutting off the

possibility of major achievement by working in a minor vein. In any case, this choice of form is consistent with her ways of displaying her talent in the years before *Glenarvon*. Though Byron's letters speak of her great gift for poetry, and Regency memorialists pay high tribute to her abilities as a painter, Lady Caroline limited herself to working in forms generally considered "small." She produced songs, occasional verses, charades, beautifully detailed miniature paintings less than an inch square—all socially acceptable outlets for feminine talents.

Though her choice of literary ends may have been conventional, her means were exotic. When Lady Caroline wrote *Glenarvon* (at night, in secret, so she claimed) she allegedly put on male attire—a page boy's costume. When she presented her manuscript to a copyist, she chose to dress her companion, Miss Welsh, as the society lady and to present herself (and the manuscript's author) as a fourteen-year-old serving boy, William Ormonde. These impersonations are blatantly suggestive, but determining exactly what they signify is difficult. There are simply too many possible meanings. Did Lady Caroline, anticipating by a quarter of a century the habit of George Sand (another female novelist who took fictional revenge on her famous lovers), cast off womanly circumscriptions and assume masculine power by changing clothes? Was she escaping from the complexities of maturity by retreating into childhood? Was she overcoming upper-class restraints, a possibility not to be discounted in someone who grew up in the aftermath of the French Revolution, perhaps the first time mob attire became modish? Was she indulging a characteristically aristocratic taste for fancy dress? All these responses, some conventional and some subversive for a person of her sex and station, seem worth arguing. All of them imply at least a measure of dissatisfaction with her situation and its constraints. But during the period of *Glenarvon*'s composition another possibility is equally plausible. Lady Caroline's pageboy disguise may have been an exercise in nostalgia for the happier days of her love affair, a period during which she had learned that the livery she enjoyed wearing possessed the extra advantage of presenting her elfin charm in the way it would appeal most strongly to Byron.

David Cecil characterizes *Glenarvon* as "a deplorable production, an incoherent cross between a realistic novel of fashionable life and a

fantastic tale of terror, made preposterous by every absurd device."[7] On strictly literary grounds, this assessment is plausible, and
everyone who writes on Lady Caroline Lamb more or less echoes
the verdict. At the core of *Glenarvon* is the education—which is to
say the ruin—of Calantha, a noble, innocent, idealistic, impulsive
beauty too fine to thrive in a hard world. Calantha marries young,
as Lady Caroline did. Her husband, Lord Avondale, though warm-
hearted, wise, and tolerant as was William Lamb, corrupts Calantha's morals by introducing her too abruptly to mundane realities, then abandoning her rudderless on the high seas of high
society, where, after some struggle, she succumbs to Glenarvon, a
Byronic seducer of unrivaled charisma, intelligence, gloom, and
guilt. Loving Calantha deeply, Glenarvon nonetheless deserts her
cruelly and callously. The world despises her. She dies of heart-
break. The men who survive her meet in a duel. In the first edition,
Glenarvon injures his adversary with provocation; Avondale rides
away with a flesh wound and a bruised ego, and when he dies it is
from sadness. In the second edition, the scene culminates with
Glenarvon plunging a dagger into Avondale's heart (which, meta-
phorically speaking, he has already done in seducing Calantha) and
departing a murderer in fact. Glenarvon dies theatrically—self-
starved, half drowned, pursued by real or imagined demons. Su-
peradded to this melodrama are other Gothic excesses: maniacs,
murderers, wicked Italians, babies switched in the cradle, revolutionaries, ghosts, an anchoress-poet turned harlot. Contrasting the
extravagantly lurid scenes of the novel (all of which are set in
Ireland, where Caroline had been sent for her sins in September of
1812) are sparkling and believable portraits of London society, with
its grandeurs, *longeurs*, hypocrisies, and absurdities, in chapters acclaimed even by the novel's harshest detractors.

It is hard to do anything but go along with critical consensus and
condemn *Glenarvon* if we take it as a whole and judge it as a novel.
That is how its author wanted it judged, ultimately. She signaled as
much by publishing it, a process requiring some persistence on
her part, and by somewhat carefully and sometimes effectively
revising the published work between first and second editions—
reducing verbiage, correcting errors, toning down the incredible
Gothicisms, cutting offensive passages, refining and altering her
chief characters, stressing the work's moral efficacy.[8] But *Glenarvon* is
a much more interesting work if we see it less narrowly, as some-

thing more than a novel. Indeed, its earliest readers purchased, perused, and condemned it not for fictions but for supposed truths—truths about Whig society, about the author and her husband, most especially about Byron. How true those truths may be is an unsettled matter. As John Galt's memorable phrase puts it, Lady Caroline was renowned for "acuteness blended with phrensy and talent"; and she once spoke of truth as "what one believes at the moment," thus sounding like a sophisticated postmodernist rather than a naive Regency writer.[9] Byron repeatedly claimed that Glenarvon's mendacity was one of the reasons for its literary weakness: "It seems to me that, if the authoress had written the truth, and nothing but the truth—the whole truth—the romance would not only have been more romantic, but more entertaining" (LJ 5:131). If we consider Glenarvon in terms of its blend of facts and fictions, conscious and subconscious ones, if we think about why it came to be written and what powerful feelings lie underneath, or sometimes burst through, the flawed surface of narrative, the book becomes a document of more meaning to its author, of more potential value to Byron and other readers. Let us begin with the circumstances of composition—themselves a muddle of truth telling and theatrical dissembling.

Why did Lady Caroline write and publish Glenarvon? For revenge, according to the most widely held belief—revenge against all who had wronged her, the Melbournes, Lady Holland, Lady Oxford, Byron. For personal repentance and the public good, as respectively asserted by Clark Olney and Lady Caroline herself in the moralizing preface to the second edition. For a mixture of these reasons, says John Clubbe, who recognizes that "the novel forced itself out of her: she had to write it much as Byron had to write his confessional poems."[10]

Glenarvon does indeed seem to have "forced itself out." We might see the expressive process as a kind of childbirth, Lady Caroline's "illegitimate" novel as the love child that resulted from her romance with Byron. From the start his attraction for her had been a literary one. The fact is acknowledged in her obituary, a composition attributed to William Lamb: "The world is very lenient to the mistresses of poets, and perhaps not without justice, for their attachments have something of excuse . . . they arise from imagination, not depravity." Lady Caroline, like the rest of fashionable London, first knew of Byron as the young traveler-poet who had written and presumably posed for *Childe Harold*. She fell in love with that potent Byronic fiction, a mask self-created but thrust on him by his admirers. The charms or deficiencies of the real man mattered little: warned by Samuel Rogers that the lionized poet had a club foot and a habit of nail-biting, the lady already in love with an idea replied, "If he is as ugly as Aesop, I must see him."[11]

Writing *Glenarvon* seems to be the product of a confessional impulse Lady Caroline shared with or derived from Byron—that and her attempt to emulate, or maybe even surpass, him. The act is comparable to the creation of *Frankenstein* a year or two later, Mary Shelley's making a "Modern Prometheus" out of parts derived from her two poet-heroes and replying in her novel to their Promethean poems. Similarly, Lady Caroline's fiction combines bits of Lord Byron with pieces of the Byronic hero in a tale with more guilt and mystification than can be found in *Childe Harold* and all the Oriental tales combined. Her need to resemble the writer she loved (and the lover she had lost) extended beyond the matters of subject and tone to manner of composition. "In one month I wrote and sent 'Glenarvon' to the press," was Lady Caroline's claim concerning the gestation of her literary progeny, a generally accepted but demonstrably false statement. Her correspondence with John Murray proves that the task cost her two or three years of labor that left the book "substantially completed" in June 1815.[12] A need to be like Byron can best account for Lady Caroline's feeling that her novel should be taken for an extemporaneous effusion in the Byron line—though spontaneity was something of a pose with him also. Publishing the results of her so-called month of composition barely two weeks after Byron's April 1816 flight from England seems like nothing so much as another act of emulation. Hobhouse and others saw Lady Caroline's ill- or well-timed novel as attacking Byron's character when it was most vulnerable; she unconvincingly but perhaps sincerely spoke of *Glenarvon* as her defense of Byron. But whatever its effect on him, the book clearly caused her to share his banishment. Publishing *Glenarvon*—flaunting the literary consequences of her infidelity before the world—may have been her Byronic gesture of self-exile, a deliberate if imperfectly calculated act she would come to regret.

Childbirth is not the only metaphor that comes readily to mind as suitable for characterizing the production of *Glenarvon*. Another apt comparison is one that Byron rejects as too tired to be worth pursuing in the English cantos of *Don Juan*: the volcano. "Poor thing! How frequently, by me and others, / It hath been stirred up till its smoke quite smothers" (DJ 13.36), the narrator says as he hunts for figurative speech to convey the repressed passion of Lady Adeline Amundeville, modeled in part on Lady Caroline. Earlier, Byron himself uses the image both to speak of Lady Caroline ("—Then your heart—my poor Caro, what a little volcano! that pours *lava* through your veins, & yet I cannot wish it a bit colder" LJ 2:170) and, in a famous phrase, to describe poetry ("it is the lava of the imagination whose eruption prevents an earth-quake" LJ 3:179). Hélène Cixous, in "The Laugh of the Medusa," resorts to the volcano as she describes feminine writing in general. Her words, however, are a particularly apt representation of what *Glenarvon* is— and, matters of gender aside, of what *Don Juan* does: "A feminine text cannot fail to be more than subversive. It is volcanic; as it is written it brings about an upheaval of the old property crust, carrier of masculine investments; there's no other way." This erup- tion, as Cixous puts it, serves "to smash everything, to shatter the framework of institutions, to blow up the law, to break up the 'truth' with laughter."[13]

Glenarvon's eruption contains little that is intentionally laughter producing; but it seems to have followed Cixous's model rather than Byron's in causing rather than preventing an earthquake. The upheaval *Glenarvon* brought about in Whig drawing rooms, at Al- mack's, Brooks's, and other haunts of the Regency powers and exquisites, came chiefly because Lady Caroline did what Cixous claims to be necessary in the second sentence of her essay: "Wom- an must write her self."[14] Lady Caroline continuously hints that in Calantha she is writing her self—and the concluding sentence of one of Calantha's many self-abasements forthrightly erases the dis- tinction between author and protagonist. " 'Yet when they read my history—' " says the heroine, conscious for the moment of her fictional status, " 'if amidst the severity of justice which such a narrative must excite, some feelings of forgiveness and pity should arise, perhaps the prayer of one, who has suffered much, may ascend for them, and the thanks of a broken heart be accepted in return' " (G 3:147).[15]

Lady Caroline's "writing her self" gives *Glenarvon* some of its best and worst features. Unwilling or unable to get beyond her own story, she offers something intense and undirected. Her view of the truth may not always have resembled other people's visions, but in *Glenarvon* (the first edition, that is) she stays true to what she saw in her upbringing, marriage, experience of society, and romance with Byron. The feelings and events presented are not edited in such a way as to fit them into the world as it is generally understood or into the realistic novel as it is generally constructed. The perspective is an eccentric one. Faithfulness to this singular view of things obliges *Glenarvon* to contain characters the common reader will find hypocritical, overblown, self-indulgent—effusions that to the ordinary ear sound incredibly naive and sentimental—incidents that are downright absurd. The problem, however, is not that *Glenarvon* fails to reflect "real life" but that life as experienced by Lady Caroline and embodied in *Glenarvon* has little in common with what most readers (even in her own day and of her own class) would find real. Sincerely recording her own congenital insincerity, foolishly publishing a transcript of her own folly, Lady Caroline makes a good confession but a bad novel. This mixed thing is perfectly characterized by a further Cixous phrase: *Glenarvon* is above all "the chaosmos of the 'personal.' "[16]

How so? One place to begin might be with names and their role in characterization. Two or three possible conventions for creating and naming characters seem to be the rule in fiction. The distinctions become clear when we look at two novels published during the same year as *Glenarvon*, Jane Austen's *Emma* and Thomas Love Peacock's *Headlong Hall*. An author aiming at lifelike characters would typically operate as Jane Austen does and provide names that may be subject to interpretation, playful or serious, but that nevertheless would pass muster in the real world. "Emma Woodhouse" and "George Knightley" may be names we can read for meaning, but they are also utterly believable. The writer whose fiction makes no pretenses of reality would be more likely to choose, as Peacock does, incredible names ("Patrick O'Prism," "Philomela Poppyseed") or to undercut credible names by explicitly announcing their significance in the literary game being played (as Peacock's playfully erudite footnotes do for "Foster," "Escot," and "Jenkinson"). Lady Caroline goes by neither Austen's rules nor Peacock's. *Glenarvon* does aim at transcribing a version of reality in its characters—that is the first objective of roman à clef. But *Glenarvon*'s names announce that they are laden with meaning in loud if not always intelligible tones. The heroine, to begin where

we should, is called "Lady Calantha Delaval." The number of syllables matches word for word with "Lady Caroline Ponsonby"—but
how much richer Lady Caroline's fictionalized name is than her
actual one! "Calantha" announces through its reference to the
heroine of Ford's The Broken Heart just what is in store for the
protagonist—and if the reader misses the allusion, Lady Augusta
Selwyn, one of the novel's best-drawn characters, facetiously spells
the matter out: " 'Come, tell me truly, is not your heart in torture?
and, like your namesake Calantha, while lightly dancing the gayest
in the ring, has not the shaft already been struck, and shall you not
die ere you attain the goal?' " (G 2:135). After thinking about the
volcanic nature of Lady Caroline Lamb and her fiction, one sees
the surname "Delaval" as something more than an attractively
aristocratic combination of syllables. The letters of "Delaval" are
"lava" enclosed—a detail especially intriguing in light of the title
that accompanies the name, for Calantha's father is duke of Altamonte. The sounds of "Delaval" are close to, though not identical
with, "devil." This heroine's name explains in various sorts of
shorthand what sort of person she will show herself to be in the
course of the novel and signals the loftiness and the intense, potentially destructive sensibility she is said to possess in the first lengthy
description of her nature:

Her feelings indeed swelled with a tide too powerful for the
unequal resistance of her understanding:—her motives appeared
the very best, but the actions which resulted from them were
absurd and exaggerated. Thoughts, swift as lightening, hurried
through her brain:—projects, seducing, but visionary crowded
upon her view: without a curb she followed the impulse of her
feelings; and those feelings varied with every varying interest and
impression. . . .
. . . All that was base or mean, she, from her soul, despised; a
fearless spirit raised her, as she fondly imagined, above the vulgar
herd; self confident, she scarcely deigned to bow the knee before
her God; and man, as she had read of him in history, appeared too
weak, too trivial to inspire either alarm or admiration.
It was thus, with bright prospects, strong love of virtue, high
ideas of honour, that she entered upon life. (G 1:75, 77–78)

Lady Caroline's background, character, and story may be Calantha's—but Calantha does not suffice to express her complexities.
Her less ladylike attributes and her unfulfilled impulses are pro-

jected into other characters. One is Zerbellini, a child who turns out to be Calantha's abducted brother and who is sent as a page to Castle Delaval by Glenarvon's alter ego, Viviani. As a boy, a change-ling, a servant, an embodied connection between Glenarvon and Calantha, Zerbellini plays a number of roles Lady Caroline acted, or fancied the idea of acting, in her real drama with Byron. A more ex-treme vision of Lady Caroline as she might have been had her ac-tions corresponded fully to her inclinations is presented in Elinor St. Clare, a character whose behavior and qualities Calantha ex-plicitly compares with her own at a number of crucial points in the novel (G 1:121, 2:27). This beautiful and wild young creature, who like Lady Caroline (and Calantha) is raised by an aunt, expresses her author's vital energy, notably absent from the ethereal though passionate Calantha, and takes Lady Caroline's capacity for out-rageous action several steps farther. "St. Clare," as she is typically styled, has Lady Caroline's fierce idealism, her talent for poetry and music, her tastes for riding, dressing in male attire, and political activism. Although she has been raised in a convent and betrothed to Christ rather than married to an earthly lord, St. Clare shows none of Calantha's scruples in yielding to Glenarvon. While Calan-tha continues to feel social constraints and keeps on with her old life after becoming fascinated with Glenarvon, St. Clare boldly renounces her old ties for the new, engrossing, disgraceful one— unlike Lady Caroline or Calantha, she goes off with the fatal object of her passions. The demands of the nineteenth-century novel being what they are, each of Lady Caroline's fictive shadows pays for her error—but the ways are different and the differences il-luminating. While Calantha, torn apart by conflicting demands and emotions, dies of a broken heart and nervous exhaustion in the middle of volume 3 (rather a serious structural problem if the novel were merely roman à clef), St. Clare endures to the denoue-ment and perishes grandly: having kept the faith with her band of Irish revolutionaries, fought like a man in battle, and burned the turncoat Glenarvon's ancestral home, she makes an equestrian leap from cliff to sea and dies theatrically, a Sappho on horseback.

"St. Clare," like "Calantha Delaval," is a name that calls out to be explicated—it is impossible not to recognize its suggestions of holiness and purity, appropriate connotations as the book begins, ironic ones later on—and also demands to be connected with other names. Within the novel St. Clare is echoed in Glenarvon's

Christian name, Clarence, in what he calls his illegitimate child by Alice MacAllain, Clare of Costolly, and in Clarendon, the surname of the poet who has enraptured Calantha's society friends, a man "gifted with every kind of merit," including "an open ingenuous countenance, expressive eyes, and a strong and powerful mind" (G 1:202). Moving from fiction to the world of fact, one finds affinities between *Glenarvon*'s St. Clare and Clare of Assisi, "Sister Moon" to St. Francis's "Brother Sun" and, like her fictional namesake, a woman whose love for a charismatic man (though a saint rather than a seducer) inspired her to join and lead a cause. It is less obvious but equally interesting that Calantha's course, like Lady Caroline's own, parallels and then at key points inverts the life of St. Clare of Rimini, who married young and lived scandalously until her conversion at the age of thirty-four, after which time she devoted herself to penance, prayer, and good works. It is also worth observing that earl of Clare was the title belonging to one of Byron's Harrow favorites, the object of an idealized schoolboy affection that Byron characterized in a letter to Mary Shelley as his only true friendship with a member of his own sex: "I do not know the male human being, except Lord Clare, the friend of my infancy, for whom I feel any thing that deserves the name" (LJ 10:34). And of course one of the small but remarkable coincidences of Byron's life was that in April of 1816, as he prepared to leave England and Lady Caroline awaited the publication of her novel, another Clare, this one female, self-named, persistent, and finally detested, entered his life: Mary Godwin's stepsister Mary Jane (Clara, Clare, or Claire) Clairmont.

These variants of *Clare* with their connections and repetitions seem fraught with significance—but the intricacy of whatever pattern there may be thwarts the recognition for which that pattern seems to call. Is the choice of *Clare* arbitrary? Doubtful, considering its repetition. Is the repetition a clumsy inadvertence? If so, Lady Caroline probably would have made changes for the second edition. A sign of links between characters? Almost certainly in the case of Clarence Lord Glenarvon and his bastard son; it is less certain but more interesting to speculate that St. Clare and Clarence indicate a deliberate connection of the book's two boldest renegades, an authorial awareness of the spiritual likeness between herself and Byron. Does Lady Caroline mean for us to see connections between her fiction and the saints' lives? Very likely, especially in light of her having added explicit references to Calantha's Catholicism to the second edition.[17] Are the variations on *Clare* a bridge between Lady Caroline's Byronic fiction and the facts of Byron's life? Perhaps. The prophetic allusion to Claire Clairmont is of course happenstance, but Byron may well have spoken to Lady Caroline, or to someone she knew, of his regard for Lord Clare. What purpose, if any, would allusion to this friendship serve? Confronting the chaosmos of the personal, one cannot be certain. The full meaning of *Clare* is far from clear—it seems to have risen less out of simple intention than out of the free play of wit as Schlegel understands it when he says that "A witty idea is a disintegration of spiritual substances which, before being suddenly separated, must have been thoroughly mixed. The imagination must first be satiated with all sorts of life before one can electrify it."[18]

Doubling and repetition work toward a more intelligible effect in Avondale and Glenarvon, the titles assigned to the novel's representatives of sinned-against William Lamb and sinning Byron. Among the surprising features of *Glenarvon*'s first edition is that these two lords, who in terms of both literary convention and real life ought to appear as opposites, are in certain ways the same man: part hero, part villain. Their titles, compound words consisting of reversed near-equivalents (*Glen* is synonymous with *dale*; *arvon* corresponds to *Avon*), exactly represent their kinship with one another and topographically suggest their shared antithetical relation to the daughter of Altamonte. However wicked Lady Caroline intended the one to seem and however admirable she wished to show the other as being, Glenarvon and Avondale respond to and affect Calantha in comparable ways: both men love and lower her.

Avondale, the good and noble husband, is nevertheless a freethinker, a man of the world. In educating Calantha, he begins her corruption: "Eager to oppose and conquer those opinions in his wife, which savoured as he thought of bigotry and prudish reserve, he tore the veil at once from her eyes, and opened hastily her wondering mind to a world before unknown. He foresaw not the peril to which he exposed her:—he heeded not the rapid progress of her thoughts—the boundless views of an over-heated imagination. At first she shrunk with pain and horror, from every feeling which to her mind appeared less chaste, less pure, than those to which she had long been accustomed; but when her principles, or rather her prejudices, yielded to the power of love, she broke from a restraint too rigid, into a liberty the most dangerous from its novelty, its wildness and uncertainty" (G 1:141).

The debasement Avondale brings upon Calantha is only theoretical—thanks to him she experiences not firsthand sin and guilt but "books of every description," more precisely characterized in the second edition as "the works of Historians, Philosophers, and Metaphysicians."[19] This progressive corruption of innocence, however, is just what Glenarvon vows to continue in the sphere of practice when, disguised as the Italian Viviani, he first encounters Calantha at a London ball: " 'Let me see her, and I will sing to her till the chaste veil of every modest feeling is thrown aside, and thoughts of fire dart into her bosom, and loosen every principle within' " (G 1:184). For the time, this is all just talk. But when he arrives in his own person back in Ireland, Glenarvon proceeds to do what he has promised. The second of the novel's three volumes is chiefly devoted to his insidious but irresistible destruction of Calantha's principles. His villainy is entirely intentional, and he insists on making Calantha fully conscious of her progressive debauchery: " 'Remember when a word or look were regarded by you as a crime,' " Glenarvon remarks when he has lured Calantha approximately halfway from her position as respectable matron to the infernal marriage vows that represent her ultimate corruption, " '—how you shuddered at the bare idea of guilt. Now you can hear its language with interest: it has lost its horror: Ah soon it shall be the only language your heart will like.' " (G 2:241).

According to common sense and the usual rubrics of fiction, the choice of parallel names for hero and villain would seem an awkward confusion; and presenting a husband's and a seducer's moral effects on the heroine as comparable would be yet more of a defect—a serious lapse from orthodox understanding of those roles. But a powerful if subconscious point is being made. Stressing the similarities between the "best" man in the novel and the "worst" one demonstrates Lady Caroline's adherence to the truths of her heart. She does not use her book as an opportunity to make Byron seem worse than he was—the crimes ascribed to Glenarvon are melodramatically incredible ones, and his charm and potential goodness remain evident to the last. Nor does she excuse William from what she perceived as his part in her downfall, much as she loved him and grateful as she was for his loyalty when the world had turned against her. A further consequence of this linkage is to generalize the corruption of Calantha, to make it resonate as a sort of archetypal act: what men, even truly loving men, do to women—and, as Byron demonstrates in Don Juan, what women also do to men.

The mythic proportions of this act are clearer because Glenarvon's debasement of Calantha is not a unique event, just as Don Juan's falling for the more experienced Julia is but the first instance of what we come to see as his life's pattern. In the course of the novel Glenarvon seduces virtually every important female character, or at least charms each one to the point where seduction would be possible should he choose it. On page 28 of volume 1, Glenarvon makes his debut as a Don Juan by pursuing and acquiring the "most beautiful woman in Florence," whose outraged husband revenges the insult to his honor by killing the lady. From there, Glenarvon's list of mistresses known to the reader expands to include Lady Margaret Buchanan, Alice MacAllain, Elinor St. Clare, Calantha, and Lady Mandeville. The women attracted to Glenarvon though not debauched by him include Calantha's cousins, Lady Augusta Selwyn, and the heiress Miss Monmouth.

In Glenarvon the function of man seems to be stealing, staining, and breaking feminine hearts—but nonetheless, the novel lets men off more lightly than it does the author's own sex. The real victims of Lady Caroline's pen are not William Lamb or Byron. Avondale's offenses are slight and more than counterbalanced by his love and virtues. Glenarvon's assorted wickednesses are either improbable or trivial and, like Avondale's, offset by what is fine in him. For believable villainy—treachery, heartlessness, cruelty, and selfishness as they are generally understood to manifest themselves—we must turn to Glenarvon's gallery of women. In Caroline's portraits of the great ladies of Whig society we find sharper outlines and less ambivalence, we sense how formidable Lady Caroline's powers of observation and understanding could be, we feel the force of Elizabeth Jenkins's assertion that "Lady Caroline had the gifts of a novelist without being able to write a novel."[20] Thanks to these gifts, even the portraits of the women she sets out to denounce retain the excellences that brought worldly success to their originals. The false Lady Mandeville, who professes friendship even as she steals Glenarvon from Calantha, is Lady Oxford to the life—the ripe beauty and winning amiability of that countess being transcribed along with her classical pedantry and notorious promiscuity. Lady Margaret Buchanan, whose hard wisdom, amorality, ambition, and attractiveness to the much younger Glenarvon make her resemble nothing so much as an extrapolation from Lady Melbourne, is the blackest English character in the story. Like many a British novelist of her day, Lady Caroline reserves the novel's darkest deed for a foreigner, the Italian La Crusca; but Lady Margaret plans that wicked act, the abduction and murder of her infant nephew to permit her son's succession to the dukedom, and she perseveres in subsequent treachery to her immediate family. Yet she is permitted heroic grandeur and the courage of extraordinary aspirations, for herself and for Calantha, of whom she says to the more conventional aunt, Mrs. Seymour, "I wish her not only to be virtuous; I will acknowledge it,—I wish her to be distinguished and great" (G 1:73–74). The other feminine portraits—Calantha's cousins (in real life the daughters of the Devonshires, Lady Georgiana and Lady Harriet Spencer), Lady Augusta Selwyn (diversely identified but perhaps likeliest to be Lady Cahir), and the most famous and brilliant of them all, the comic apotheosis of Lady Holland as the Princess of Madagascar, dominatrix to her reviewer-slaves at Barbary House—demonstrate that Lady Caroline could achieve, if not sustain, the blend of selectivity and truth to life that makes for successful satire.

As for the depiction of Calantha herself, one cannot fairly accuse Lady Caroline of self-indulgence. Instead, she is "her own best psychologist,"[21] as her biographers implicitly acknowledge by relying on *Glenarvon* to supplement primary sources of information on her life. Insight and candor characterize the following representative passage, an assessment of Calantha's character in London society: "Calantha was esteemed generous; yet indifference for what others valued, and thoughtless profusion were the only qualities she possessed. It is true that the sufferings of others melted a young and ardent heart into the performance of many actions which would never have occurred to those of a colder and more prudent nature. But was there any self-denial practised; and was not she, who bestowed, possessed of every luxury and comfort, her varying and fanciful caprices could desire! Never did she resist the smallest impulse or temptation. If to give had been a crime, she had committed it; for it gave her pain to refuse, and she knew not how to deprive herself of any gratification" (G 1:193). For Lady

Caroline as she wrote Glenarvon, one of these indispensable grati-
fications was self-expression, a process that poured forth much
that is powerful and promising. But only occasionally did she go
beyond self-expression to shape the truths that had emerged into
that more or less "made" thing fiction is generally seen to be.

As Byron was beginning Don Juan, Glenarvon would have been useful
enough as a reminder that though confession and literature may be
related, they are not identical: that eruption of the personal, however fascinating, is not enough. But the novel had more to offer
than a negative example. The character of Glenarvon is a "half-real
hero" like Don Juan, if in quite a different way. Both the truths and
the myths that comprise Lady Caroline's homme fatal can be seen as
calling for refutation, even if Byron could not dignify her publication with a direct reply. Don Juan and the Byronic narrator both
serve as such a refutation, one that resembles Lady Caroline's
portrait in its shifting proportions of fact and fancy. Glenarvon's
relationships with women in particular demanded a response—
for Byron was very far from seeing himself as the Byronic seducer
Glenarvon depicts. Apart from Glenarvon's predations, though, Lady
Caroline's comments on love, marriage, and the differences between men and women in the Great World are much in the vein of
Byron's observations on these topics in Don Juan. If Byron found her
opinions worth echoing and deliberately echoed them, he was
a cosmopolite in realms beyond nationality. Even if the resemblances between his pronouncements and Lady Caroline's show
nothing more than a shared position, we must reassess popular
conceptions of them both, must recognize the good sense coexist-
ing with her absurdities and the sensitivity behind his cynicism.

    Byron told Madame de Staël, Thomas Moore, and others that
Glenarvon could not be a good portrait because he had not sat
long enough for a likeness to be caught; but in fact Lady Caroline
captured some of his salient features and combined them with the
Byronic legend to striking effect. Glenarvon's story is not Byron's,
but many specific details, sometimes combined or applied in new
ways, do come from Byron's life and legend. Glenarvon's appearance and manner are Byron's as they were generally perceived by
those who read him into Childe Harold and the Oriental tales: "It was
one of those faces which, having once beheld, we never afterwards
forget. It seemed as if the soul of passion had been stamped and

printed upon every feature. The eye beamed into life as it threw up its dark ardent gaze, with a look nearly of inspiration, while the proud curl of the upper lip expressed haughtiness and bitter contempt; yet, even mixed with these fierce characteristic feelings, an air of melancholy and dejection shaded and softened every harsher expression. Such a countenance spoke to the heart" (G 2:31–32).

Like the public image of "Byron," a mask or misconception half revealing and half revising the man behind it, Glenarvon resembles without being identical to Byron the man. The son of a mother "of doubtful character" (Mrs. Byron's character was unimpugned, but her temper and mental balance were questionable), Glenarvon inherits a ruinous abbey from a disreputable grandfather (as opposed to Byron's succeeding his great-uncle, the "Wicked Lord"). He rents the estate during his minority to a lord whose name is de Ruthven (Lord Grey de Ruthyn leased Newstead Abbey) and spends his youth in traveling widely (mostly in Italy rather than Byron's Greece and Turkey). Lady Caroline draws in Byron's fondness for monk's robes, his skull cup (associated with drinking blood, not wine, in the novel), and his love of Mediterranean climes. From *Childe Harold* and the Oriental romances she takes the Byronic sense of a guilty secret and a soul "scorched with living fire" (G 1:240); uncannily anticipating Byron's Swiss and Italian years, she associates Glenarvon with storms and boats. She shrewdly and accurately captures Byron's special blend of liberal politics and conservative social attitudes. Glenarvon is an aristocrat keen on his hereditary privileges, but also a charismatic revolutionary, inflaming Irish radicals of the country round his estate: "whilst many of those who had adopted the same language had voluntarily thrown off their titles, and divided their property amongst their partizans, he made a formal claim for the titles his grandfather had forfeited; and though he had received no positive assurance that his claim would be considered, he called himself by that name alone, and insisted upon his followers addressing him in no other manner" (G 2:80). Lady Caroline's presenting her Byronic hero as a revolutionary is a stroke of fiction that might at first seem downright prophetic, for Byron's involvement with the cause of liberty in Italy and Greece was still years ahead. But her affair with Byron had taken place during the short period when he had involved himself in parliamentary politics, speaking for the sort of Whig views Lady Caroline's childhood hero Fox had represented, a young lord defending his provincial populace (Nottingham frame-breakers, not Irish tenantry) from repressive Tory policies.[22] It was resourceful and apt that Lady Caroline should make her promising revolutionary a part of the continuing conflict that she would have seen at first hand during her 1812 stay in Ireland.[23] It is interesting that she should have resolved the contradiction in her hero's nature in favor of his aristocratic side. Regaining his title and lands, engaging himself to an English heiress who like Annabella Milbanke found reclaiming a handsome genius "a task too delightful to be rejected" (G 3:103), taking command of an English ship, Glenarvon sails in league with Lord Avondale's uncle and betrays his former comrades in revolution.

Similarly, the passionate progress of Calantha's involvement with Glenarvon closely follows the pattern of Lady Caroline's romance with Byron, though details are often rearranged. Calantha and Glenarvon first meet at a ball (Glenarvon, however, is in double disguise as Viviani masquing as a monk). Glenarvon, like Byron, notices his lady's exquisite talent and pleasure in dancing—but in wanting to partner her in this expression of "the animal spirits of youth" he is the exact opposite of Byron, who during their liaison prohibited Lady Caroline's waltzing. Editing out Byron's limp and imagining him as a potential dancing partner signal Lady Caroline's strong impulse to idealize her lover and their love—and perhaps a concurrent urge to revenge herself on him by publicly repairing the flaw. The most successfully dramatic real gestures of their courtship also appear in the fictional one. Three examples are Calantha's recognition that the face of this fallen angel is her destiny (G 2:31), Glenarvon's presenting a rose to the lady who values, as he claims, "all that is new or rare . . . for a moment" (G 2:113), and Glenarvon's grudging avowal of Avondale's excellences in the Shakespearean comparison "He is as superior to me as Hyperion to a satyr" (G 2:153). The circumstances of Glenarvon's announcing "I am no longer your lover" and advising his cast-off mistress to "correct your vanity, which is ridiculous; exert your absurd caprices upon others; and leave me in peace" (G 3:82–83) exactly match Byron's informing Lady Caroline of his new liaison in a letter dispatched from Lady Oxford's Armidian bower—and the words of dismissal are generally believed to have been Byron's, though only phrases of the published piece are to be found in his extant correspondence, and those phrases are in separate letters (LJ 2:222, 242). Art, in *Glenarvon*, thus consists of rearrangement rather than invention—and in chronicling the "fatal passion," Lady Caroline's rearrangement is limited to details. The pace and tone of the literary affair are if anything too faithful to the torturous and incredible real one—the result of this fidelity being that volumes 2 and 3 (the parts of the book given over to the liaison) are nearly unendurable.

Because *Glenarvon* is in its odd way a truth-telling book and because no biographies or memoirs of Byron had yet appeared,[24] the vast and curious readership beyond Byron's circle of personal acquaintance would have had no reason not to accept Lady Caroline's portrait as an accurate one. Accordingly, Byron may have wished more strongly than he would admit for a public way of setting the record straight and detaching himself from Lady Caroline's creation. *Don Juan*, with its teasing, self-conscious air of half-real confession, would offer just such an opportunity. Perhaps, to take a small and specific example, Glenarvon's opportunistic betrayal of his revolutionary confederates is one reason why Byron is so quick to make plain his own sympathies for Ireland and hatred for political turncoats in the Dedication of *Don Juan*. In like manner, perhaps the sanely philosophical, quietly facetious tone habitually adopted by the *Don Juan* narrator is among other things a reaction to Glenarvon's drunken air of high-proof Byronism, lavishly poured and never diluted by the laughter and detachment that were always and engagingly possible for Byron the man. Whether or not the reason is rebuttal, the character of Don Juan shares nothing with Glenarvon but aristocratic birth, attractiveness to women, and mobility (a quality to which we shall return). The Anglo-Irish lord's devious, introspective bad nature is in all other respects a polar opposite of the Spaniard's naive, unreflective good one.

All this being said, we must recognize that *Don Juan*'s rereading of *Glenarvon* does not always involve refutation. Even in the matters just discussed, there have been affinities as well as oppositions. The confessional mode of *Don Juan* parallels *Glenarvon*'s, though the tone is completely different; and Byron resembles Lady Caroline in distributing himself throughout his work rather than simply voicing his views and qualities in one persona, whether Juan, the narrator, or someone else.[25] Apart from Don Juan's relations with the sequence of resourcefully amorous, more or less older women who hunt him down, Byron's depictions of the interactions of society men and women in love and marriage are very close to what Lady Caroline offers in Glenarvon. And for good reason: Byron was too intelligent a reader of life and literature not to profit from the authoritative insights of others, and he knew that Lady Caroline's understanding of the English Great World was better than his own, her view of that world being from a less marginal position. Byron entered the first circles on sufferance and through talent. Lady Caroline had been born and bred a "first-rate." Her birth and Devonshire House breeding were part of her charm for most who knew her, and certainly for Byron. Besides adding to her fascinations, these attributes gave her in fact what was only a pretense with Byron—the stunning indifference to public opinion possible only for those with supreme social (if not personal) confidence.

Twice in Glenarvon Lady Caroline explicitly voices this confidence, and with it her understanding of how rare it was in the Great World. Both passages closely resemble stanzas from Don Juan's English cantos. First is a paragraph following the description of Calantha's character quoted earlier. Unlike Calantha, the creature of mobility who follows her ever-variable feelings, the typical, less secure denizen of the Great World is imprisoned beneath a layer of artifice: "Such character [as Calantha's] is not uncommon, though rarely seen amongst the higher ranks of society. Early and constant intercourse with the world, and that polished sameness which results from it, smooths away all peculiarities; and whilst it assimilates individuals to each other, corrects many faults, and represses many virtues" (G 1:76).[26]

The unnatural, frozen correctness that Lady Caroline describes is the prevailing impression given by the upper-class English among whom Don Juan finds himself in the latter cantos. London society's "polish'd horde— / Form'd of two mighty tribes, the Bores and Bored" (DJ 13.95) comes immediately to mind here—as does the Amundevilles' country-house party, a gathering "polish'd, smooth, and cold / As Phidian forms cut out of marble Attic" (DJ 13.110). In a later passage discussing Calantha's early days in metropolitan society, Lady Caroline speculates on the reasons for this chilly want of ease found in the Great World's higher but not highest circles: "Perhaps too anxious a desire to please, too great a regard for trifles, a sort of selfishness, which never loses sight of its own identity, occasions this coldness among these votaries of fashion. The dread of not having that air, that dress, that refinement which they value so much, prevents their obtaining it; and a degree of vulgarity steals unperceived amidst the higher classes in England, from the very apprehension they feel of falling into it" (G 1:203–4). Here Lady Caroline demonstrates that though she was indifferent to popular opinion she could, on occasion at least, keenly penetrate the workings and prejudices of the fashionable world's collective mind. Her reading of manners and morals in Regency society is as perceptive as anything later offered by Madame de Staël in the English chapters of her admirable *Considérations sur les principaux événements de la Révolution française* or Bulwer Lytton's survey of the pre-Reform period, *England and the English*.

The English cantos of *Don Juan* strike me as drawing often and effectively on the fruits of Lady Caroline's understanding as reflected in *Glenarvon*. I shall return to some of the ways and subjects later, in the essay devoted to Don Juan in England, but here will focus on the most important cluster of topics receiving similar treatment in *Glenarvon* and *Don Juan*: love, marriage, and how both fit in with the truths of human nature. If Lady Caroline's and Byron's works view seduction antithetically—her novel presenting it as a masculine enterprise and his poem emphasizing its potential to be a feminine one—their pictures of matrimony are comparable. Neither *Glenarvon* nor *Don Juan* holds out much hope for happy marriage. In *Glenarvon*, husbands and wives make one another miserable either by dying or by living, as is the case throughout *Don Juan*. In *Glenarvon's* world, the safest sort of alliance is a mutually beneficial arrangement like that of Lady Augusta Selwyn, who in the course of explaining her convenient union to Calantha also voices the case against marriages based on feeling. Lady Augusta's speech is a beautifully calculated blend of candor and sophistry—a prime example of how fine Lady Caroline's ear for conversation could be:

"After all, a wife is only pleasant when her husband is out of the way. She must either be in love, or out of love with him. If the latter, they wrangle; and if the former, it is ten times worse. Lovers are at all times insufferable; but when the holy laws of matrimony give them a lawful right to be so amazingly fond and affectionate, it makes one sick."

"Which are you, in love or out of love with Mr. Selwyn?"—
"Neither, my child, neither. He never molests me, never intrudes
his dear dull personage on my society. He is the best of his race,
and only married me out of pure benevolence. We were fourteen
raw Scotch girls—all hideous, and no chance of being got rid of,
either by marriage, or death—so healthy and ugly. I believe we are
all alive and flourishing somewhere or other now. Think then of
dear good Mr. Selwyn, who took me for his mate, because I let him
play at cards whenever he pleased. He is so fond of cheating, he
can never get any one but me to play with him." (G 1:211–12)

Don Juan echoes this cheerfully struck bargain in the mechanical
marriages that "might go on, if well wound up, like watches" (DJ
15.40) and the arrangement of the Duke and Duchess of Fitz-
Fulke: "Theirs was that best of unions, past all doubt, / Which
never meets, and therefore can't fall out" (DJ 14.45).

In Don Juan as in Glenarvon, marriages founded on love cannot
succeed so well as those less hopeful ones based on convenience.
The problem lies partly with the institution, partly with human
nature. The latter portion of the difficulty is bound up with mobility, that natural quality surviving in Calantha though repressed in so
many of her peers. Glenarvon too is a mobile being, ever and
intensely devoted to the favorite of the moment, "of a disposition
to attend so wholly to those, in whose presence he took delight,
that he failed to remember those to whom he had once been attached" (G 3:95). The intelligent worldling Lady Augusta acknowledges such variability as the general way of the human heart: "Now
dont you know that every thing in nature is subject to change:—it
rains to day—it shines to-morrow;—we laugh,—we cry;—and the
thermometer of love rises and falls, like the weather glass, from the
state of the atmosphere:—one while it is at freezing point;—another it is at fever heat.—How then should the only imaginary
thing in the whole affair—the object I mean which is *always purely
ideal*—how should that remain the same?" (G 1:264).

The narrator of Don Juan makes much the same case for mobility
at several points, one being as canto 2 closes and he is at pains to
account for how Juan, having vowed constancy, can so soon have
forgotten Julia for Haidée. Throughout the canto, Byron has shown
how eager humans are to see nature as a sort of backdrop for their
personal dramas: the shipwrecked sailors and passengers interpret
rainbows or showers, the appearance of a white seabird or a turtle,
as providential props. Their true relation to nature and its workings

is the inverse of what they perceive. Humanity conforms to natural laws rather than nature behaving according to human ones. Acknowledging this reality, Byron's narrator, like Lady Augusta, sees mobility as a sort of inner weather, the climate of the soul for those honest enough to acknowledge it: "The heart is like the sky, a part of heaven, / But changes night and day too, like the sky" (DJ 2.214). He also shares Lady Augusta's sense that in permitting the object of feeling to change, one stays true to the feeling itself. "This sort of adoration of the real / Is but a heightening of the 'beau ideal'" (DJ 2.211). All vows are hollow, then—and it is interesting to see how closely Glenarvon's hollow vows to Calantha resemble Juan's to Julia. "'May God destroy me in his vengeance,'" cries Glenarvon eagerly, "'if, though absent, I do not daily, nay, hourly think of thee, write to thee, live for thee!'" (G 3:8). This melodramatic, consciously false profession sounds a good bit like Don Juan's self-deceptive shipboard effusion, seven windy lines of unnatural sentiment comically juxtaposed, in the couplet, by all-too-natural feeling:

> 'And oh! if e'er I should forget, I swear—
>   But that's impossible, and cannot be—
> Sooner shall this blue ocean melt to air,
>   Sooner shall earth resolve itself to sea,
> Than I resign thy image, Oh! my fair!
>   Or think of any thing excepting thee;
> A mind diseased no remedy can physic—'
> (Here the ship gave a lurch, and he grew sea-sick.)   (DJ 2.19)

Just as these false declarations of masculine constancy resemble one another, so *Glenarvon's* and *Don Juan's* generalizations on the nature of feminine attachment are parallel in their reflection of Regency society and its values. Count Gondimar speaks thus of Calantha's susceptibility to extramarital suitors: "'But the hour of perdition approaches; the first years of peace and love are past; folly succeeds; and vice is the after game. These are the three stages in woman's life'" (G 1:238). Don Juan's statement of this position is more epigrammatic but equally cynical:

> In her first passion woman loves her lover,
>   In all the others all she loves is love,
> Which grows a habit she can ne'er get over,
>   And fits her loosely—like an easy glove.   (DJ 3.3)

The love woman comes to love for its own sake is consistently presented in *Glenarvon* as slavery for both sexes. (Lady Caroline also applies the metaphor to marriage, so perhaps it would be more precise to characterize love as indenture, slavery over a finite period.) Early in the book, the naive Calantha fails to see that love, even without vows, takes away liberty. She admits to loving Avondale but tells him that "dear as he was, her freedom was even dearer . . . that she never would become a slave and a wife" (G 1:130). Whereas she fails to see that love itself removes that freedom, Avondale does understand. Though notably proud and independent, he acknowledges the potential tyranny of the woman who has his heart: "you shall be my mistress—my guide—my monitress—and I, a willing slave" (G 1:132). Throughout the novel, in the case of one character after another, love makes itself known through images of enslavement—of chains, shackles, subservience, obedience. Only Glenarvon is free from this human bondage. Perhaps that is the secret of his power and charm. It is, in any case, the message of the song he sings when Calantha first sees him in propria persona and directly finds herself enamoured.

> "This heart has never stoop'd its pride
> To slavish love, or woman's wile." . . .
> "Then hope not now to touch with love,
> Or in its chains a heart to draw,
> All earthly spells have fail'd to move."   (G 2:32)

What woman worth the name could fail to take up Glenarvon's challenge? And if the condition Byron's Lambro confronts in his nation's affairs also holds true in personal politics—that one must be either a slave or an enslaver—what woman would not find herself under the yoke of this demon-lover? The connection between love and slavery pervades *Don Juan* as well. Juan's heated assertion that " 'Love is for the free!' " (DJ 5.127) chiefly shows his naiveté and his indignation at being forced into harem-girl garb. The poem's prevailing sense is that "free love" robs the lover of his or her freedom, that "*Wedlock* and a *Padlock* mean the same" literally in the East but figuratively everywhere (DJ 5.158), that, as the quotable John Johnson tells Juan, "Most men are slaves, none more so than the great, / To their own whims and passions, and what not" (DJ 5.25).

The advantage that men hold over women in this sorry state is

one of wider options, a matter recognized and comparably demonstrated in *Glenarvon* and *Don Juan*. The problem with the Avon-
dales' marriage (and with the Lambs' in life and with the Amundevilles' in *Don Juan*) arises in part because, for men, love is not
enough. It may enslave for a time, but the world holds other
fascinations: military affairs for Avondale, political ones for Lamb
and Amundeville. Women, especially married women, have no
such recourses when the chains of old love grow heavy. There is
nothing to do but love again. Lady Caroline puts the point this way:
"That which causes the tragic end of a woman's life, is often but a
moment of amusement and folly in the history of a man. Women,
like toys, are sought after, and trifled with, and then thrown by
with every varying caprice" (G 3:90–91). Donna Julia's valedictory
letter from the nunnery to which she has been dispatched makes a
similar contrast:

> 'Man's love is of his life a thing apart,
>   'Tis woman's whole existence; man may range
> The court, camp, church, the vessel, and the mart,
>   Sword, gown, gain, glory, offer in exchange
> Pride, fame, ambition, to fill up his heart,
>   And few there are whom these can not estrange;
> Man has all these resources, we but one,
> To love again, and be again undone.'   (DJ 1.194)

Though we might be inclined to suspect the rhetoric of so splendid a deceiver as Julia has shown herself, the case she makes is
echoed throughout *Don Juan*. When the Byronic narrator says "Alas
the love of women" (DJ 2.199), Byron, sympathizing with the position Lady Caroline has voiced in her novel, means it—for the
moment.

If the nature of human feelings as experienced by both genders
is to change, or to change their object, there is bound to be a
fundamental opposition between marriage and love, a contract
and a feeling. Even when love persists, as it does for Henry and
Calantha Avondale (who like Henry and Adeline Amundeville
have the best marriage we are privileged to see in their milieu,
though still a highly imperfect one), it cannot satisfy. The two
parties are looking for different things in their relationship, as is
indicated by this exchange, which holds within it many phrases or
positions voiced and amplified in *Don Juan*. We come in on the

debate just as Calantha has concluded a lengthy case for husbands giving more guidance and attention to wives with the generalization " 'Marriage is the annihilation of love.' "

" 'The error is in human nature,' said Lord Avondale smiling— 'We always see perfection in that which we cannot approach:— there is a majesty in distance and rarity, which every day's intercourse wears off. Besides, love delights in gazing upon that which is superior:—whilst we believe you angels, we kneel to you, we are your slaves;—we awake and find women, and expect obedience:—and is it not what you were made for?'—"

" 'Henry, we are made your idols too—too long, to bear this sad reverse:—you should speak to us in the language of truth from the first, or never.—Obey—is a fearful word to those who have lived without hearing it; and truth from lips which have accustomed us to a dearer language, sounds harsh and discordant. We have renounced society, and all the dear ties of early friendship, to form one strong engagement, and if that fails, what are we in the world?—beings without hope, or interest—dependants—encumbrances—shadows of former joys—solitary wanderers in quest of false pleasures—or lonely recluses, unblessing and unblest.' " (*G* 1:272–73).

The language and assertions of this exchange will be worth keeping in mind later, when we look at Byron's attitude toward English marriage and what it does to both sexes, but especially women. The ideas Lady Caroline advances here are intelligent, but none is extraordinary, nor are the words in which she casts those ideas unusual. What is striking is that much of what she says in this dismissed and "damnable" novel is also found, essentially unchanged, in Byron's great poem.

The publication of Don Juan (serial as it was) did not comprise the last act in Byron's and Lady Caroline's drama, nor did it offer the last word in the literary conversation that has been considered here. Even after her fall from grace through offenses in life and literature alike, Lady Caroline had not learned discretion. Her reaction to Don Juan resembled that mixture of amusement, awareness of brilliance, and acknowledgment of impropriety voiced by Hobhouse, Moore, and other such men of the world rather than the revulsion deemed appropriate to such respectable females as would admit to being readers. She told John Murray, "you cannot think how

clever I think 'Don Juan' is, in my heart," though, qualifying that
praise, she conceded the poem to be "neither witty, nor in very
good taste."27 Like some other readers with poetical talents of their
own, she was in fact so taken with Byron's accomplishment that
she apparently had to emulate it—in two anonymous effusions, *A
New Canto* (to *Don Juan*) and *Gordon: A Tale*. The latter, two cantos'
worth of critical comment on *Don Juan*, effectively demonstrates
how tedious ottava rima can be when it lacks the beautifully modu-
lated variety of tone and topic found in *Don Juan*. The first of *Gordon's*
cantos, amplifying the sense of Lady Caroline's letter to Murray and
taking much the same line as was taken by Hobhouse and company, recognizes the poet's genius and deplores the immoral ends
it achieves. The second canto, rather more dramatic if less coherent, offers an argument between the (male) narrator and a
demonic visitor on the merits of Byron's poem and concludes with
the view of hell *Don Juan* promises to display in its "canto twelfth."
Gordon's final poetic gesture, to serve Byron just as he served Southey in *Don Juan*, stands as clear proof that it is generally wiser not to
try reenacting a trick superbly executed by someone else:

> "This was" the author's "earliest scrape, but whether
>   "I shall proceed with his adventures, is
> "Dependent on the public altogether,
>   "We'll see, however, what they say to this."
> To *see* what people *say* is awkward rather,
>   At least in my view, if not so in his.
> "The first four rhymes are" Byron's "every line,
> "For God's sake, reader! Take them not for mine."28

   Gordon can be seen or said to exhibit some of *Glenarvon's* worst
features rather than a selection of *Don Juan's* best ones, but *A New
Canto* is a far more impressive achievement. Where *Gordon* discusses, the *New Canto* impersonates. Instead of vying with Byron by
attempting an ottava rima review of *Don Juan*, Lady Caroline "becomes" him and "continues" *Don Juan*, a venture made easier by
temperamental mobility, the acuteness obsession can confer, and
the superb ear that served her well in the society conversation of
Glenarvon and in the lines she wrote for music. Through the act of
poetic impersonation she implicitly reveals a shrewd and pro-
found understanding of *Don Juan* and Byron alike. A good indication of Lady Caroline's perceptiveness is her sometimes uncanny

way of anticipating, in this response to the first two cantos of Don Juan, some of the themes, images, and preoccupations that would later become important in Byron's poem.

Like Gordon, A New Canto takes as a point of departure Byron's promise that his twelfth canto will show "The very place where wicked people go"—but here the form this revelation takes is not a glimpse into hell but the coming of the apocalypse to London and the world beyond it, a fiery catastrophe not unlike the one Byron will imagine destroying, à la Cuvier, the Regency world he has known (DJ 9.37–38). Lady Caroline's apocalypse enlarges—and redirects the heat of—the carefully staged Brocket bonfire at which she burned facsimiles of Byron's letters and love gifts while white-clad village girls chanted verses of her devising. In A New Canto the verses punish, through the assumed voice and vision of Byron, the canting English public that had condemned the "immorality" of both Glenarvon and Don Juan. It is a vigorous and perhaps intensely gratifying fantasy, this business of Lady Caroline becoming one with Byron: in the imagined role of Caroline-as-Byron she can at once enjoy the active satisfaction of dealing out vengeance herself and the more passive one of being avenged by the poet she still loved too well. She can both worship and mock at Byron's shrine.

Writing as Byron empowered Lady Caroline in a way that her page-boy disguise could not. Even as it represses her Devonshire House lisp, the narrative strategy of A New Canto frees her pent-up strength and passion. Caroline-as-Byron frankly and vigorously relishes the global damnation that awaits flagrant and hypocritical sinners alike. As the New Canto begins, there is no time or place for moralizing or sentimentalizing: the end of the world is a one-performance-only extravaganza to be witnessed in the spirit with which Byron had observed a public guillotining at Venice, "as one should see every thing once—with attention" (LJ 5:229–30).

Caroline-as-Byron chooses as the fittest place from which to view the apocalypse St. Paul's, the edifice that, in ways we have already seen, epitomizes London and England in Letters from England and Don Juan:

> When doomsday comes, St Paul's will be on fire—
> I should not wonder if we live to see it—
> Of us, proof pickles, Heaven must rather tire,
> And want a reckoning—if so, so be it—
> Only about the Cupola, or higher,

If there's a place unoccupied, give me it—
To catch, before I touch my sinner's salary,
The first grand crackle in the whispering gallery.

The ball comes tumbling in a lively crash,
And splits the pavement up, and shakes the shops,
Teeth chatter, china dances, spreads the flash,
The omnium falls, the Bank of England stops;
Loyal and radical, discreet and rash,
Each on his knees in tribulation flops;
The Regent raves (Moore chuckling at his pain)
And sends about for Ministers in vain.

The roaring streamers flap, red flakes are shot
This way and that, the town is a volcano—
And yells are heard, like those provoked by Lot,
Some, of the Smithfield sort, and some *soprano;*
Some holy water seek, the font is hot,
And fizzing in a tea-kettle *piano.*
Now bring your magistrates, with yeomen back'd,
Bawls Belial, and read the Riot-Act!—[29]

"Fair maids and ugly men," "the dainty and the shabby," "high
dames" and "the wander'ng beggar" are caught up in this natural
event more democratic than anything the most radical reform bill
could legislate. The spectacle grows increasingly cosmopolitan.
"There'll be at Petersburgh a sudden thaw" (NC 213); Norway's
Baltic copper mines "Swell, heave, and rumble with their boiling
ore, / Like some griped giant's motion peristaltic" (NC 219); and
"The Turkish infidel may now restore / His wives to liberty, and ere
to Hell he go, / Roll in the bottom of the Archipelago!" (NC 214)
Freed by poetic impersonation from the various constraints on her
talent, Lady Caroline here becomes in art the "little volcano" she
was so notably capable of being in life. The lava of emotion and
imagination, to return to that metaphor shared by Byron and
Cixous, bursts through the crust of multiple conventions, sparing
only the pose of impersonation. Caroline-as-Byron is free to savor
the "Delicious chaos" (NC 213) that bewilders and appalls more
conventional souls, free to write as Byron might and in fact, in later
cantos, would. If, as Margot Strickland has suggested, Lady Caroline was, without knowing it, "a captive Celtic woman artist,
struggling to free herself from oppressive Anglo-Saxon male domi-

nation,"[30] it is no small irony that speaking in the voice of the half-English, half-Scots lord she had loved with self-enslaving intensity should ultimately prove her successful means of self-expression.

Once all things and people, from St. Paul's and the Peak of Derbyshire to Alexander's Winter Palace, from Napoleon to an unnamed "bright beauty" with raven tresses (NC 215) to the "rank elders, fearful of denials" who "pick Susannahs up in Seven dials" (NC 214), have been consigned to incendiary damnation, the narrator's anger seems to cool.

> Perhaps the thing may take another turn,
> And one smart shock may split the world in two,
> And I in Italy, you soon may learn,
> On t'other half am reeling far from you.   (NC 215)

Starting in this fashion, the last ten stanzas of the poem offer a more modest cataclysm, one where Caroline-as-Byron presents the everlasting separation between Lady Caroline and Byron in the grand platonic image of sundered halves, a world cracked apart at "Some wicked capital, for instance Paris" (NC 215). In this second vision, the narrator soothes those "poor nervous souls" earlier affrighted by the inflammatory muse. We see "spotless spirits, snowy white" rising serenely from the ruined world (NC 215). As is the case with George III in Byron's *Vision of Judgment*, personal virtues do purchase salvation—but not for the narrator, burdened with "never quench'd desire, / Still quench'd, still kindling, every thought devout / Lost in the changeful torment." This "changeful torment" is perhaps the dark side of mobility shared by Lady Caroline and Byron, and also, it is implied, by the audience addressed: "Return we to our heaven, our fire and smoke" (NC 216).

And there amid the fire and smoke we find the blazing author of *Don Juan* (Byron as Caroline-as-Byron reads him) requiring and despising the fame that has proved to be his hell on earth:

> Mad world! for fame we rant, call names, and fight—
> I scorn it heartily, yet love to dazzle it,
> Dark intellects by day, as shops by night,
> All with a bright, new speculative gas lit.
> Wars the blue vapour with the oil-fed light,
> Hot sputter Blackwood, Jeffrey, Giffard, Hazlitt—
> The Muse runs madder, and, as mine may tell,
> Like a loose comet, mingles Heaven and Hell.

> You shall have more of her another time,
> Since gulled you will be with our flights poetic,
> Our eight, and ten, and twenty feet sublime,
> Our maudlin, hey-down-derrified pathetic.
> For my part, though I'm doomed to write in rhyme,
> To read it would be worse than an emetic—
> But something must be done to cure the spleen,
> And keep my name in capitals, like Kean.   (NC 216)

The *Don Juan* echoes (of cantos written) and prophecies (of cantos yet to come) are complex and multiple here. Among other things we see, in forms more blatantly self-mocking than Byron himself would choose, *Don Juan's* double-minded attitude toward fame and "flights poetic." The language conveying that ambivalence is also typical of *Don Juan*, as is the self-swallowing conclusion, an utterance blending celebrity with indigestion and neatly reprising the sense of the words opening *A New Canto*, "I'm sick of fame— I'm gorged with it." The reflexive metrical comments and attacks on critics have already appeared in *Don Juan*—the images of gaslight, lamps burning blue, and Heaven mingled with Hell are yet to come, in the English cantos. The varied affinities between these heated lines and *Don Juan* demonstrate both Lady Caroline's accurate reading of Byron and her intense identification with him—the latter implied throughout but finally announced, in the telltale pronoun shift from "my" to "our" for the first half of the final stanza.

Impersonation was from childhood a particular forte of Lady Caroline, so it seems highly fitting that one of her replies to *Don Juan* should be long-distance ventriloquism in ottava rima. Equally daring and appropriate to her dramatic nature was a visual reply, her enacting Don Juan surrounded by a throng of devils at an Almack's masquerade. This bit of bravado inspired Byron to tell his and Caroline's correspondent Murray, "What you say of Lady Caroline Lamb's Juan at the Masquerade don't surprise me—I only wonder that She went so far as 'the *Theatre*' for 'the *Devils*' having them so much more natural at home" (LJ 7.169). Gestures of this sort guaranteed that Lady Caroline, like Byron, would gain the goal acknowledged by Caroline-as-Byron in the last line of the *New Canto*. Lady Caroline Lamb's name, like Lord Byron's and Edmund Kean's, has been kept in capitals. And the victory was more than typographical; it was cosmopolitan. Just as the still-infatuated Lady Caroline "kept" BYRON in the British "capital" he had left behind, so her sayings and doings, most especially *Glenarvon*, kept CARO LAMB with him, in the capitals and provincial towns of his exile.

V

England in
Don Juan

If the world is the aggregate of all that is dynamically
affective, then the cultivated man will never succeed
in living in just one world.

Friedrich Schlegel, *Athenaeum Fragments*

The last three essays have shown several pragmatic reasons not to put "just one world" into literature if that one world is one's own, several different ways of telling English truths but telling them slant. In *Letters from England*, Southey assumed a Spanish mask that safely distanced him from his pronouncements on the mother country and also gave his opinions at least a semblance of cultural comparison. The English pantomime managed to be topical, timely, and irreverent under the Examiner's watchful eye by presenting home truths and personages in fantastic scenes and manifestly unreal guises. Even Lady Caroline Lamb showed some prudence (if not enough) in displacing the tumultuous half-realities of *Glenarvon* from England, where they occurred, to Ireland, where she was sent that they might not continue.

We have seen that *Don Juan*, like *Letters from England*, *Glenarvon*, and the English pantomime, is made from *domestica facta*. Like the other works, it strategically ranges beyond the microcosmic source of its materials. As its preliminaries suggest, the poem is not so much about its Spanish protagonist and the lands in which he finds himself as about its British author, the British narrator through whom he speaks, and the island home they both know best of the many scenes and societies depicted—not Britain isolated so much as Britain compared with other places, peoples, and times. How Byron introduces the matter and mores of Regency England into a narrative set elsewhere, as Don Juan's story is from its outset until the sixty-fifth stanza of canto 10, will be the subject of this chapter. Why Byron does so is evident in this chapter's epigraph. The choice is more principled than practical. Having already offended his native land enough to feel himself an outcast and to act out that perceived exile, Byron had no compulsion to be anything more or less than direct in commenting on the British microcosm—but as romantic ironist and as urbane aristocrat he surely would feel the philosophical force of Schlegel's case for cosmopolitanism. Whether or not he had firsthand knowledge of the fragment or the Schlegelian opinion it crystallizes (and he may well have, for Friedrich's brother A. W. Schlegel was at Coppet when Byron stayed there in 1816), the position was one he shared. Byron's most famous endorsement of worldly experience, a statement that fleshes out Schlegel's elegant abstraction, comes in a letter to Douglas Kinnaird: "As to 'Don Juan'—confess—confess—you dog—and be candid—that it is the sublime of *that there* sort of writing—it may be bawdy—but is it not good English?—it may be profligate—but is it not *life*, is it not *the thing*?—Could any man have written it—who has not lived in the world?—and tooled in a post-chaise? in a hackney coach? in a Gondola? against a wall? in a court carriage? in a vis a vis?—on a table?—and under it?" (*LJ* 6:232) "Good English"—"life"—"the thing": as adequate a summation of *Don Juan* as five words are likely to convey.

Byron's choosing cosmopolitanism rather than insularity suggests things about him, but also about his ideal reader, a nonexistent being whose perfect blend of birth, breeding, erudition, experience, wit, feeling, vigor, tolerance, conviction, and various other excellences was lacking in his real readers, even those men of the world to whom he addressed his epistolary glosses on the poetic endeavor: Moore, Murray, Hobhouse, Kinnaird. I would suggest that the dominant voice heard in *Don Juan* belongs to a British version of Schlegel's "cultivated man." Though the poem may be "remarkably unprescriptive of its reader"[1] in the sense of offering richly diverse things to a heterogeneous audience, much of the time this British cosmopolite utters words intended chiefly, or at any rate immediately, for other cultivated men of his own society and time. The poem characteristically speaks about women rather than to them, alludes to posterity instead of addressing it, shows a wide knowledge of disparate nations and classes that is itself a crucial characteristic of that exclusive club of cultivated Englishmen to which Byron belongs and in which he is at pains to place his narrator and to find some of his most important readers, if not all of them. To validate his and the narrator's credentials as fellow initiates, Byron must display from the start his understanding of the milieu in which his ideal reader resides as well as those circles through which his fictive protagonist moves. Because "soundness" in certain crucial insular matters is a prerequisite for anyone aspiring to pronounce on wider concerns, England must be brought into Don Juan long before Don Juan is brought into England. How to do so? Largely, of course, through the famous digressions. But in Don Juan cultural comparison is yet more pervasive than digressions alone would allow it to be. Other strategies are necessary. All of them, along with the digressions, can be seen as varieties of parabasis—a phenomenon that now calls for a few explanatory words.

Parabasis, literally a "coming forward," is a feature of Greek Old Comedy—a suspension of action that takes place at or toward the middle of the play as the chorus, alone in the orchestra and unmasked, advances to present the author's sincerely and strongly held opinions, whether on art, politics, religion, or other timely matters. The parabasis shatters dramatic illusion: as Gilbert Norwood puts it, "such a passage—or rather such a conglomerate of songs and non-dramatic recitative—is *prima facie* inconceivable in the centre of a drama."[2] But suspending the play's action and thereby stressing its illusory nature effectively contributes to the comic whole. Schlegel drew upon the paradox inherent in this theatrical convention to account for the simultaneous creation and destruction that constitute irony: irony, as Schlegel sees it, is "permanent parabasis." Hans Eichner points out that the Greek word *parekbasis* is also Schlegel's preferred term for that literary technique we tend to call "digression"[3]—and digression is one way for Byron's alter ego the narrator to step forward unmasked (while still masking the author) in Don Juan. There are smaller, less obvious ways of highlighting the fictive nature of the poem's narrative—providing glimpses of the stage manager behind the pantomime scenes, the essential Englishness underlying the apparent internationalism. One such means is through distinctively English mispronunciation of foreign names and other words, a strategy examined in the discussion of opening signals. Another is the continual presence of literary allusions, tags that incrementally demonstrate

Byron's status as not just a well-bred cosmopolite but also a well-read one. It would be digressive here to deal at length with particular allusions—anyone requiring general confirmation of how fast, dense, and various the literary quotations, anecdotes, references, and parodies spill forth can find the proof required on most any page of McGann's resourceful notes to the Oxford Don Juan. For now let it suffice to say that Shakespeare, the Bible, Horace, Milton, and other venerable ingredients contribute significantly to Byron's simmering literary stew—as can less-familiar or less-respected materials, among them the three I have discussed at length: Southey, Caroline Lamb, the spectacular theater of commedia and pantomime.

Some of Don Juan's allusions are obvious. Others are exceedingly subtle. Still others, I suspect, are virtually undetectable—Byron's literary dandyism manifesting itself in exclusive jokes unperceived by anyone but their perpetrator. The obvious allusions (for instance, the "poetical commandments" of canto 1) give clear warning of what Byron's game will be. The subtler ones lead readers who recognize them to admire Byron and congratulate themselves for mental agility, thereby forging a community of wit, a select society of minds thinking alike. Shared allusions, in other words, can be Byron's way of telling England's cultural elite that "I am one of you"—and his readers' way of recognizing that, whatever place and time they inhabit, they can for a moment think like Byron. Private allusions (or perhaps they should be called elusions) set a limit on this consensus of author and audience. They are the poet's way of not only keeping even his finest readers from full competence but also preventing those readers from achieving any clear sense of the ground and extent of their incompetence, in this way thwarting their chance of having, like Socrates, at least the sure knowledge of ignorance that is the first step away from it.

English interjections, from the lengthiest digressions to the most inobtrusive touches of diction, are moments of parabasis in that they take us out of the world contrived for Don Juan's adventures and back to the "real" one Byron and his characterized reader have in common. Let us first see how the feat is accomplished in the second, third, and fourth cantos, where the narrative element is comparatively strong, the tendency to digress is less pronounced than elsewhere, and there is as yet no embodiment of English values within the tale itself. Here, in blending shipwreck, piracy, idyllic love, and slavery, Juan's story is as engaging as it ever will be. Even so, we are detached from the narrative and removed from its locale by frequent and artfully placed parabases—English intrusions on a Mediterranean tale.

Canto 1 ends with a parabasis—the previously quoted and discussed couplet on Southey's borrowed rhymes and Byron's feigned fear that the lines be taken for his—and canto 2 begins with parabasis. Before the narrative resumes there is of course no way to digress from it; instead, the poem hovers between England and the Mediterranean, between fiction and teasingly real "Byroniana." We start off facing a generalization that is either obtuse or mockingly insincere—and given the nature of the narrator as revealed in the first canto, the latter seems likelier:

> Oh ye! who teach the ingenuous youth of nations,
>   Holland, France, England, Germany, or Spain,
> I pray ye flog them upon all occasions,
>   It mends their morals, never mind the pain.   (DJ 2.1)

The second half of the stanza returns to Juan, whose "best of mothers and of educations" (equally evident insincerity) had in the previous canto failed to preserve the morals and modesty of which he has been divested "in a way, that's rather of the oddest" (insincere again, the "way" referred to being entirely natural and ordinary). Thereby a contrast is set up between the north and the south—and set up as could be done only by someone who knows both well enough to ridicule their different hypocrisies, as an "Englishman resident in Spain" or a "Spaniard who had travelled in England" might do.

Because the narrator has already made a perverse point of being wrongheaded in this canto's first few assertions, the audience is conditioned to reverse his next claim, a retrospective suggestion that a "public school" would have been just the thing to have cooled Juan's adolescent fancy (DJ 2.2). Having made that reversal, the reader who knows something of Byron is encouraged to think of the poet's "hot youth," not much damped down by Harrow. The ensuing coy reference to Juan's "lady-mother, mathematical, / A ——— never mind" (DJ 2.3) likewise sends us back to Byron's personal history and specifically to Annabella, though if charged with mental manipulation of this sort he could plead innocent in just the same way that his narrator could deny bitch being the word meant to fill his pause, even though it is the noun most readers will instinctively supply[4] given that the context is a witty, racy poem, the referent is a female inclined to be selfish, devious, and hypocritical, and the next person to be characterized is graced with an animal epithet ("his tutor, an old ass").

Turning to Juan's story and then away from it, the narrator dispatches his protagonist to Cadiz, then uses this shift of scene to call attention to his own traits. Not the least of these is digressiveness, for after a single line of narrative, the poem devotes three stanzas to characterizing its narrator:

> I said, that Juan had been sent to Cadiz—
>   A pretty town, I recollect it well—
> 'Tis there the mart of the colonial trade is
>   (Or was, before Peru learn'd to rebel)
> And such sweet girls—I mean, such graceful ladies,
>   Their very walk would make your bosom swell;
> I can't describe it, though so much it strike,
> Nor liken it—I never saw the like:
>
> 6
>
> An Arab horse, a stately stag, a barb
>   New broke, a cameleopard, a gazelle,
> No—none of these will do;—and then their garb!
>   Their veil and petticoat—Alas! to dwell
> Upon such things would very near absorb
>   A canto—then their feet and ancles—well,
> Thank heaven I've got no metaphor quite ready,
> (And so, my sober Muse—come, let's be steady—
>
> 7
>
> Chaste Muse!—well, if you must, you must)—the veil
>   Thrown back a moment with the glancing hand,
> While the o'erpowering eye, that turns you pale,
>   Flashes into the heart:—All sunny land
> Of love! when I forget you, may I fail
>   To——say my prayers—but never was there plann'd
> A dress through which the eyes give such a volley,
> Excepting the Venetian Fazzioli.

We understand here that the narrator has traveled widely. He "recollects" Cadiz and must have been to Venice, having seen its distinctive local costume; and the procession of exotic beasts implies even more extensive journeying. We infer that his experience of women is equally wide and appreciative, Spanish women being admired in a comparative way. This connoisseur of places and women is someone whose handling of the English language and poetic conventions is both masterful and light. At once serious and playful, he demands that characterizations be accurate and that figurative tropes be precisely chosen and employed only when necessary, yet he trifles with his "chaste" and "sober" muse as if she herself were some "sweet girl"—even violating the integrity of her stanzas by leaving a parenthesis open when the couplet has closed. Rhetorically ingenious, he succeeds in having things both ways— as evidenced by his including images (like the quadraped menagerie in stanza 6) to reject them, and his pausing before, then censoring, unsuitable sentiments ("may I fail / To——say my prayers") to emphasize them. The experiences, values, and personality conveyed through this description overlap with Byron's but cannot be proved his alone in that none of the details are unique to him— they might portray any number of intelligent, amorous, and eloquent English travelers.

So might most of the other British parabases in this canto and the two following. Only a few details truly single out Byron among cosmopolitan English aristocrats. The assertion in canto 2 that Juan is a strong swimmer alludes, as Byron could not resist doing when circumstances were appropriate, to his own notable exploit in that line—"He could, perhaps, have pass'd the Hellespont, / As once (a feat on which ourselves we prided) / Leander, Mr. Ekenhead, and I did" (DJ 2.105)—a "real" moment whose reality is undercut by its own miniature parabasis, when the mythic Leander is brought into the company of Ekenhead and Byron. The descriptions of Juan's sufferings at sea, the facts of which come from various sources, explicitly acknowledge just one literary progenitor, *A Narrative of the Honourable John Byron* . . . : "his hardships were comparative / To those related in my grand-dad's Narrative" (DJ 2.137). Apart from these cases, though, the narrator's momentary intrusions of English matters and tastes do not uniquely characterize Byron, though they certainly fit him as well or better than they do anyone else.

The most important of such instances is a digression that rises out of Juan's linguistic apprenticeship in Romaic, his personal tutor on the pirate's island being the pirate's daughter Haidée. The circumstances remind the narrator of what delightful incentives to learning (and not learning) he has enjoyed in similar situations:

> They smile so when one's right, and when one's wrong
>   They smile still more, and then there intervene
> Pressure of hands, perhaps even a chaste kiss;—
> I learn'd the little that I know by this:

165

> That is, some words of Spanish, Turk, and Greek,
>   Italian not at all, having no teachers;
> Much English I cannot pretend to speak,
>   Learning that language chiefly from its preachers,
> Barrow, South, Tillotson, whom every week
>   I study, also Blair, the highest reachers
> Of eloquence in piety and prose—
> I hate your poets, so read none of those.

166

> As for the ladies, I have nought to say,
>   A wanderer from the British world of fashion,
> Where I, like other "dogs, have had my day,"
>   Like other men too, may have had my passion.

In this passage the narrator supplies some details that accurately suggest Byron: travel, international adventures with women, wide reading, status in the Great World. Merrily blended with these specifics are others so blatantly uncharacteristic of Byron's situation (the claims of not having an amiable woman to teach him Italian, of having gained what small skill in English is his from parsons rather than poets, of having "nought to say" about the ladies) that they call to mind Byron's great love of mystifying an audience and thus suggest him equally as well as the accurate details do. But however successful this passage may be in turning the reader's mind to Byron in particular, it could with equal justice be applied to many another member of that class of Englishmen to which he belongs.

Attitudes distinguishing a cultural type, not merely Byron, similarly emerge when a generalization that real women surpass their stone likenesses conjures up the narrator's memory of "an Irish lady, to whose bust / I ne'er saw justice done," (DJ 2.119)—or when meditation on the costly nature of love makes him muse, "I won-

der Castlereagh don't tax 'em" (DJ 2.203)—or when professed
hatred of "that air / Of clap-trap, which your recent poets prize"
(DJ 2.124) impels him to forego tantalizing suspense and identify
Haidée and Zoe directly and honestly. These last three examples
introduce a particular British, if not uniquely Byronic, frame of
mind into the Oriental tale of Juan and Haidée. The persona spin-
ning this Mediterranean romance is someone who can claim acquaintance with society beauties such as Lady Adelaide Forbes (the
likely inspiration of the sculptural digression)[5] and their portraits.
He is someone who implicitly disapproves of Foreign Secretary
Castlereagh and his taxes. He is someone who opposes imported
poetical systems and provincial self-congratulations of the kind the
Lakers, Bowles, and other debased moderns inflict upon their
readers—and the word he chooses to characterize their efforts is
apt, economical, down to earth, and distinctively English.[6] The
perspective from which such a being surveys the world is liberally
Whig yet a bit beyond all parties, classically Augustan yet individu-
alistically eclectic, elitist in several senses—it is a British viewpoint
but certainly not the common one.

The more conscious we are of this perspective from which the
narrator looks on his world and assembles his story, the less power
the narrative has to absorb us. It is especially important that we are
distanced from the story at the crucial beginnings and endings of
cantos—a strategy begun in canto 1 and continued without variation in the three succeeding ones. We have already seen how the
narrator draws attention away from Juan and Spain, toward himself, Byron, and their English context in the first stanzas of canto 2.
This canto ends as so many do with the narrator digressing into the
apparently personal. He begins by recognizing—as the reader already must have done—how his protagonist, like other versions of
Don Juan and like Glenarvon in a passage quoted in the last chapter, has forgotten his absent love because of the present one. A
general explanation of such behavior follows. Then comes application of the law to a particular case, the narrator's own:

> I hate inconstancy—I loathe, detest,
>   Abhor, condemn, abjure the mortal made
> Of such quicksilver clay that in his breast
>   No permanent foundation can be laid;
> Love, constant love, has been my constant guest,
>   And yet last night, being at a masquerade,

I saw the prettiest creature, fresh from Milan,
Which gave me some sensations like a villain.

210

But soon Philosophy came to my aid,
    And whisper'd "think of every sacred tie!"
"I will, my dear Philosophy!" I said,
    "But then her teeth, and then, Oh heaven! her eye!
I'll just inquire if she be wife or maid,
    Or neither—out of curiosity."
"Stop!" cried Philosophy, with air so Grecian,
(Though she was masqued then as a fair Venetian.)

211

"Stop!" so I stopp'd.—But to return: that which
    Men call inconstancy is nothing more
Than admiration due where nature's rich
    Profusion with young beauty covers o'er
Some favour'd object; and as in the niche
    A lovely statue we almost adore,
This sort of adoration of the real
Is but a heightening of the "beau ideal."

At this point the narrator is playing a complex game, the old
platonic one of appearance and reality. The "real" Venetian lady
costumed as the muse of philosophy is herself only a particular
mortal embodiment of that universal and immortal essence impersonated through her disguise: notice that though the lady is at the
masquerade, Philosophy is designated the actual role player, "being masqued then as a fair Venetian." Similarly, the narrator is a false
face perfectly fitting (and also patterned on) Byron, the expatriate
reveling, as his letters of the period announce, in the pleasures of
Venice—pleasures dependent for their full flavor upon the contrasting recollected tastes of England.[7] But "Byron" in the letters
and in this digression is a representative man of his class and
nation. Several signs to this effect are evident in what Mikhail
Bakhtin would call the "hybrid utterances"[8] of the final four stanzas, where diction, figurative language, and allusion all undercut
the plausibility of the poem's fictive world. The usual means of
shattering such an illusion is to emphasize the artificial nature of
the literary work—here the method is to highlight Don Juan's connections with "reality" known and shared by Byron, his narrator,

and his implied reader. Among the specifics better suited to Regency England than Lambro's isle are "beau ideal," a French phrase indispensable to the vocabulary of the Great World, and "killing" used in its English slang sense ("graces quite as killing") with a British coin, the "shilling," as its rhyme (DJ 2.213). Calling a tearful existence "the English climate of our years" (DJ 2.214) and alluding to Burton by labeling this discussion of melancholy an "anatomy" (DJ 2.216) similarly enhance the aristocratic English author and narrator and diminish the exotic Juan and Haidée, who are the merest of contrivances as the canto winds up:

> In the mean time, without proceeding more
>   In this anatomy, I've finish'd now
> Two hundred and odd stanzas as before,
>   That being about the number I'll allow
> Each canto of the twelve, or twenty-four.   (DJ 2.216)

Canto 3 begins and ends with just this sort of nonchalant yet insistent undermining of the story, characters, setting, and literary conventions. "Hail Muse! *et cetera.*—We left Juan sleeping" is the brilliantly laconic start of canto 3, which leaves the hero to his happy unmarried slumbers for eleven stanzas, while love and marriage are examined and found analogous to wine and vinegar. The generalization holds in all climes and at all times. Petrarch, Dante, Milton, and by implication Byron himself illustrate different facets of the incompatibility of love and marriage. But the peculiar institution analyzed seems to be modern English marriage. Both terms and ideas are close to those found in *Glenarvon*, where, as we have seen, "In her first passion woman loves her lover" (DJ 3.3) and "a woman planted— / ... After a decent time must be gallanted" (DJ 3.4) and "love and marriage rarely can combine, / Although they both are born in the same clime" (DJ 3.5) and "Men grow ashamed of being so very fond" (DJ 3.7).

The narrator suspends the idyll of Juan and Haidée after only some sixty stanzas in which the narrative advances hardly at all— stanzas presenting Lambro's Odyssean return to a "house no more his home" and his almost voyeuristic presence at the lovers' richly described feast—and for the last quarter of the canto turns to various poetical and metapoetical concerns, most immediately offering the famous "isles of Greece" lyric sung to Haidée, Juan, and their guests by a poet "With truth like Southey and with verse

like Crashaw" (DJ 3.79). This lyric and its context richly complicate
the Dedication's fairly simple notion that bad poetry rises from bad
politics and vice versa. "The isles of Greece" is the song of a crass
opportunist "preferring pudding to no praise" (DJ 3.79). Yet it is a
work of genius. Not because of its political message, for that "glorious idea crumbles on closer inspection," as Malcolm Kelsall convincingly demonstrates[9]—but because it superbly achieves its generic task. A drinking song, it presents all that such a work is meant
to: alternating exaltations and abasements that are sometimes personal and sometimes universal, sentiments and ironies now pleasing, now pleasantly painful. "The isles of Greece" blends oppositions to achieve the complexity that distinguishes a singularily
beautiful lyric, or wine, from the ordinarily agreeable many. But my
main concern here is with the poet rather than his poem. Though
solidly grounded on Lambro's island, this "sad trimmer" draws
our attention away from the world in which he sings and back to
the real one with its real islands, especially the Venetian one where
Byron composes to please himself and the British one where
Southey, like the Greek poet, "earn'd his laureate pension" (DJ
3.80).

Characterizing his nameless modern poet, Byron is at his ironic
and cosmopolitan best. He inscribes the portrait with more meaning than a reader impatient for resumed action, distracted by the
lyric interlude, or intent on finding a key to real people behind the
poem's fictions is likely to detect. Obviously the "turncoat" is
meant to mirror Southey, and by extension Wordsworth and Coleridge, the trio of Lakers whose common excursion from the liberal
sentiments of their youth is to be explicitly denounced a few
stanzas farther on (DJ 3.93–95). But there is more. To start, there is
the mention of Richard Crashaw, not just a metaphysical poet
whose distinctive verse might evoke ridicule in a more austere age
and a man whose name can make a comic rhyme for "Pacha."
Byron introduces Crashaw because he, like Southey and the unnamed poet, is a kind of turncoat: the son of a noted Puritan cleric,
he converted to Roman Catholicism. Like another changeable
poet, the Byron of Don Juan, he also left England for Italy and
abandoned English verse forms for contemporary Italian models.
Thus through his likeness to Crashaw the Greek poet serves as a
personal bridge connecting Southey with the Byronic narrator,
who is very close to Byron at this point in the poem, and whose

"hot youth—when George the Third was king" (DJ 1.212) provides a phrase echoed in the description of this Greek poet's "singing as he sung in his warm youth" (DJ 3.83). In fact, many of the descriptions of the Greek lyricist seem to embody Byron's sort of adaptability more than Southey's.[10] A few examples:

> He was a man who had seen many changes,
>   And always changed as true as any needle;   (DJ 3.80)

> He had travell'd 'mongst the Arabs, Turks, and Franks,
>   And knew the self-loves of the different nations; (DJ 3.84)

> His muse made increment of any thing,
>   From the high lyric down to the low rational: (DJ 3.85)

Standing behind all these changeable English poets is the venerable Horace, who having praised the republic could praise Augustus—and having shifted his ground could admit as much. As Kelsall has observed, the Horatian admission itself appears in Don Juan[11]—aptly quoted at the start of the stanza where the Byronic narrator comments on how he has changed since his "hot youth": " 'Non ego hoc ferrem calida juventa / Consule Planco' " (DJ 1.212).

Presenting a number of actual turncoat poets in one unnamed fictional lyricist is an act of construction analogous to the Grimaldi Clown's ingenious arrangement of assorted objects into visual similes or an overascription like Caroline Lamb's choice of St. Clare, a name resonant with too many possible meanings to permit its working into a scheme of roman à clef. Byron's mixture of models brilliantly demonstrates that "impurity" need not debase and can actually strengthen a literary fabrication. Paradoxically, the existence of several possible models, rather than just one, confers self-sufficient integrity on the created character: because the singer of "The isles of Greece" is not purely Southey, or Byron, or Crashaw, or Horace, he can be pure poet. His essence, undiluted by the extraneous biographical attributes of any single personality, is composed of two elements: verbal talent and changeability. Through the essential example provided by the unnamed poet Byron surprises us into seeing the basic similarity between mobility, an excusable and sometimes even admirable quality in the poem, and treachery, one of the most despicable traits presented. Mobility unites many of the most important real and fictive people of Don

Juan: the Lakers, Byron, the narrator, Don Juan, John Johnson, Julia, Lady Adeline Amundeville. Noticing this affinity between amiable characters and contemptible ones, we are driven to search for a telling distinction. We find one, I think, in the fact that a shift of position can be disinterested or interested, natural or calculated, a matter of temperament or a means of opportunism, an affirmation or a denial of what is best in the mixed nature of the mobile being.

I hope that this look at the singer of "The isles of Greece" has demonstrated how helpful to appreciating *Don Juan*, in fact how downright indispensable to understanding certain aspects of the poem, is the cosmopolitan "cultivation" spoken of in this chapter's epigraph from Schlegel—the traveling beyond our personal boundaries that brings us closer to being Byron's ideal readers. The unnamed versifier whom we have been considering is a character completely enclosed in *Don Juan*'s fictive world; and he is almost an abstraction—the Poet pared down to a pair of defining traits (talent and mobility) along with those minimal attributes no human being can lack (a time, a place, a gender). But is this picture of the Poet a good likeness? And what is its significance? We are better able to judge if we can follow the inductive process Byron has implied in abstracting this modern Greek manifestation of the Poet from at least four real-life poetic chameleons, if we bring to the story information from other worlds, particularly from the classical and English literary traditions. Information, both intensive and extensive, is especially necessary as canto 3 closes and canto 4 begins. The stanzas spanned by this part of the poem (DJ 3.87–111 and 4.1–7) constitute the Byronic parabasis that most closely resembles the composite poetic device as Aristophanes, for instance, would have employed it. We part from the fictional world of Lambro's island with stanza 87's summation of the Greek poet's performance ("Thus sung, or would, or could, or should have sung, / The modern Greek, in tolerable verse")—briefly return to "our tale" in the first six lines of stanza 101, which merely tell us that the feast has ended and the lovers are alone at twilight—then pick up "Young Juan and his lady-love" after the couplet of the seventh stanza of canto 4 brings the digression to an explicit close ("Meanwhile Apollo plucks me by the ear, / And tells me to resume my story here").

This parabasis is in many ways a difficult one to explicate. Its range of topics is extraordinarily wide, even for Don Juan. It proves as dense as the most heavily name-dropping sentences of the prose Preface—and its density is even harder to penetrate because the allusions are as often as not implied ones, literary tags in addition to names or titles.[12] Even its position in the poem poses a problem the reader must solve. If we recognize the parabasis as a logically continuous passage, we must admit that its continuity, its spilling over from the end of canto 3 to the start of canto 4, violates the poem's structure. At the same time, we must acknowledge that the integrity of the parabasis is itself violated by the conspicuous and self-contradictory utterances closing one canto and opening the other: the ostensibly arbitrary shutdown of canto 3 ["I feel this tediousness will never do— / 'Tis being too epic, and I must cut down / (In copying) this long canto into two" (DJ 3.111)]—and the insistently introductory note struck by the first lines of canto 4: "Nothing so difficult as a beginning / In poesy, unless perhaps the end."

One original canto or two? Signs point both ways—the logical continuity suggesting the former state, the poetic and rhetorical separation indicating the latter. As it happens, the two cantos were at first a single longer unit.[13] Byron did, as he claims, divide the one sprawling canto into two parts. But why say that he has done so "in copying"—not the true moment of bisection, as the first line of canto 4 makes perfectly evident? Why make the self-nullifying announcement "They'll never find it out, unless I own / The fact" (DJ 3.111)? Breaking laws is an assertion of power; the more wanton the crash through barriers, the more graphic the display of force. By conspicuously flouting the rules ordinarily applicable to the shape of a rhetorical structure, whether a canto or a parabasis, Byron offers concrete evidence that the imaginative force called the poet need not respect the conventions that have risen in its arena of creation. In the next few paragraphs we shall see that the power of words and the lies of poets are two pivotal, interrelated concerns of the parabasis. Byron's playful inconsistencies in closing one canto and opening another enact on the level of poetic structure the very truths verbally asserted in the parabasis.

As we have seen, the Byronic narrator begins his parabasis by dismissing the "modern Greek" and his "tolerable verse" from the stage of the poem. Assessment of the Greek's achievement leads to generalization about all poets:

If not like Orpheus quite, when Greece was young,
    Yet in these times he might have done much worse:
His strain display'd some feeling—right or wrong;
    And feeling, in a poet, is the source
Of others' feeling; but they are such liars,
And take all colours—like the hands of dyers.   (DJ 3.87)

The dyer's hand stained by the colors it employs, affected by the effect it contrives, may be the most famous part of this passage, but there are other details well worth discussion. One such matter is the appositive *liars* and its homonym *lyres*. We have already seen that the lie and the lyre taken together characterize the poet of "The isles of Greece." Because he is modern yet a countryman of Orpheus, an essence distilled from several real poets, the nameless singer can serve as Everypoet, a representative being connecting his high mythic prototype with Horace, Crashaw, Pope, Dryden, Byron—and also with debased contemporary practitioners of the art such as the detested Lakers, whose "names at present cut a convict figure, / The very Botany Bay in moral geography" (DJ 3.94). If we recognize that all poets are liars with lyres, we shall avoid certain erroneous assumptions, among them the unfounded faith that inferior poetry lacks the power to do harm and the equally false belief that great poetry straightforwardly reveals simple truth. Once we acknowledge that comparatively poor poetry may some- how endure and need not be completely impotent, we can under- stand why attacks on "bad poets" belong in Don Juan, despite Hob- house's suggestion that "assault of the poor creatures so infinitely below you in poetical character would look to the world perfectly wanton and harmless except to your own great reputation which places you above even the chastisement of such grovellers."[14] And having generalized about the difficulty of finding truth in orphic utterances, where the "lie" may derive from the poet's misspeak- ing, the audience's misapprehending, or both, Byron has given us fair warning that even his own poetic assertions should not be uncritically accepted at face value.

Byron's remarks on poets and their productions are calculated to be universally relevant but particularly applicable to contemporary British realities. The parabasis announces timeless convictions but also provides a timely defense of Don Juan and an attack on those modern British poets who fall short of, and themselves assail, the standards it embodies, Augustan values inherited from Pope and Dryden. The power of poets' words justifies both the defense of "good" poets and the attack on "bad" ones: "feeling, in a poet, is the source / Of others' feelings" (DJ 3.87) and "words are things, and a small drop of ink, / Falling like dew, upon a thought, produces / That which makes thousands, perhaps millions, think" (DJ 3.88). Ensuing stanzas offer ample evidence that words make truths and poets kindle feelings. "Troy owes to Homer that whist owes to Hoyle" (DJ 3.90); how the present generation sees Marlborough, Milton, and Burns depends in some measure on what features have been stressed by their respective biographers, Coxe, Johnson, and Currie (DJ 3.90, 91, 92). Having acknowledged that the writer's selectivity produces a new reality by determining the readers' image of whomever or whatever is being animated or reified through words, Byron takes prompt advantage of his right to select. As he sees it, the Lakers (most prominently Wordsworth) have misrepresented the Augustans (especially Dryden and Pope).[15] The Lakers' views, however obscure and erroneous Byron may think them, have reached print and thus have a chance to "make thousands, perhaps millions, think." But if Byron's own words can discredit the thinkers, he can counteract their thoughts. Accordingly, he selects and exaggerates a few salient features to represent the Lake-dwellers in his poem:

> All are not moralists, like Southey, when
>   He prated to the world of "Pantisocrasy;"
> Or Wordsworth, unexcised, unhired, who then
>   Season'd his pedlar poems with democracy;
> Or Coleridge, long before his flighty pen
>   Let to the Morning Post its aristocracy;
> When he and Southey, following the same path,
> Espoused two partners (milliners of Bath.)   (DJ 3.93)

Because Wordsworth is the one Laker who has most directly threatened the contemporary reputations of Dryden and Pope (and also perhaps because Byron accurately perceives him, with more talent than Southey and more productivity than Coleridge, as having the most potential to cut a figure for posterity), he bears the brunt of the literary attack, though the epic *longeurs* induced by Southey's epics do receive a stanza's attention (DJ 3.97). The case against Wordsworth is based on specific and fairly fresh evidence, the poems singled out for ridicule being the "drowsy frowzy" Excursion (its second edition having been published in 1820), "The Waggoner" (published in 1819), and "Peter Bell" (published in 1819). Wordsworth's shortcomings are presented not as debatable matters of taste but as downright deficiencies. In The Excursion Wordsworth "builds up a formidable dyke / Between his own and others' intellect" (DJ 3.95)—surely a flaw if words are meant to make others think. In "The Waggoners," he is charged with plodding, provincial complacency (DJ 3.98). In "Peter Bell" he reveals a woeful lack of cultivation and sense. Byron's argument focuses on a detail that might, in less resourceful hands, furnish material for the merest quibble:

> He wishes for "a boat" to sail the deeps—
>   Of ocean?—No, of air; and then he makes
> Another outcry for "a little boat,"
> And drivels seas to set it well afloat.   (DJ 3.98)

In contrast to Wordsworth, the Byronic narrator, a man of common sense and uncommon cultivation, has no trouble finding an array of more felicitous possibilities:

> If he must fain sweep o'er the etherial plain,
>   And Pegasus runs restive in his "waggon,"
> Could he not beg the loan of Charles's Wain?
>   Or pray Medea for a single dragon?
> Or if too classic for his vulgar brain,
>   He fear'd his neck to venture such a nag on,
> And he must needs mount nearer to the moon,
> Could not the blockhead ask for a balloon?   (DJ 3.99)

Notice how the ground of criticism shifts away from strictly poetic concerns here: Wordsworth's choice of the "little boat" shows him not so much a bad poet as a fuzzy thinker, something likelier to arouse the contempt of a larger segment of Byron's audience. Furthermore, the narrator's catalogue of alternative means of transport manages to impute to poor Wordsworth various deficiencies not directly relevant to the detail under present consideration. By implication the author of "Peter Bell" is ill-grounded in the classics, inadequately equipped by training or temperament for horsemanship, even ignorant of technological developments. At the end of the indictment, the ideal reader of Don Juan is meant to conclude that Wordsworth notably lacks certain qualities cherished by that ruling-class culture to which both poet and audience belong. Wordsworth and "Trash of such sort" may sneer "at him who drew 'Achitophel' " (DJ 3.100), but the reader is not likely to side with the sneerer after what the parabasis has done to him. Byron's portraits of the Lake poets and their productions are not entirely fair likenesses—though his earlier "poets are liars" is a statement of *caveat lector* that may relieve him of any need to strive for objectivity. Whether or not the likenesses are fair, they have lasted—and in a sense they have actually triumphed over more faithfully rendered portraits. Byron's gift of words is such that readers who know Southey, Wordsworth, and Coleridge to have been less than adequately portrayed in these lines, who even understand in just what ways the quoted passages fall short of doing justice to the maligned trio and their poetic productions, may still think of the Lakers in Byron's vivid phrases and images. A great poet's lies (or contorted truths) do put ideas in other heads, *Don Juan* again serving down the ages as the best practical demonstration of the theoretical truth it asserts.

The indignant eloquence directed against Wordsworth and company will ring truer still if the reader is favorably disposed toward its speaker. Thus the beautiful and often discussed "Ave Maria!" stanzas (DJ 3.102–9), which in some ways seem at odds with the bitterly contemptuous denunciation that precedes them, can be seen as a useful phase in the complex argument that constitutes *Don Juan's* chief parabasis. Byron has just shown himself able to hit hard and aim well—now he seems to soften and strategically reveals his romantic and idealistic side, his best weapon against those "casuists" who "are pleased to say, / In nameless print—that I have no devotion" (DJ 3.104). Wit is not exactly banished from this charming interlude, which so movingly portrays the hour of prayer and love as Byron experienced it with Teresa Guiccioli in the Ravenna pines; but sentiment and apparently candid self-revelation take center stage. The reader, especially if familiar with details of Byronic biography, is made to sympathize with the narrator. Once that sympathy is achieved the artful speaker, as if embarrassed at his uncharacteristic lapse into honest emotion, takes refuge in facetiousness: "But I'm digressing," he says,

> Sure my invention must be down at zero,
>   And I grown one of many "wooden spoons"
> Of verse (the name with which we Cantabs please
> To dub the last of honours in degrees).   (DJ 3.110)

If anything, this retreat heightens the compliment implied in the intimacy of the "Ave Maria!" interlude—and just as that earlier section flatters the reader who appreciates the biographical aptness of its details, so this passage builds on what is implied to be common ground. The reader, as if a favored fellow *alumnus cantabrigensis*, feels complicity with Byron when relied on to understand university slang and classical terms and concepts (passim, Ποιητικης, and the Aristotelian party line on poetic length), when privileged to hear that the one long canto has been "*too* epic" and will be cut in two, when flattered with the confidence that "They'll never find it out, unless I own / The fact, excepting an experienced few." As the canto closes and the parabasis enters its last phase, true confessions curtailed at just the right moment and "old boy" consensus blended of antics and esoterics prove superbly effective at ensuring that Byron, his narrator, and the reader stand together as a community of the cultivated—amateur classicists against corrupt moderns, cosmopolites against yokels, a discerning "we" against an imperceptive "they."

Thus when the introductory generalizations on intellectual pride and how experience chastens it have begun canto 4 very effectively indeed (despite the fact that there is "Nothing so difficult as a beginning"), the narrator speaks from Byron's personal viewpoint—a vantage point made highly sympathetic to the reader in the closing stanzas of canto 3. The tone is serious without being heavy. Wit and pertinent allusion serve, as they so often do in *Don Juan*, to make us smile even as we recognize sober truth:

> As boy, I thought myself a clever fellow,
>   And wish'd that others held the same opinion;
> They took it up when my days grew more mellow,
>   And other minds acknowledged my dominion:
> Now my sere fancy "falls into the yellow
>   Leaf," and imagination droops her pinion,
> And the sad truth which hovers o'er my desk
> Turns what was once romantic to burlesque.
>
> 4
> And if I laugh at any mortal thing,
>   'Tis that I may not weep; and if I weep,
> 'Tis that our nature cannot always bring
>   Itself to apathy.   (DJ 4.3–4)

These lines sing out "He is an Englishman" almost as clearly as if they were W. S. Gilbert's song to that effect. The barding—the professed attempt at the national stiff upper lip (failure at complete stoicism being permissible because the speaker is a poet, hence an Englishman of feeling)—the apt mythological reference to Thetis dipping Achilles in the Styx that follows the quoted lines—all are appropriate to the voice of the expatriate Cantab who closed canto 3. That cosmopolite now launches into metapoetic commentary, elegantly making his defense of *Don Juan*, like his attack on Wordsworth's art, an integral part of the poem. The following stanzas clearly indicate the responsive nature of *Don Juan*:

> Some have accused me of a strange design
>   Against the creed and morals of the land,
> And trace it in this poem every line:
>   I don't pretend that I quite understand
> My own meaning when I would be very fine,
>   But the fact is that I have nothing plann'd,
> Unless it were to be a moment merry,
> A novel word in my vocabulary.
>
> 6
> To the kind reader of our sober clime
>   This way of writing will appear exotic;
> Pulci was sire of the half-serious rhyme,
>   Who sang when chivalry was more Quixotic,
> And revell'd in the fancies of the time,
>   True knights, chaste dames, huge giants, kings despotic;
> But all these, save the last, being obsolete,
> I chose a modern subject as more meet.
>
> 7
> How I have treated it, I do not know;
>   Perhaps no better than they have treated me
> Who have imputed such designs as show
>   Not what they saw, but what they wish'd to see;
> But if it gives them pleasure, be it so,
>   This is a liberal age, and thoughts are free. (DJ 4.5–7)

Byron's sensitivity to British criticism—and the previously published cantos 1 and 2 had provoked plenty of it—is evident in his pose of offhandedness. But the self-deprecation is also a strategy for retaining the sympathies of the implied reader. After suggesting that Wordsworth is pompous and abstruse, yet dogmatic and provincial, Byron is at pains to avoid the appearance of putting on side. He must convey the impression of modesty, lucidity, tolerance, intense and wide experience—traits that will aid him in his desire to please the cosmopolitan reader, broaden the insular one (that cultural imperialist whose habit of dealing with "exotic" modes and matters is to domesticate them, as the poem's rhyme here has done with the word Quixotic) and speak convincingly to both of timely matters—false knights (and baronets and lords), dissolute ladies, pygmies who fancy themselves gigantic, and of course "kings despotic." All Europe may provide examples for this "half-serious" poem, all continents and subsequent ages may ultimately furnish readers, but the immediate English audience is the one Byron can move in a manner he can calculate and toward ends he can envision. That "kind reader of our sober clime" must be made willing to accept the narrator's home truths.

Accordingly, Don Juan's associative arabesques typically establish connections between English things, words, situations, and practices and corresponding matter drawn from the wide world beyond. Sometimes English tastes or values are normative, as in canto 3 and 4, where the ordeals of shipwreck and marooning illustrate Don Juan's (and all humanity's) basic need for food and drink. "Ceres and Bacchus" take all forms in these cantos: we see near-starvation, cannibalism, restorative seaside breakfasts in the island cave, and finally the exquisite delights of a banquet. Byron subtly but persistently connects all this feast and famine with the reader's prosaic world of eating and drinking. His means is repeated mention of those stereotypical English favorites tea and beef.[16]

Similarly, when in canto 5 Don Juan finds himself surrounded by and bedecked in unfamiliar Oriental splendor, distinctively British words or comparisons keep the reader from being drugged by the opiate of mere exotic description. When Juan, disguised as a harem girl, trips on his petticoat, Byron uses the so-called tyranny of rhyme to justify his employing a Scots vernacular pronoun: "whilk" instead of "which"—a choice he repeats in unrhymed position at the start of the next stanza: "Whilk, which (or what you please)" (DJ 5.77–78). The palace's massive portals may be guarded by implike dwarf-mutes, but the doors have hinges "smooth as Rogers' rhymes" (DJ 5.89). Juan's uncritical admiration of the "strange saloon" that lies behind the doors brings up a critical issue—the Horatian matter of *nil admirari*—that Byron makes peculiarly English, and peculiarly his own, by pinning a particular British identity (that of his publisher) on his reader, casting the matter in terms of English literature, and transforming the translation:

> "Not to admire is all the art I know
>   (Plain truth, dear Murray, needs few flowers of speech)
> To make men happy, or to keep them so;
>   (So take it in the very words of Creech)."
> Thus Horace wrote we all know long ago;
>   And thus Pope quotes the precept to re-teach
> From his translation; but had *none admired*,
> Would Pope have sung, or Horace been inspired? (DJ 5.101)

When Don Juan balks at kissing the sultana's foot, the narrator stresses that the specifics may be foreign but the general situation is not: "There's nothing in the world like *etiquette* / In kingly chambers or imperial halls, / As also at the race and county balls" (DJ 5.103). And when Juan spurns the sultana's advances (surely an alien adventure for most readers) Byron directly asks that her wrath be imagined in terms of an experience more familiar in Regency society:

> Ye! who have kept your chastity when young,
>   While some more desperate dowager has been waging
>   Love with you, and been in the dog-days stung
> By your refusal, recollect her raging!   (DJ 5.130)

The convergence of cultures achieved by intellectual and verbal arabesques of this sort does not merely alert Byron's fellow Britons to the home truths pointed out by Juan's international escapades— it also enriches passages concerned with primarily British matters. A five-stanza digression on bluestockings, where an elaborately false tone of regret masks Byron's real disappointment that female readers failed to appreciate "Donny Johnny" (DJ 4.108–12), nicely illustrates this point.[17] Here, "Oh!" "Ah!" and other exclamations alternate with rhetorical questions in a mock-mournful address to the no-longer "benign ceruleans of the second sex" (DJ 4.108). Byron is up to his old tricks of combining pseudobiographical recollection ("What, can I prove 'a lion' then no more?" "I know one woman of that purple school, / The loveliest, chastest, best, but—quite a fool"), literary quotation, misquotation, and allusion (bringing in Shakespeare, Wordsworth, and Southey), and witty reference to scientific developments (the cyanometer, a contrivance seemingly well-named for measuring the "intensity of blue" in each learned lady). But the passage's most brilliant effect involves superimposing a mythic past on the literary coteries Byron remembered from his Years of Fame following the publication of *Childe Harold*:

> What, must I go to the oblivious cooks?
>   Those Cornish plunderers of Parnassian wrecks?
> Ah! must I then the only minstrel be,
> Proscribed from tasting your Castalian tea!   (DJ 4.108)

Along with lining portmanteaus, wrapping pastries was a fate for which literary works gone aground were destined in Byron's day—so the cooks are not only themselves "oblivious" to the merits of *Don Juan*, they also act to promote its oblivion in the wider world. There is considerable delight in seeing Byron's skill at fusing Parnassus, the inland mountain of Apollo and the Muses, with the rocky coast of Cornwall, so deadly to ships, then blending the Cornish pillagers of shipwrecks with the metropolitan purveyors of Cornish pasties and other baked goods. The hybrid phrase "Castalian tea" adds further refinements. The idea of brewing tea for salon frequenters from the waters of the Parnassian spring Castalia suggests, as does "Cornish plunderers of Parnassian wrecks," a distinctively English debasement of something sacred—a sacrilege both literally and symbolically appropriate to the circumstances. But because the name *Castalia* commemorates a nymph who flung herself into the spring as she fled from the embraces of Apollo, this phrase has the further advantage of pertaining to the human relationship here being deplored, the shrinking of fastidious literary nymphs from the robust delights Byron/ Apollo has offered them in *Don Juan*. Lest this last significance escape a reader whose grasp of Greek geography is inadequate to the occasion, Byron offers a second chance at the insight in his digression's final line: "Oh, Lady Daphne! let me measure you!" (DJ 4.112). Here, the coldly virtuous nymph is the one who avoided Apollo's importunities by becoming a bay tree, with foliage subsequently sacred to the god and coveted by his followers the poets. Like brewing tea from Castalian water, Byron's metamorphosing

Daphne into an English nobleman's daughter diminishes what was purely mythic. At the same time, such linkage can be seen as exalting what was merely mundane. The Great World where Byron is no longer the darling of Lady Daphne and her kind is nothing so great when compared with the realm of Apollo, but the fact that the two spheres can be compared increases Regency England's appeal. Again, though, it is the cosmopolitan, the habitué of both worlds, who must make the connection.

In each of the cases so far examined, introducing English matters to *Don Juan* has involved a sort of parabasis, and thus has carried us, however momentarily, out of the fictive world in which the narrative has been unfolding. But Byron had at his disposal two "dramatic" means of bringing such matters in, of taking up English phenomena without suspending the tale. One way, transporting Don Juan to England, will be the subject of the next chapter. The other way, bringing an English person into *Don Juan*, is what Byron chose to do at the start of canto 5, as Juan finds himself part of the slave market's international merchandise. Also there for sale is John Johnson, whose likeness to Southey's "Newbury Renegado" and whose role in persuading Don Juan to enact the role of Juanna have already been mentioned. This estimable fellow becomes Don Juan's, if not *Don Juan's*, introduction to the English character and the values and behavior that comprise it.

The extraordinarily ordinary English name John Johnson suggests, among other things, that its possessor will be a representative figure. Johnson's appearance is correspondingly that of a good English type:

> A man of thirty, rather stout and hale,
> With resolution in his dark gray eye,
> Next Juan stood, till some might choose to buy.
>
> 11
> He had an English look; that is, was square
>   In make, of a complexion white and ruddy,
> Good teeth, with curling rather dark brown hair,
>   And, it might be from thought, or toil, or study,
> An open brow a little mark'd with care.   (DJ 5.10–11)

Cecil Y. Lang convincingly argues that this description affectionately portrays Byron's boxing master from bygone days, that John

Johnson is based on his near-namesake "Gentleman" John Jackson.[18] The details of Johnson's appearance also tally in a general way with Byron's own looks when his health was sound (though the matter of "good teeth" may have been wishful thinking—his letters from Italy remind English friends to send "Waite's red tooth powder" with a persistence that suggests some anxiety). Johnson's cool attitude toward his former wives, at which we looked in the second essay, is, like the dental superiority, a quality Byron would be glad to have—or to have attributed to him. The premature pose of world-weariness and the ability to view his own plight with detachment and humor are Byronic features we by this point in the poem have learned to recognize as equally characteristic of the narrator. In fact Johnson turns out to be, like Byron and the narrator, an exemplary specimen of the contemporary English philosopher as delineated in chapter 6 of *England and the English*, no systematic idealist but a practical student of conduct in a material world.[19] The congruence between Johnson's perspective and the narrator's becomes evident early in canto 5, where Johnson, whose cynicism does not prevent him from making the best of circumstances, tries to comfort Juan with these words of wisdom:

> "But after all, what is our present state?
>   'Tis bad, and may be better—all men's lot:
> Most men are slaves, none more so than the great,
>   To their own whims and passions, and what not." (DJ 5.25)

Two stanzas later the narrator is generalizing about the pleasure of "purchasing our fellow creatures" in much the same way:

> And all are to be sold, if you consider
>   Their passions, and are dext'rous; some by features
> Are bought up, others by a warlike leader,
>   Some by a place—as tend their years or natures;
> The most by ready cash—but all have prices,
> From crowns to kicks, according to their vices.   (DJ 5.27)

As these similar observations suggest, the worldly English empiricist Johnson embodies a certain side of the Byronic narrator, though that narrator is of course a much more complex and intriguing entity. By dint of his presence in the fictive world of the poem, Johnson is able to impart some of his and the narrator's shared practical wisdom to Don Juan. And Juan sorely needs it, for, paradoxically, his life as choice-making creature has begun with his enslavement. His previous "choices" have been variously determined—by instinct and sentiment (affairs with Julia and Haidée), internalized code (courageous endurance of shipwreck, rash defiance of Lambro), biological necessity (reliance on Haidée's nurturing, resistance to the "bella donna" on the slave ship), or mixtures of these impulses. Now, in Constantinople, Juan is stripped of his former social identity yet put into social situations calling for more difficult decisions than his previous experience has offered. As Bunyan supplied Faithful and Hopeful to help Pilgrim through the tight spots of his Progress, so Byron provides Don Juan with a comrade whose attributes, if assimilated, will help him deal with the new challenges of increasingly adult experience.

John Johnson proves himself indispensable to Juan on three occasions, in situations that ascend in complexity. As Baba conducts the purchased Europeans through the imperial precincts, young man's bravado spurs Juan to suggest that he and Johnson "knock that old black fellow on the head" and make their escape. Here (DJ 5.44), Johnson's simple reminder of realities suffices to correct Juan's course. Having bashed the eunuch, how would they get out? And how would getting out improve their situation? And anyway, why make any attempts before getting the badly needed sustenance of a meal?

When the two enslaved Westerners face further threats to their identities in the Turkish costumes Baba chooses for them and the circumcision he recommends (DJ 5.67–69), Johnson's prudence instructs Juan through example. The matter of circumcision raised by Baba evokes Johnson's cagiest courtesy and provokes an intemperate explosion from Juan. The stanzas presenting their responses offers telling contrast of temperaments. Johnson, significantly, manages to have the first and the last word:

> For his own share—he saw but small objection
>   To so respectable an ancient rite;
> And, after swallowing down a slight refection,
>   For which he own'd a present appetite,
> He doubted not a few hours of reflection
>   Would reconcile him to the business quite.
> "Will it?" said Juan, sharply; "Strike me dead,
> But they as soon shall circumcise my head!

72

"Cut off a thousand heads, before——"—"Now, pray,"
　　Replied the other, "do not interrupt:
You put me out in what I had to say.
　　Sir!—as I said, as soon as I have supt,
I shall perpend if your proposal may
　　Be such as I can properly accept;
Provided always your great goodness still
Remits the matter to our own free-will."   (DJ 5.71–72)

Johnson's diplomatic evasiveness demonstrates to Juan, always impetuous and often naive but not stupid, that a manly man need not always face coercion with direct resistance. It is Johnson's example rather than Baba's threats, I think, that leads Juan to acquiesce in his temporary transformation to Juanna. With "some slight oaths" here, some sighs there, tugs, trips, and other awkwardnesses, Juan deliberately shows that he is neither accustomed to nor pleased by putting on female apparel. But by the time the disguise is complete, he has entered into the game with the good grace that is always wise when opposition is fruitless. Johnson, rightly reading Juan's change of mood, parts from him with mixed advice and badinage; and Juan has become enough like his practical mentor to return the volley in his new and temporary character:

"We needs must follow [says Johnson] when Fate puts from shore.
　　Keep your good name; though Eve herself once fell."
"Nay," quoth the maid, "the Sultan's self shan't carry me,
Unless his highness promises to marry me."   (DJ 5.84)

In the preceding situations, Johnson's values clearly were suited to effecting a satisfactory outcome. But the Englishman's material philosophy will not suffice to handle everything Fate presents, as is evident in canto 8 when, on the battlefield of Ismail, Juan rescues Leila, a beautiful Turkish child. Though both Juan and Johnson are gentlemen, as Johnson immediately recognized in the slave market (DJ 5.13), and both are soldiers of fortune for the present time, they look at the problem posed by the act of rescue from different places on the human continuum. Here, as before, Don Juan shows himself hobbled by lofty ideals—but this time Johnson's pragmatism will not, unalloyed, answer the needs of the moment.

Fighting against his own comrades, the Cossacques, to save a child of the enemy is chivalrous instinct on Juan's part. When he has foiled the child's assailants, Juan gazes into her eyes and sees her with his heart, which responds with "pain, pleasure, hope, fear, mixed / With joy to save, and dread of some mischance / Unto his protégée" (DJ 8.96). What he sees and how he feels combine to give Juan, at this highly inconvenient moment, one of his most soberly responsible impulses in the whole poem. He vows to suffer anything for Leila's safety: " 'At least I will endure / Whate'er is to be borne—but not resign / This child, who is parentless and therefore mine' " (DJ 8.100). "Borne" is interestingly double here—if read as "born" it suggests acceptance not merely of the humane responsibilities implicit in "protégée" but of parenthood's added burdens. And like a loving parent, Juan accepts more responsibility for her than any mortal can actually take for another: " 'I saved her—must not leave / Her life to chance' " (DJ 8.99). Though he has only just encountered the girl and in spite of the fact that he is in the midst of slaughtering her countrymen, he vows to cherish her existence above his own: " 'I'll not quit her till she seems secure / Of present life a good deal more than we' " (DJ 8.100). Such an attachment, instantly formed, unrealistic in its aim, and inconsistent with Juan's present role and situation, is clearly emotional rather than reasonable.

Avowing his new responsibilities, Juan calls on Johnson to " 'Look / Upon this child' " (DJ 8.99). The older man sees Leila with his eyes, not his heart, and accordingly perceives her youth and beauty, not the attendant associations that have won Juan's allegiance. The child's physical attributes alone are not enough to distract Johnson from his present pursuit of victory and the booty that goes with it:

> . . .—"Juan, we've no time to lose;
>   The child's a pretty child—a very pretty—
> I never saw such eyes—but hark! now choose
>   Between your fame and feelings, pride and pity" (DJ 8.101)

In the last line quoted, the narrator characterizes the alternatives presented to Johnson's lucid Augustan mind in witty, alliterative pairings of the sort now most famous from Jane Austen titles: "fame and feelings," "pride and pity." Choosing between such alternatives will not be not a simple matter for Johnson, who has by no means enlisted in the ranks of those he earlier called "the world's stoics—men without a heart," the purely material creatures who have learned that "To feel for none is the true social art" (DJ 5.25). As an empiricist, Johnson slights the importance of neither fame nor feelings, neither pride nor pity—but the way he balances the conflicting claims clearly shows which have primacy: " 'I should be loth to march without you, but, / By God! we'll be too late for the first cut' " (DJ 8.101).

The shared act of looking at Leila and the different reactions to that look epitomize Juan's and Johnson's contrasting perspectives on the world and reveal the blind spots hampering each viewpoint. Juan has strong, proper feelings but is incapable of translating them into reasonable action; Johnson shows willingness to make the expedient choice without heeding higher claims. The solution either man would reach alone is unpalatable. Juan would perversely give up fame, fortune, and perhaps his life to save a child whose safety would in no way be guaranteed by his sacrifice. Johnson, having eschewed ordinary morality in the special arena of battle, would succumb to ordinary cupidity—a debasing decision, for although in the brutal panorama of war one life may mean little, one man's share of the booty means infinitely less. But when Johnson's rational and Juan's emotional approaches combine rather than oppose one another, a solution satisfactory on emotional, moral, and pragmatic grounds becomes possible. Emotion serves as catalyst to this solution, but reason is chief agent. Faced with an "immovable" Juan, Johnson, "who really loved him in his way" (DJ 8.102), comes up with a practical plan of action that will allow him to have his own way while respecting Juan's feelings. The Englishman

> Picked out amongst his followers with some skill
>   Such as he thought the least given up to prey;
> And swearing if the infant came to ill
>   That they should be all shot on the next day;
> But, if she were delivered safe and sound,
> They should at least have fifty roubles round. (DJ 8.102)

Johnson's way of love is certainly different from Juan's—it is reasonable love, a partially unemotional emotion, yet another of the poem's many demonstrations that strength can reside in mixture or impurity. Johnson's skill in reading his followers and in recognizing that Juan cannot be talked out of his attachment to the Turkish child comes from gauging heads and hearts, then selecting the tools (here, threats and bribes mixed with assurance of justice) best suited to move them to his ends. Ironically, Johnson's blend of warm regard for Juan, sangfroid, and cold cash makes for the success of Juan's noble gesture.

In the resolution of this dilemma we see that a truly resourceful person would combine, as Johnson comes to do, the natures (which is also to say the moral nationalities) of Don Juan and John Johnson—and the names suggest as much. Juan is literally the Spanish John—hot, emotional, acting on instinct. Johnson is the English Juan—cool, rational, acting on intention. Each sort needs some attributes of the other for physical and spiritual survival in a world larger than either one's native country. Each, in effect, needs to be a cosmopolite. Just as Juan without Johnson's reason to guide him and Johnson without Juan's feelings to consider can be seen as at or near the ends of human nature's continuum, so the world in which Don Juan is traveling seems to have gradations of climate enclosed by extremes. Juan's origin, Spain, is hot and emotional as he is. Johnson's origin (and Juan's final destination in the poem as we have it), England, is the proper sphere of calculation and money, cold in climate and temperament, as the narrator is fond of stressing. Traveling between these extremes, Juan increasingly comes to need Johnson's particular strengths—for the passage from Spain to Greece, Turkey, Russia, and England (and like it the journey from boyhood's end at sixteen to young manhood at twenty-one) is progressively chilly in moral terms, ever less the realm of the heart and more the kingdom of the head.

Though Juan can take on some of John Johnson's practical wisdom, that material philosophy for which the English mind of Byron's day showed itself well adapted, he remains essentially different from his mentor. The difference is partly a matter of nationality, partly a function of age. But most crucially it is, like the difference between the "good" poets and the "bad" ones discussed earlier, a consequence of two distinct varieties of mobility, contrasting types offering one representation of what, for Lilian Furst, is "a central axis of the irony" in Don Juan—"the tension between spontaneity and self-consciousness."[20] Like Southey's "Newbury Renegado," Johnson, whether in the palace or on the field of battle, is able to see possibilities and make choices, his keen eye always looking for the path of least resistance, his intellect unprejudiced by a strong moral or emotional stance. Juan's way is not so much to choose as to react to his environment, to take on the color of his surroundings without assessing the implications of his position. As we have seen, he can be convinced to change his course when such a change does not conflict with his feelings, but (with the notable exception of his stint of female impersonation) he does not seem able to come independently to that choice. Once convinced to take any course of action, Juan becomes the new character he plays, his mind undistracted by alternatives. At Ismail, for example, once Johnson has devised the acceptable scheme for saving Leila, Juan will "march on through thunder" (DJ 8.103) and give over his energies to fighting with the same intensity that only moments earlier animated his newly embraced paternal role. His manner of fighting, however, indicates that Johnson's practical approach has not yet become part of his character. Like his Cossacque comrades, Juan is moved by impulse rather than strategy to spare a "brave Tartar Khan" and his five brave sons (DJ 8.104–6), then to assail these admirable enemies with renewed ferocity when the hopelessly outnumbered band refuses mercy (DJ 8.107–19).

Thus even when they partake of one another's natural and national influences, Johnson and Juan do not become identical cosmopolites. For good and for ill, Johnson is a finished being—self-propelled, self-directed, consciously manipulative. Within limits, Juan is an evolving and maturing personality. As the poem goes on, we shall see that he becomes more calculating but never downright Johnsonian, though as he moves toward the country-house heart of England, ever farther from his native climate and into an increasingly alien one, the roles he lives call more and more for cool, rational, worldly sense. As Don Juan's last cantos unfold, Johnson is no longer physically with him, but Juan survives and prospers because he has subsumed something of the older man and the culture he represents. Don Juan's England as we shortly shall see it is very much Johnson's country. Only a Juan who is also part Johnson—a Schlegelian "cultivated man" who like the composing poet and his projected narrator is able to see, feel, and think—can hope to make his way in such a world.

VI

Don Juan
in England

The notion that the English national character is sublime is unquestionably the doing, in the first instance,
of innkeepers; but novels and plays have fostered it
and thereby made a by no means contemptible contribution to the science of sublime ridiculousness.

—Friedrich Schlegel, *Athenaeum Fragments*

This chapter brings squarely and directly before us the matter of
how England, that southern part of the "tight little island" where
Don Juan's author and narrator started out and where its protagonist
and narrator end up, looks from Byron's panoramic and cosmopolitan perspective. Some readers may wish that we had arrived
here sooner—but in various ways we have been exploring the
edges of the topic all along. Robert Southey's Espriella is "Don Juan
in England" insofar as he is a Spanish observer and traveler among
the alien Britons. Caroline Lamb's Glenarvon is "Don Juan in England" insofar as he is a British lady-killer of mythic proportions.
Popular theater, as we have seen, brought the legendary don to
London and made him the toast of the town some years earlier
than Byron's poem did. The poem itself, as the last chapter has
shown, occupies itself with English matters prior to presenting
English episodes: *Don Juan* is in England long before Don Juan is.

Given the English preoccupations of the digressions and other
moments of parabasis, Byron must have considered the possibility
of sending Juan himself sailing toward the white cliffs early on. It
might seem tempting to see the last lines of the 207th stanza of
Canto 1 as a statement of farsighted purpose: "Besides, in canto
twelfth, I mean to show / The very place where wicked people go."
When canto 12 does come round, the narrator takes on the traits

necessary for admission to such a place—"But now I'm going to be immoral; now / I mean to show things really as they are" (DJ 12.40)—and his mise-en-scène for such "immoral" showings is "that microcosm on stilts / Yclept the Great World" (DJ 12.56), London's heartless heart of fashion. But the international and intellectual voyage of *Don Juan* is more errant than mapped and charted, and it would be going too far to think that as he ended his first canto Byron had a firm sense not only of a poem that would contain a twelfth canto but even of what that twelfth canto would treat. Nonetheless, the idea of sending Juan to England may have appealed, even taken on something like inevitability, once Byron had decided to extend Juan's adventures beyond the Spanish incident, a self-contained story after the fashion of *Beppo*. If, as I have argued, Byron knew Southey's *Letters from England*, that piece of cultural observation would offer both a precedent to follow and an achievement to surpass; and the Don Juan spectacles popular on the British stage from 1817 on would suggest the comic potential of such a pilgrimage. In any case, one of *Don Juan's* more astute contemporary critics, J.G. Lockhart, advised just this course of action in his pseudonymous response to the early cantos, *John Bull's Letter to Lord Byron*: "You know the society of England—you know what English gentlemen are made of; and you know very well what English ladies are made of; and, I promise you, that *knowledge* is a more precious thing, whatever you at present may think or say, than any *notion* you or any other Englishman ever can acquire either of Italians, or Spaniards, or Greeks."[1]

Byron read and relished John Bull's letter, which he pronounced "diabolically well written—& full of fun and ferocity" and suspected to be the work of Hobhouse, Peacock, or Isaac D'Israeli, in late June of 1821 (LJ 8:145—letter of 29 June to Murray). Ironically enough, "John Bull's advice came just when Byron had promised Teresa Guiccioli that he would not continue Don Juan (LJ 8:145— letter of 4 July to Murray). But John Bull's expressed preference for knowledge over notions was a view Byron shared; and though the resumed cantos do not carry Don Juan to England straight away, they get him there effectively and treat his stay there intensively.

The English cantos (which for my purposes will mean canto 10, where Juan arrives at Dover, to canto 16, the last one completed) are more admired than studied. Perhaps sheer fatigue sets in for some readers by the time they reach the long poem's last, longest, and most complex episode. Perhaps other readers feel that they already have seen Juan in every human situation worth their scrutiny and have heard in digressions the narrator's thoughts on every English subject warranting comment. Perhaps still other readers are frustrated when the poem becomes even less than it has been the story of Don Juan's adventures and more the intricately detailed portrait of a culture—that portrait itself being no simple likeness but a brilliantly accomplished pastiche. Those readers who persevere, though, are rewarded with the great pleasure of watching Byron's talent exert itself in what John Bull rightly identified as its ultimate arena, on home ground where the poet's cosmopolitan intelligence makes sense, fun, and myth of that small world best known to him. The rich and densely topical English cantos amply repay readers who take account of their cultural context, and the greater portion of this chapter will concern itself with some of the particulars of this part of the poem. First, however, some general remarks about the shape and nature of the English cantos, and the state in which we find Don Juan and the narrator when they begin.

When we last took leave of Don Juan, on the battlefield of Ismail, he had yielded to John Johnson's practicality without exactly adopting that commonsensical stance as his own. Once the battle is over and his blood has cooled (as it is sure to do on a journey north to Petersburgh), Juan joins the party of pragmatists. Johnson may have vanished from the poem, but his sanely empirical way of facing life has become part of Don Juan: in effect, the older man "anglicizes" the spirit of his protégé. When Juan arrives at Catherine's court, his innocent idealism has been replaced by conscious purpose and self-interest that enable him to profit by all he has experienced and all he will encounter.

> There was a something in his turn of limb,
>   And still more in his eye, which seemed to express
> That though he looked one of the Seraphim,
>   There lurked a Man beneath the Spirit's dress. (DJ 9.47)

To put it simply and prosaically, Don Juan has grown up. His natural openness to experience has given way to an equally attractive and far more coherent state, a moral transition that can be more concisely and accurately characterized in French nouns than English ones: *naïveté* has given way to *honnêteté*. Whereas headlong passions or other, milder feelings threw Juan blindly into earlier love affairs, he commences his liaison with Catherine with his eyes open, his heart closed. Their relationship is mutually convenient. The empress covets Juan's "face, / His grace, his God-knows-what" (DJ 9.67); he has learned, since his high-minded rejection of Gulbeyaz, how flattering and agreeable a potentate's attentions can be. Thus Juan and Catherine, in the way of the world, fall not into love but "into that no less imperious passion, / Self-love" (DJ 9.68). The narrator ruefully admits that Juan's new pragmatism does not improve his character or his morals:

> Don Juan grew, I fear, a little dissipated;
>   Which is a sad thing, and not only tramples
> On our fresh feelings, but—as being participated
>   With all kinds of incorrigible samples
> Of frail humanity—must make us selfish,
> And shut our souls up in us like a shell-fish.   (DJ 10.23)

The hard encasement that is a consequence of worldly wisdom comes up again as Byron launches Juan on the Arctic Ocean of English society:

> A little *"blâsé"*—'tis not to be wondered
>   At, that his heart had got a tougher rind:
> And though not vainer from his past success,
> No doubt his sensibilities were less.   (DJ 12.81)

Hard surfaces may not afford the maximum of sensibility, but they do lend themselves to polish. When we see Juan in London, the formerly rough diamond glitters artfully. His mobility, once merely instinctive, has become tactical as well:

> Juan—in this respect at least like saints—
>   Was all things unto people of all sorts,
> And lived contentedly, without complaints,
>   In camps, in ships, in cottages, or courts—
> Born with that happy soul which seldom faints,
>   And mingling modestly in toils or sports.
> He likewise could be most things to all women,
> Without the coxcombry of certain She Men.   (DJ 14.31)

This sort of mobility, which will take its ultimate fictive form in the dazzling Lady Adeline Amundeville, remains essentially a matter of personal temperament (witness Byron's smug epistolary contrast of his own adaptability to the rigors of travel with his companion Hobhouse's inflexibility).[2] But experience improves upon the gift nature has conferred—and the innately mobile Don Juan, once he has reached British shores, has already played and learned from many parts, lover and hero, slave and imperial favorite, and on varied stages, in Spain, Greece, Turkey, and Russia. The great value of the cosmopolitan mobility he has achieved is neatly characterized by that arbiter of English behavior Lord Chesterfield: "A conformity and flexibility of manners is necessary in the course of the world; that is, with regard to all things which are not wrong in themselves. The *versatile ingenium* is the most useful of all. It can instantly turn from one object to another, assuming the proper character of each."[3]

When we see Juan in England, the mature nonchalance of a Chesterfield or an Alcibiades enhances his versatility. Juan rides splendidly to hounds one day and asks the next morning " 'If men ever hunted *twice?* ' " (DJ 14.35). He dances with grace without losing the gentleman in the ballet master (DJ 14.38). The art that conceals art is his Trojan horse—and perhaps its greatest benefit is that it enables him to win without appearing to play, to insinuate without insinuation, to serve his own interests without seeming to threaten those of others. The twenty-one-year-old Juan's dignified amiability, exquisite ease, and perfect tact are, in short, the very social gifts a twenty-four-year-old Byron may have wished for when he "woke up famous" and found all society at his door.

Anne Mellor has observed that in the English cantos Juan and the narrator "psychologically move closer together," a convergence that becomes incarnate when the two meet at the electioneering banquet in canto 16.[4] Similarly, the distance between the narrator and "Byron" (the man whose experiences comprise the raw materials of these cantos and whose imagination transforms reality to art) is smaller than it has been at some other times in the poem. The complete congruence of Byron's circumstances and attitudes and his narrator's is evident in the following commentary directly following Don Juan's first sight of "Albion's chalky belt":

> I have no great cause to love that spot of earth,
>   Which holds what might have been the noblest nation;
> But though I owe it little but my birth,
>   I feel a mixed regret and veneration
> For its decaying fame and former worth.
>   Seven years (the usual term of transportation)
> Of absence lay one's old resentments level,
> When a man's country's going to the devil.   (DJ 10.66)

The narrator's position and Byron's are likewise identical in canto
10's digression on Francis Jeffrey (stanzas 11–19). The stanzas contain a precise description of how Byron's anger over the Edinburgh's
review of Hours of Idleness turned to enduring respect for the editor.
There are equally accurate indications of Byron's perennial dislike
for another old Scots enemy, Brougham ("A legal broom's a moral
chimney-sweeper, / And that's the reason he himself's so dirty"), of
his parentage and childhood rearing ("But I am half a Scot by birth,
and bred / A whole one"), and of the wistfulness for "Auld Lang
Syne" that counterbalances and blends with the disapproving sentiments voiced above to create the half-satiric, half-elegaic perspective that we shall find to be the prevailing viewpoint in the English
cantos. When Juan sets foot on British soil, Byron's British memories need no longer be displacements, or intrusions shattering the
narrative through parabasis, as they do in the passages just discussed. The composing poet's real experiences, circumstances,
and acquaintances—along with the features, values, and preoccupations of his native culture—now furnish material for the poem's
episodes as well as its digressions. Don Juan moves through scenes
and situations formerly experienced by the author and his narrator.

This is not to say that the author's and narrator's relationship to
English subject matter is more straightforward than it has been
earlier in the poem. Definition by contrast is still Byron's means of
proceeding, but the contrast is subtler than before. He distinguishes less between pure national types than between sorts of
cosmopolitanism. Juan the poised, polished, experienced alien
confronting England is no longer a being defined by one culture,
but neither are the English aristocrats among whom his time will
be passed. (It is no coincidence that "Amundeville," the Norman
surname of Juan's principal patrons in society, is roughly equiv-

alent to the Greek compound "cosmopolis.") And as we have
already seen, the Byronic narrator is a cosmopolite whose worldly
versatility surpasses young Juan's. The difference was a relatively
simple contrast between innocence and experience in the poem's
early cantos; but as the continentally traveled Juan gains knowledge of the narrator's island home, the distinction between their
varieties of cosmopolitanism becomes more complex. For Juan,
England is the here-and-now; for the narrator, Byron, and the reader,
it is a then-and-now evident in the here. Because of the suggestive integrity of the particulars Byron and his narrator offer us, Don Juan's
England proves to be what Goethe's Italy is for Bakhtin in his essay
"The Bildungsroman and Its Significance in the History of Realism
(Toward a Historical Typology of the Novel)"—a "chronotope," a
place permitting us to range through time in space, to see the past
in the present.[5] The chronotopic nature of Don Juan blends a time
when the narrative is taking place (1792 or so), a period from
which most of the real details are drawn (1811–16, Byron's years in
the Great World), and the moment of composition (1822–23).[6] In
addition, the story unfolds against two monumental, association-
encrusted backdrops—London and Norman Abbey—whose
structures can be seen as the story of England written in stone.

Saturating place with time, permeating things and locations with
the history of a culture, is no easy business; and in the English
cantos the narrator is less flippant than he has been about his epic
task. "I now mean to be serious" (DJ 13.1), says the narrator—and
later on, "my Muse by no means deals in fiction: / She gathers a
repertory of facts" (DJ 14.13). But though he shows himself serious, factual, and inventive in presenting the English microcosm
through which Don Juan moves, the narrator professes that the
Great World he has engaged to present is not intrinsically important or interesting:

> The portion of this world which I at present
>   Have taken up to fill the following sermon,
> Is one of which there's no description recent:
>   The reason why, is easy to determine:
> Although it seems both prominent and pleasant,
>   There is a sameness in its gems and ermine,
> A dull and family likeness through all ages,
> Of no great promise for poetic pages.   (DJ 14.15)

The narrator goes on to regret, in words reminiscent of some we have already examined in Glenarvon's pronouncements on ruling-class monotony of manner, the tyranny of convention that puts "A sort of varnish over every fault" (DJ 14.16) and smooths out more desirable differences as well. Such deprecation of the fashionable world is itself a fashionable attitude, a signal that the speaker belongs to the group—and has been a member long enough to become jaded. It also is the narrator's shrewd way of enhancing his artistic achievement, for the task of making an unlikely subject sparkle on "poetic pages" must be recognized as harder than doing the same for innately attractive material. In any case, a backward glance shows that the narrator's assertion has proven dead wrong over time, perhaps in part because of Byron's brilliant success in bringing the aristocratic milieu of late eighteenth- and early nineteenth-century England to life. From the "silver-fork" novelists (Bulwer-Lytton, Disraeli, and a school of lesser fry who followed in Don Juan's wake) to Georgette Heyer and the present-day writers of "Regency romance," resuscitations of the Great World have retained their appeal for a popular readership—and in the hands of a Thackeray or a Byron this microcosm, whether we call it "Vanity Fair" or the "Paradise of Pleasure and Ennui" (DJ 14.17), is evoked in such a way that "the compact wholeness of the real world is sensed in each of its images."[7]

The "real world" ruled by the third and fourth Georges and conjured up by the selective images of the English cantos was, beneath the "calm patrician polish" that Byron and Lady Caroline saw as allowing so little variety in high life, undergoing great change, as became increasingly evident in the post-Waterloo years. The Napoleonic wars had thinned the ranks of the nobility and offered the glorious survivors a means toward new titles (such as duke of Wellington). The Industrial Revolution had begun to create a new aristocracy of wealth, eager and able to get ahead. Society, growing more fluid, also became more self-conscious and vulgar.

On one hand the climbers, finding it easier to imitate the trappings of aristocracy than to cultivate noble character and simpler to achieve a superficial ease than to master the social discipline that makes for genuine poise, became devotees of sham. On the other hand, the aristocrats battled to maintain the old distances and in their campaign to do so resorted to exclusivism that was often trivial and silly. They let it be understood that Hyde Park at five in the afternoon was the private precinct of the wellborn. London's clubs flourished as never before. Gentlemen of quality watched the world from White's bay window and lost their fortunes in the card rooms of Brooks's, Boodle's, and Watier's; that is, until Mr. Crockford, having relinquished his fishmongery for a more lucrative trade, erected the splendid if rather democratic club where, according to Captain Gronow, he won "the whole of the ready money" of the generation.[8] The opera had become generally accessible, so Almack's assumed its place as "the seventh heaven of the fashionable world." Here the Ton assembled for waltzes, weak tea, and bread and butter: austere amusements and refreshments that mocked the luxuries of the new rich. A minimal subscription charge made Almack's universally affordable, but a despotically selective group of sponsors ensured that admittance to the ballroom was valued as the ultimate social accolade. Exclusiveness manifested itself individually as well as collectively. Young men, whether established or aspiring, cultivated dandyism. Whether they adopted the classical severity of Brummell or the rococo style of Count d'Orsay, the dandies acknowledged through their unremitting attention to detail that in a changing society the distinction conferred by station could not suffice alone.

Despite its prevailing names, the Regency or "day of the dandies" was an age when influential women dominated society. The Duchess of Devonshire, Lady Holland, Lady Jersey, Lady Melbourne, and the like were, within their limited realm, unchallenged powers during the age of Wellington and Brummell. Byron calls this state of affairs "gynocrasy" in the English cantos, where the ironic contrasts between appearance and reality, pretense and passion, that characterize Regency society as a whole culminate in the well-wrought woman, who embodies both the last word on worldly excellence and the dangerous results of affirming artifice at the expense of natural impulse. In the English cantos what Anthony Paul Vital asserts of Don Juan in general is especially true: the narrator "treats of women and their power with the respect (and, at times, the lack of respect) that he grants other 'things existent'—he opens them to analysis and so also to the potential of having their comic failures uncovered."[9]

Taking "things existent" as his subject in this way, Byron might be seen as appealing to a wide contemporary English public, for heightened consciousness of social nuances gave those climbing

up and those looking down a shared literary interest. The en-
trenched aristocrats could reinforce class solidarity through reading a work by, for, and about their own kind; the aspiring middle
classes could find in the same work vicarious social experience and
practical guidance in fashionable behavior. But even if it were not
for the immorality sure to make squeamish members of this public
reject Byron's vision of "things really as they are," the poem's
cosmopolitanism would exclude such insular readers unless they
were willing to look beyond present realities.[10] Within the poem
Don Juan can take such a broad view: he is able to see the Regency's Great World, an island on an island, in a wider geographical
and social context. The Great World's relative insignificance is yet
more evident to the narrator and Byron, who have traveled in time
and space beyond the microcosm under scrutiny. In canto 9, Byron
takes up Cuvier's theory of successive creations, each new order
feebler than its predecessor and each ended by catastrophe, and
imagines a future

> When this world shall be former, underground,
>   Thrown topsy-turvy, twisted, crisped, and curled,
> Baked, fried, or burnt, turned inside-out, or drowned,
>   Like all the worlds before,   (stanza 37)

a time when George IV might be "dug up" as a fossil find, a
Mammoth or Titan to the diminished beings of the new creation.[11]
The geological investigation depicted in this passage is not far from
what Byron does in the English cantos: he unearths a world dead
to him in certain senses, yet in other senses vitally interesting, even
engrossing. Condensing past and present, distilling real people
into essences that can be combined, Byron makes a myth, albeit a
subversive one, of the very facts he preserves. Having belonged to
and gone beyond the culture of his homeland, he has equipped
himself adequately both to describe and to transform it.

The shape that description takes is a classical one. In *Byron and
Joyce through Homer*, Hermione de Almeida persuasively demonstrates the "epic equivalence" of *Don Juan* and *Ulysses* as modern
descendants of the *Odyssey*. At this point, the key inference I would
draw from her study of affinities and indebtedness is that Byron's
epic resembles Homer's in being a journey home. *Don Juan* is a
homing of several sorts—a return to origins on the part of Byron,
the narrator, and even in a sense Don Juan if we see our "ancient

friend" as offspring of the English pantomime, but also a homing in on the truths and traits of that native culture which has always been important to Byron's poem and on which his attention is now sharply focused. In cantos 10–16, the wayward path Don Juan's adventures have previously pursued becomes straight and increasingly narrow. It takes him from the shores of England to London to the West End to the highest circles in the fashionable district— from there to a house party composed of a chosen few from that elite and finally, in the last complete canto, to a single day as lived at Norman Abbey.

Byron's Cuvier-like retrieval of words, themes, matters, and characters that have been buried is not confined to his remembrance of British things past in the portion of Don Juan that now concerns us. The ninth, tenth, and eleventh cantos, which have as their business Don Juan's sojourn as Catherine's minion in Russia and his travel as her envoy to England, consistently echo, in incidental and significant ways, the beginning of the poem. When those introductory signals that implied what Don Juan would be and how it would proceed are heard again, their reprise suggests a fresh start for the poem, one that Byron explicitly announces several times in the English cantos. Like the implicit signals, these announcements of intent display similarities to and differences from what has gone before.

We find such a resonant new beginning in the opening stanza of canto 9, a passage whose effect depends on our recollection of the initial stanza of the Dedication, where the narrator addresses "Bob Southey." In canto 9, name-changing liberties of this sort combine with the linguistic imperialism evident in the pronunciation "Don Joo-un" as the narrator invokes "Wellington" or "Vilainton"—a hero, he implies, worthy of the praise a laureate like Southey might be expected to bestow. Wellington is, like Southey, a Tory, a turncoat (in the sense that after having freed Europe from Napoleon he has "repaired Legitimacy's crutch"), and the recipient of his nation's largesse ("great pensions" as opposed to the laureate's petty ones). Each patronized Englishman is in turn a fit sponsor for the poetic unit over which his name presides: as Southey represented the union of bad poetry and bad politics (the focus of Byron's Dedication), so Wellington can be seen as the English epitome of love and war, the passionate enterprises dominating canto 9 and taking yet more impressive human form in their Russian female embodiment, Catherine the Great. Having employed the shiftiness of language to mock the names of the two Englishmen at the start of the respective stanzas begun by their names, Byron uses a monosyllabic pun to close each stanza and deflate each of the men he has invoked:

Like "four and twenty blackbirds in a pie;" (Dedication, stanza 1)

Humanity would rise, and thunder "Nay!" (DJ 9.1)

In each line, the final noun establishes an implicit comparison between the "eminent" Southey and Wellington and less-than-admirable beings who in the recent past have filled identical or analogous roles: Pye, Southey's predecessor in the laureateship and a thoroughly mediocre poet, and Ney, the French field marshal whose nation rewarded him, on the restoration of the Bourbons, with execution.

Canto 10 brings with it many echoes of earlier moments in *Don Juan*. Shunning "the common shore" and skimming "The Ocean of Eternity" (DJ 10.4), the narrator demonstrates his poetic superiority to the narrow vulgarians he wishes would "change [their] lakes for ocean" in the Dedication. "But at the least I have shunned the common shore" also offers, at long range, a gloss on the epigraph *communia dicere*, guidance as to what particular sense of this phrase is applicable to the interests of an aristocratic and cosmopolitan poet. Words, situations, and people from Don Juan's early days also return. Donna Inez, remarried and mother of a second son (who will no doubt be treated to an upbringing as fine as Juan's), indirectly reenters the poem by means of a cant-filled letter eloquently affirming her unchanged nature (DJ 10.31–33). Juan sighs and pines (DJ 10.37–38) as he did when wandering adolescent and lovesick in the woods, but now the malady is surfeit of Catherine's favors rather than deficiency of Julia's. Sentimental images and phrases from Juan's early amours in sunny climes appear, with ironic difference, at the start of his Russian adventures: the "Moon" and "June" rhymes (DJ 10.9) recall the Julia episode; the phrases "cheek which seems too pure for clay" (DJ 10.8) and "But Juan was not meant to die so soon" (DJ 10.9) bring back the Grecian ghost of Juan's purest love to haunt the scene of his sordid Russian liaison. And that liaison, like the adulterous affair with Julia, breaks off prematurely, with Juan being dispatched on a regime of travel by an imperious older woman—Catherine filling both Julia's and Inez's parts here.

Off the ailing "Russ Spaniard" goes through Poland, Germany, and Holland, with a diplomatic mission in London at the end of the road. In eyeshot of his destination, as he gazes down on the metropolis from Shooter's Hill, Juan is inspired with what is, along with the shipboard farewell to Julia, one of his longest speeches in the poem. Like the inflated postures of that sentimental valediction, this speech is a tissue of absurd idealizations, especially when we consider Juan's assertions in light of what the narrator has said of the great nation being addressed. Like the nautical valediction, this specimen of exalted rhetoric is rudely interrupted, though by a human force rather than a natural one:

> "And here," he cried, "is Freedom's chosen station;
>   Here peals the people's voice, nor can entomb it
> Racks, prisons, inquisitions; resurrection
> Awaits it, each new meeting or election.
>
>   10
> "Here are chaste wives, pure lives; here people pay
>   But what they please; and if that things be dear,
> 'Tis only that they love to throw away
>   Their cash, to show how much they have a-year.
> Here laws are all inviolate; none lay
>   Traps for the traveller; every highway's clear:
> Here"——he was interrupted by a knife,
> With, "Damn your eyes! your money or your life!" (DJ 11.9–10)

Juan's intrepid response to the highwaymen is a gunshot, not a verbal reply—for as is true with his mother Inez, his understanding of English does not range beyond "their shibboleth, 'God Damn!' " (DJ 11.12). A few stanzas later, when Juan is waylaid by the "tender tribe" of bluestockings, their linguistic accomplishments also hearken back to Inez's: "They talked bad French of [*sic*] Spanish" (50). And finally canto 11 (where Don Juan himself is an envoy) ends in a formal envoi for *Don Juan*, as canto 1 does and no others do. As in canto 1, the send-off clearly echoes and then wittily transforms the " 'Go, little book!' " cribbed from Southey's *Lay of the Laureate*:

> Thus far, go forth, thou Lay! which I will back
> Against the same given quality of rhyme,
>   For being as much the subject of attack
> As ever yet was any work sublime,
>   By those who love to say that white is black. (DJ 11.90)

Whereas Southey's envoi claims that "if" his book's "vein be good" the world will "find" (and presumably approve) it, Byron's boldly asserts that his cantos are of the highest sort and that they will receive attention. Southey, conventional and modest, speaks tentatively of his poem but trustingly of the audience that will receive it: Byron, subversive and candid, doubts the world but not his work.

McGann's editorial notes to Don Juan suggest that "The English Cantos should be divided into two parts: Canto X, st. 54 [actually 64] to Canto XIII, st. 54 (which concentrate on London and English city life); Canto XIII, st. 55 to the end (which observes English manners in the setting of Norman Abbey)."[12] This division, widely customary in the English picaresque, is to be found in various works resembling Don Juan: Tom Jones, Glenarvon, Letters from England— even in the English Don Juan extravaganzas if we think of individual stage spectacles as parts of one story. Besides allowing for classical contrast of urbs and rus, this arrangement permits Byron to vary the perspective in his cosmopolitan critique of English ways and institutions. As Don Juan approaches and then experiences London, he serves as a representative foreigner, much as Southey's Don Manuel does. Apart from the encounter with the highwayman and the arrangement of guardianship for Leila (a practical necessity in terms of the poem's further development, because a Don Juan encumbered with a ward could not freely enter into the amorous intrigues demanded of him by legend and literary precedent), Juan's early experiences of England are generic. His critical reactions supplement the narrator's, but they could be observations from the perspective of virtually any well-traveled alien sharing his cultural background. Later, when Juan arrives at Norman Abbey, he is actively involved in the complex dealings of a particular, and precisely particularized, circle—and he renders highly individualized judgments on the people and situations he encounters there.

The contrast in Don Juan's respective ways of treating town and country is plausible for several reasons. Any new arrival will begin, as Juan does, by reading an unfamiliar culture's collective features: partly because the broadest generalities are most immediately apparent, partly because the specific relationships through which one develops a sense of nuance and detail have not yet been established. The fact that Juan's sustained experience of England

begins in London, then moves to the country, adds further credibility to the poem's shift of perspective: the capital city's crush and
confusion can be seen as overwhelming both Juan's individuality
and the distinctiveness of the people he meets. At Norman Abbey
the players are fewer—and because "Good company's a chess-
board" or puppet theater (DJ 13.89) each guest has presumably
been invited to fill a particular role. In the country-house world
where two or three wits (or bluestockings or dowagers or finan-
ciers) are to be encountered rather than two or three dozen, it
would be easier to distinguish individuals even if Juan did not have
insights gleaned from his metropolitan experience to guide him in
understanding the various English types they represent.

As Juan and Leila travel toward London, the narrative takes note
of the details of England that would strike the first-time visitors to
British shores as impressive: white cliffs, green fields, well-paved
roads, high prices—all English particulars of the kind Espriella's
account records. Like Southey's Spanish protagonist, Juan and
Leila reveal their foreignness not just by noticing features a native
might take for granted but also by reacting in un-English ways to
what they see. The alien nature of their response to England is
clearest when Leila the Mohammedan and Juan the Catholic ob-
serve Canterbury Cathedral and its relics. The young travelers ob-
serve what any tourist would—the Black Prince's helm, "Becket's
bloody stone," and such—but do not understand that what they
see is (or is supposed to be) the spiritual center of a national faith.
Leila, having learned that the edifice is "God's house,"

> only wondered how
> He suffered Infidels in his homestead,
>   The cruel Nazarenes, who had laid low
> His holy temples in the lands which bred
>   The True Believers.   (DJ 10.75)

Juan responds first as a soldier, second as a Catholic:

> The effect on Juan was of course sublime:
>   He breathed a thousand Cressys, as he saw
> The casque, which never stooped, except to Time.
>   Even the bold Churchman's tomb excited awe,
> Who died in the then great attempt to climb
>   O'er kings.   (DJ 10.74)

Leila's "misapprehension" (entirely natural in light of her experience of Christians at Ismail) is not further developed in the poem;
but Juan's inability to see English faith here, in the cathedral repre-
senting to Anglicans what St. Peter's stands for to Roman Catholics,
is worth keeping in mind. Perhaps we are meant to conclude that
Juan fails to sense a living religion in the archbishop of Canterbury's church because there is little if any to be sensed, because the
church has become a secular monument. Such a response would
be consistent with developments later in the poem, when Juan's
Catholicism will be one of his bonds of sympathy with Aurora
Raby, who like him and unlike the other guests at Norman Abbey
must see the monastery stripped from the Roman church and
conferred on the Amundevilles by Henry VIII as something more
than a historical curiosity. At present, Byron makes use of the
contrast between Catholic orthodoxy and English values as one of
several ways of presenting the cultural insularity summed up in the
nation's capital. Faithless from Juan's Catholic perspective, the English Protestants have profaned holy ground by putting God's
property to worldly uses. In the same way, the English language, a
verbal reflection of dominant cultural attitudes, has trivialized supernatural terms and by implication the cosmic realities they signify. Byron brilliantly demonstrates this point by making "Hell"
and "Paradise"—"Hell" and "Paradise" emptied of transcendental
power and rendered utterly mundane—important ingredients in
his evocation of London.

Smoky London as Juan first glimpses it from Shooter's Hill
seems to be "the 'Devil's drawing-room'" (DJ 10.81); and its likeness to Hell is stressed in various ways, not the least of them being
Byron's reminder to attentive readers (DJ 12.2) that as he writes this
part of the poem in 1823 he is thirty-five, the age of Dante narrating
the Inferno, and his insistence that the English cantos constitute a
"sermon." But the connection between London and Hell is well
established before Juan rides into town. Speaking in canto 8 of
Juan's lack of malice in battle, the narrator observes that "if he
warr'd / Or loved, it was with what we call 'the best / Intentions'"
(DJ 8.25)—"Those ancient good intentions, which once shaved /
And smoothed the brimstone of that street of Hell / Which bears
the greatest likeness to Pall Mall" (DJ 8.26). The fact that "Hell" and
"Pall Mall" rhyme without our having to mispronounce one or the
other is a small but telling sign that in England the gap between

appearance and reality is a feature so basic as to pervade all levels of the culture. But my reason for mentioning the passage here is to point out the digression's connection between London and the satanic city of Pandemonium—a likeness more extensively developed in the narrative of the English cantos. When Juan, with his broad experience of bad Continental roads, sets out for London, he finds the highway, like that leading to Hell, smooth and easy (DJ 10.71). The streets of the metropolis, Pall Mall again being singled out for specific mention, are also well paved (DJ 11.24, 29)—and illuminated by flames, though these come from gaslights rather than the ghastly lamps one might encounter in either Hell or the Paris of Juan's day, where "on their new-found lanthorn, / Instead of wicks, they made a wicked man turn" (DJ 11.26). Following Pall Mall's fashionable, smoothly paved, brightly lit course, Don Juan, characterized in hell-bent terms as "our young diplomatic sinner," continues on the course that will conduct him to his own London abode, "past some Hotels, / St. James's Palace, and St. James's 'Hells'" (DJ 11.29).

The words, phrases, and images at which we have been looking establish an explicit connection between King George's capital and Satan's; but the effect achieved is the reverse of what one might expect. The likeness between Hell and London fails to invest the latter with cosmic evil—rather, it domesticates and trivializes the former. If a "Hell" is seen as nothing worse than a gambling resort and if the infernal streets are said to resemble those in London's Clubland, essential evil and unhappiness do not vanish; but what was sublime becomes ridiculously ordinary. The great, grim netherworld with its brimstone lake and howling damned souls shrinks to petty human scale when Byron stocks it with the technological innovations and drawling fashionable folk found in Regency London. The concept of Hell, like the pronunciation of Don Juan, is imported, then cut to English measure.

Hell's antithesis, Paradise, mentioned often in this part of Don Juan, undergoes similar diminution. Again, Byron's rhetoric points out the insular English attitude that domesticates the unfamiliar and narrows the cosmic to the comprehensible. When Juan makes his way to the depths of Hell / Pall Mall through suburban streets distinguished by the infelicity of their names—among the "Groves, so called as being void of trees" and the "Mounts Pleasant, as containing nought to please, / Nor much to climb"—we find

" 'Rows' most modestly called 'Paradise,' / Which Eve might quit without much sacrifice" (DJ 11.21). Later, the unnatural "English winter—ending in July, / To recommence in August" has for its appositive "the postillion's Paradise" (DJ 13.42). And in three rhetorically homologous phrases, Byron characterizes the Kentish countryside crossed by travelers to London as "A Paradise of hops and high production" (DJ 10.76), a West End ballroom as "An earthly Paradise of 'Or Molu' " (DJ 11.67), and the smoothly monotonous Great World itself as "This Paradise of Pleasure and Ennui" (DJ 14.17).

All these usages deny Paradise its metaphysical reality and make it promise, at best, exceedingly trivial benefits in place of its traditional ones; but let us linger for a moment over the celestial components mentioned in the three prepositional phrases quoted above. Hops. High production. Or Molu. Pleasure. Ennui. Several significant features of the metropolitan English culture in which Don Juan is now immersed are discernible in this oddly assorted collection, features presented repeatedly and intensively in the English cantos. Throughout the final seven cantos, we see that England is a material world—at all levels of society, from the bottom (hops being used to make beer—along with beef and tea, the proverbial mainstay of the populace) to the top ("Or Molu" being a highly fashionable element of elite decor).

One of Don Juan's distinctive excellences is its ability to make thematic use of the most prosaic-seeming particulars, such as ormolu or Kentish hops and the beer in which those hops are used. In pursuing the latter topic, our first text might be "A Paradise of hops and high production" (DJ 10.76) joined with the first lines of the next stanza: "And when I think upon a pot of beer— / But I won't weep!—" (DJ 10.77). The final change for the worse in Byron's ubi-sunt catalogue furnishes another text: "—I have seen malt liquors / Exchanged for 'thin potations' by John Bull— / I have seen John half detect himself a fool.—" (DJ 11.85). And finally there is this passage, where a single country girl with "the problem of a double figure" (DJ 16.61) awaits Lord Henry's magisterial pronouncements:

> But this poor girl was left in the great hall,
>   While Scout, the parish guardian of the frail,
> Discussed (he hated beer yclept the 'small')
>   A mighty mug of moral double ale.   (DJ 16.67)

The contemporary relevance of these passages and the part they play in Byron's portrait of Regency England become apparent in light of certain developments in British brewing in the late eighteenth and early nineteenth centuries. First, the price of a pint of beer had been in the eighteenth century stable enough to become traditional, "part of the nature of things in that limited horizon of certainty which every society takes for granted." Riots accompanied an upward adjustment of price in 1766—but the new price of 4d. held until 1799, from which time "no price lasted long enough to be defended as traditional." When the prices of such ingredients as hops and malt rose, a further means of preserving profit was the dilution of beer or the replacement of costly ingredients by cheaper ones. During the early nineteenth century, English farmers suffered several disastrous harvests—in 1799–1801 and in 1817–18 hops, for instance, went from export to import status. Furthermore, until Waterloo the Napoleonic disturbances made continental sources of ingredients less than reliable. Not surprisingly, a regular science of "beer doctoring" arose—a practice widespread enough to provoke an article in Byron's regular reading matter the *Edinburgh Review*.[13]

Turning back to the *Don Juan* passages, we can see that in Byron's retrospective view it is ironical to call Kent a "paradise" (or eternal home) of hops—and that in the era spanned by the poem "high production" was not necessarily connected with the time-honored way of using those hops. Hence the narrator's near lachrymose thoughts on beer rise not only from expatriate nostalgia but also from a mental comparison of good old English beer with the debased modern product. This sense of England's present inferiority and past vigor ties in with the Cuvier notion of successive, ever weaker creations—and it recurs in the lines from the ubi-sunt stanzas, where the diminished nature of beer is a symptom of social degeneracy even the bluff common man can detect. The link between brewing truths and social ones is forged, and polished with considerable irony, in the passage about the lusty but injudicious peasant girl brought to Norman Abbey for justice. The same "guardian" of parish values who denounces beer for being "single" (or "small," or weakened) condemns the girl for her "double" condition. Interestingly, one of the important words in the early nineteenth-century beer disputes, *pale* (referring to one of the kinds of malt and the product brewed from it) figures twice and in two different ways in this small fable. Later in the stanza quoted, we hear that the arraigned culprit must wait "until Justice could recall / Its kind attentions to their proper pale." A few stanzas earlier, she is described as "extremely pale, / Pale as if painted so; her cheek being red / By nature" (DJ 16.64)—thus contrasting with the sophisticated society ladies who resort to rouge and coquetry, both enhancements unknown and unnecessary to this natural being. The behavior of those "cold coquettes" is itself described in a beer-trade term as "not quite adultery—but adulteration" (DJ 12.63).

The England whose beer and belles are alike in their debasement is a realm of calculation, where "high production" is the concern of almost everyone Juan meets, from his Dover landlord to Tom the highwayman to the hoteliers of St. James and the milliners equipping "drapery misses" on credit—and on up the social ladder to the scheming parents and fortune-hunting beaux and belles, the place-hunting politicians, and the Regent with such expensive, publicly subsidized tastes as the Brighton Pavilion (DJ 14.83). It is a realm of artifice. Just as ormolu presents an appearance of gold but a reality of copper and tin, so the cosmetically enhanced facades of society ladies counterfeit beauty, health, and emotional simplicity (See DJ 11.48; 12.62; 13.111; and for ironic contrast 16.64, quoted above). Their deceptive cordiality offers more light than heat ("Those Polar summers, all sun, and some ice" in DJ 12.72), the chill beneath the smile itself being a misleading impression, because this cold-bloodedness in turn conceals sensuality (implied in the comparison to "virtuous mermaids, whose / Beginnings are fair faces, ends mere fishes" in DJ 12.73).

The imported word "Or Molu" (especially when spelled as Byron chooses to spell it) suggests, as Ennui and the many other French words in the English cantos do, two contradictory truths about the Great World and the culture it epitomizes. Peter Manning sees the fashionable cacophony of Franglais as a Regency reenactment of the Babel myth's enduring validity and further recognizes that Byron, brilliantly playing with both languages, escapes the restrictions of any one culturally prescribed set of moves in the game.[14] The other way of escape involves "playing" with neither language—and hence the second truth. Ennui, grande passion (DJ 12.77), debonnaire (12.85), recherché (13.28), and other imported words are foolish when they are nothing but embellishments to idle chatter. French, however, can be and has been seriously, usefully incorporated into English—and the English language has accordingly gained in richness what it has lost in purity. The weakness of the Great World's argot is its shallow cosmopolitanism, but one strength of English is its being a truly cosmopolitan tongue. So although the Great World's frivolous babble mocks a unity lost, it also suggests—with accuracy if not depth—an integration gained. The difference, linguistically speaking, can be seen in the respective degrees of assimilation exemplified by two of the nouns presently being discussed: "Pleasure" (or *Plaisir* across the English Channel) and "*Ennui*."

The yoking of "Pleasure and Ennui" to characterize that fashionable Paradise in which Juan now finds himself offers another clue to the workings of the English cantos. We know from trite truisms that the pursuit of pleasure becomes *ennuyant*. But in the English cantos with their unrelenting attention to Society, that "polished horde / Form'd of two mighty tribes, the *Bores* and *Bored*" (DJ 13.95), Byron proves that pursuit of *les ennuyants* can be pleasant. Byron's means of generating that pleasure is the cosmopolitan play of writing—a species of levity neatly suggested by the compound word *Foolscap*, which appears just four times in *Don Juan*: thrice in the urban part of the English cantos and once in an earlier digression. Here are the relevant lines themselves, first a question from the address to "Lady Daphne" and the other bluestockings, who have banned Byron from their Castalian tea:

> What, can I prove "a lion" then no more?
> A ball-room bard, a foolscap, hot-press darling?   (DJ 4.109)

Next, that striking image of St. Paul's Cathedral, the final detail of Juan's panorama from Shooter's Hill:

> A huge, dun cupola, like a foolscap crown
> On a fool's head—and there is London Town!   (DJ 10.82)

Then, a renewed recollection of the lost Years of Fame, though here Byron ascribes more stature to his former role than was discernible above in "ball-room bard" and "foolscap, hot-press darling":

> Even I—albeit I'm sure I did not know it,
>   Nor sought of foolscap subjects to be king,—
> Was reckoned, a considerable time,
> The grand Napoleon of the realms of rhyme.   (DJ 11.55)

And finally a description of middle age (which we soon discover to mean the Dantean thirty-five years), that period

> . . . when we hover between fool and sage,
> And don't know justly what we would be at,—
>   A period something like a printed page,
> Black letter upon foolscap, while our hair
> Grows grizzled, and we are not what we were. (DJ 12.1)

Readers who hold that repetitions have conscious or unconscious significance will find it interesting to see that the word *foolscap* comes into *Don Juan* only when Byron is concerned with a certain range of matters, all having something to do with time or scenes now past for him—still more interesting to see the intricate connections established by his arabesque of association. In all the passages quoted, *foolscap* denotes writing paper (the term is said to have risen out of a cap-and-bells watermark employed by certain early papermakers) but also simultaneously suggests the jester's crown literally characterized by the compound word. The word *foolscap* thus is intrinsically a piece of verbal play; but what Byron does with it in these four passages proves infinitely more sophisticated.

In presenting the dome of St. Paul's as the sort of paper hat English revelers are particularly fond of putting on for Christmas, birthdays, and other festivals, he wittily combines both primary meanings of *foolscap*—and in addition he captures a minor but distinctive cultural trait, implies the collective folly of the metropolis, and perhaps shows something of how English Protestantism (here represented by the largest of its cathedrals) looks to the Catholic outsider Juan. "Black letter upon foolscap" achieves a different visual effect—the mixture of dark and white characterizing middle-aged hair, a sign, it may be, of the mingled nature said to distinguish that era when "we hover between fool and sage." Folly and sagacity, power and vulnerability, seem inextricably allied in the postures of a "ball-room bard" or a "grand Napoleon of the realms of rhyme." Byron simultaneously deprecates his former celebrity and regrets its passing; he acknowledges both the triviality and the importance of reigning over "foolscap subjects"—a reign achieved over one sort of "subjects" (readers) by imaginative deployment and arrangement of "subjects" in another sense (themes and topics). In the mixed foolery and seriousness of recording his

personal and cultural past in black on white, the middle-aged
cosmopolite, a man between worlds in so many senses, finds the
one world that will suffice. He finds it by making it. England and
youth are past for Byron—the reign of George III and Regency are
now past for all his readers, George IV having been crowned (not
with foolscap) in 1821. But a poetical Napoleon can fashion a chronotope from what is past—that condensation becoming more
richly vital in some ways than the real materials from which it is
distilled. And so it is with Regency London in the English cantos.
By lamenting its loss, Byron makes it endure. By candidly presenting its repellent characteristics along with its attractive ones, he
makes it engage the readers' attention. The grand stanzas at the
close of canto 11 are nothing less than an apotheosis of the Great
World whose realities are said to be so little, narrow, dull, and
dead. The glamour and glory, we might conclude, are reflected:
they originate not in the "foolscap subjects" but in the kingly poet.
Yet he is the "inclusive figure of his age,"[15] and so the era must
partake of his triumph. Byron conjures up and reanimates that
vanished milieu in the ubi-sunt passage appearing in part below—
or perhaps it would be better to say that he represents a milieu that
has stayed alive within him because, all professions aside, he has
loved it all too well. In McGann's words, "Here at the outset of the
final movement of Don Juan, he parades before us the touching
tableau of his emotional commitments, and all those butterflies he
has loved and hated, sought and scorned:"[16]

76

"Where is the world," cries Young, "at eighty? Where
    The world in which a man was born?" Alas!
Where is the world of eight years past? 'Twas there—
    I look for it—'tis gone, a Globe of Glass!
Cracked, shivered, vanished, scarcely gazed on, ere
    A silent change dissolves the glittering mass,
Statesmen, chiefs, orators, queens, patriots, kings,
And dandies, all are gone on the wind's wings.

77

Where is Napoleon the Grand? God knows:
    Where little Castlereagh? The devil can tell:
Where Grattan, Curran, Sheridan, all those
    Who bound the bar or senate in their spell?

Where is the unhappy Queen, with all her woes?
  And where the Daughter, whom the Isles loved well?
Where are those martyred Saints the Five per Cents?
  And where—oh where the devil are the Rents!

78

Where's Brummell? Dished. Where's Long Pole Wellesley?
    Diddled.
    Where's Whitbread? Romilly? Where's George the Third?
Where is his will? (That's not so soon unriddled.)
    And where is "Fum" the Fourth, our "royal bird?" . . .

Where are the Grevilles? Turned as usual. Where
My friends the Whigs? Exactly where they were. . . .

80

Where are the Lady Carolines and Franceses?
    Divorced or doing thereanent.

Seventy years are no longer needed to constitute an age, says the narrator, who has seen so much change in seven years that he now doubts any human permanence "Except the Whigs *not* getting into place" (stanza 82):

83

I have seen Napoleon, who seemed quite a Jupiter,
    Shrink to a Saturn. I have seen a Duke
(No matter which) turn politician stupider,
    If that can well be, than his wooden look.
But it is time that I should hoist my "blue Peter,"
    And sail for a new theme:—I have seen—and shook
To see it—the King hissed, and then carest;
But don't pretend to settle which was best.

84

I have seen the landholders without a rap—
    I have seen Johanna Southcote—I have seen
The House of Commons turned to a tax-trap—
    I have seen that sad affair of the late Queen—
I have seen crowns worn instead of a fool's-cap—
    I have seen a Congress doing all that's mean—
I have seen some nations like o'erloaded asses
Kick off their burthens—meaning the high classes.

85

I have seen small poets, and great prosers, and
    Interminable—*not eternal*—speakers—
I have seen the Funds at war with house and land—
    I've seen the Country Gentlemen turn squeakers—
I've seen the people ridden o'er like sand
    By slaves on horseback—I have seen malt liquors
Exchanged for "thin potations" by John Bull—
I have seen John half detect himself a fool.

These stanzas essentially encapsulate the urban segment of the English cantos, where Byron's task has been to anatomize the evanescent realms of illusion that are "Great" Britain and its epitome the "Great" World. The methods we have seen at work in these cantos have included gathering a "repertory of facts" about the milieu, using Don Juan to provide the generalized reactions of a traveling alien, implying certain cultural traits, and then weaving connections among those facts, reactions, and traits through recurring images and words. To this point, Byron has not yet done much characterizing of individuals or making of fiction; but both of these enterprises will come into play as the scene shifts from London to Norman Abbey and both the narrator and Don Juan supplement their anatomical study of English culture at large with a resumed interest in storytelling. At Norman Abbey the real English details collected by that tenacious muse Memory will be transformed and combined with other, older materials—most notably classical myth and popular legend. What will result is a superbly successful episode distinguished by such "novelistic" qualities as a large set of complex characters, detailed social commentary, and intricacy of plot—an episode at once autobiographical in its source of details and highly imaginative in its handling of those details, as close as Byron will get to telling his own story and to using the Don Juan tradition in its familiar shape.

The Norman Abbey episode, going back as it does not only to patterns previously enacted in *Don Juan* but also to Byron's days in the Great World, can be seen as a sort of meditation on things that return—a poetic equivalent of Proust's *A la recherche du temps perdu* or Anthony Powell's *Music of Time* series of novels. The action leads up to what is literally the tale of a revenant, the ghost of the Black Friar stalking the cloisters that once belonged to his order. The Black

Friar is merely the most obvious returning phenomenon, though. Byron brings back, revised and improved, his ancestral estate of Newstead Abbey and the society people he knew during the Years of Fame. Those lost people are themselves revenants in two further senses. They resemble Juan's earlier acquaintances and with him reconstitute patterns of experience already established. Furthermore, the narrator, who in these cantos is likelier than ever before to dredge up tags, names, and situations from his classical education for the reader's benefit, suggests that the people and patterns brought back are English incarnations of the ancient truths of character and situation embodied in Greek and Roman myth.[17]

The altered focus of the English cantos becomes apparent toward the end of the "Town" section, as canto 13 begins with a leisurely, specific account of Juan's acquaintance with a particular pair of fashionable aristocrats, the Amundevilles. Juan and Lord Henry meet in the course of "diplomatical relations" and form "a basis of esteem" that passes for friendship in the world (DJ 13.15). The friendship prospers at "noble routs, / And diplomatic dinners" (DJ 13.24) until Juan becomes "a recherché, welcome guest" at the Amundevilles' town house in "Blank-Blank Square" (DJ 13.28)—the sort of guest to be carried off to the country once July or August arrives and Parliament closes, signaling the manifestly artificial end of the "London winter" and the start of the season the "twice two thousand, for whom earth was made" (DJ 13.49) spend on their estates.

Besides devoting time to the early days of the acquaintance that promises to become something headier for Juan and Adeline, Byron takes pains to amplify on the tastes, qualities, possessions, occupations, and inner lives of the Amundevilles throughout the episode in which they figure. Not even Don Juan, over the whole course of the poem, receives much more analytical attention than is devoted to Lady Adeline. Lord Henry, though less fascinating than his wife is to the narrator, turns out to be, after Juan, the most carefully drawn of the poem's male characters—fictive male characters, that is, Southey, Wellington, George IV, Napoleon, Plato, and Horace receiving much the same intensity of treatment that Lord Henry does. This degree of attention, along with the narrator's assurances that the densely specific English cantos are fact filled, suggests that Lord Henry and Lady Adeline are real. They are and they are not. Byron bases the Amundevilles, and other members of the Norman Abbey house party, on actual English people—and speculating on the originals has always been an attractive venture for readers.[18] My own inclination is to see William and Lady Caroline Lamb as the principal sources of the Amundevilles; but as is the case with Donna Inez, the poet of "The isles of Greece," and John Johnson, no single model suffices to account for the fictive presences. Byron's portraiture, if portraiture we are to call it, is highly imaginative. It searches out essences and presents them through an eclectic array of particulars.

This abstracting and recombining is a process entailing some risks in a "realistic" narrative—notably that details will not be adequately assimilated or that contradictions or gaps will impair the credibility of a character constructed from real materials and meant to seem round. There are a few such problems, small ones, with the Amundevilles—most important being an unresolved contradiction in Lord Henry's station. (Being styled "Lord Henry" signifies that he is a younger son of a duke or marquess—yet he is the incumbent of what is manifestly the ancestral Amundeville estate.) But of course Byron's aim in taking on "things really as they are" (or have been) is not to provide a biographical study in ottava rima. Nor are the English cantos, despite the narrator's repeated assertions, all that much of a sermon on the folly and wickedness of English aristocrats he has known. As various critics have noticed, the depictions are much gentler than a true satirist's would be. Malcolm Kelsall offers the political explanation that the great Whig lord and his country estate offer, as they have done before and will do afterward in literature, a cultural ideal during an age when Europe has seen repressive centralized regimes and revolutionary tumults that bring no real progress: "Like it or not, therefore, Lord Henry and Norman Abbey represent the best that is on offer." Frederick L. Beaty, who agrees with Kelsall that the Amundevilles represent English aristocracy at its best, observes that Byron may well have mellowed through his "empathy with gifted people who have been prevented from fulfilling their capabilities and from achieving happiness because they have yielded to the snares of a repressive, stultifying society." J. Michael Robertson recognizes that Byron's "sometimes uneasy but usually ingenious union of two principles," the basically antithetical codes of aristocracy and individualism, is bound to produce "a partial discrimination of contending values"—an ironist's mingled and sometimes self-refuting mixture of admiration and deprecation. For Jerome J. McGann the productive conflict here, as elsewhere in Byron's poetry, is between love and illusion: because Byron has "loved what vanishes," neither savage indignation nor detached superiority is consistently available to him.[19]

In the country-life portion of the English cantos, the social theme emerges through a presentation of Byron's own past—a past recaptured and transformed. Norman Abbey, the seat of the Amundeville family, is Newstead revised and improved:

> An old, old monastery once, and now
> Still older mansion, of a rich and rare
>   Mixed Gothic, such as Artists all allow
> Few specimens yet left us can compare
>   Withal   (DJ 13.55)

—"embosom'd in a happy valley, / Crown'd by high woodlands, where the Druid oak / Stood . . ." (DJ 13.56)—before it, "a lucid lake, / Broad as transparent" (DJ 13.57)—adjacent, "A glorious remnant of the Gothic pile" that had been the friars' (DJ 13.59). This mansion and its estate, revealing England as it has been through the ages, constitute a sort of time-lapse portrait in the media of stone and land. At the same time, they present Byron's personal history as he might have liked it, the house being more aesthetically distinguished than it actually was—the ancient woods being preserved in verse when they had in fact been cut down and sold by his predecessor the "Wicked Lord."

Inside, the mansion is "vast and venerable" (DJ 13.66)—also much more luxuriously furnished than was the house the young Byron inherited and leased to Lord Grey de Ruthyn. Of the contents, the narrator chooses to describe the ancestral portraits, which serve like the architecture to give visible form to the Amundevilles' place in English history: "Steel Barons, molten the next generation / To silken rows of gay and garter'd Earls," blooming Lady Marys and "Countesses mature in robes and pearls" (DJ 13.68), judges and bishops, "attornies-general" (DJ 13.69) and generals. After these "hereditary glories" on canvas comes a parade of Old Masters—Carlo Dolce, Titian, Salvatore, Albano, Vernet, Spagnoletto, Lorraine, Rembrandt, Carravagio, Teniers (DJ 13.71–72)—again, exaggeration mingled with fantasy. The portraits suggest a degree of national eminence to which the Byrons, important though they had been, did not rise until the poet's day; and the heterogeneous but distinguished picture collection is one that Byron might have liked but never owned. After this selective whirlwind tour of the galleries, the aristocratic narrator professes to fear that "Dan Phoebus takes me for an auctioneer" and with apparent consideration and modesty tells the reader, "I spare you then the furniture and plate" (DJ 13.74). This expression of personal tact and literary taste (it is high time for a change from visual description) also manages to imply that the uninventoried goods might be on a level with the superb and diverse picture collection, as the furnishings of Byron's Newstead were not.

This look at the physical background for Don Juan's last episode clearly shows that reviving and rewriting the personal past could be at once satisfying for the poet and effective for his poem. This happy convenience holds true for the supporting cast of characters—the Regency wits, guardsmen, metaphysicians, and peeresses brought together at the Norman Abbey house party but never assembled at Newstead, where so large a group of fashionable folk could not have been very comfortably accommodated. In portraying the remembered celebrities of his Years of Fame, Byron can extract the essential qualities of each distinguished character and suppress the unnecessary details that clutter or undercut the prevailing impression: he has no need to acknowledge the stammer of this rich and handsome naval hero, the feeblemindedness that qualifies the charms of that impeccably connected heiress, the habitual parsimony that makes the society of a brilliant conversationalist with the most humane principles less attractive than it might be. The names—Longbow, Strongbow, Miss Giltbedding, Kit-Cat, Jack Jargon, Dick Dubious, Countess Crabbey, and so on—indicate how schematic a purpose these characters, like the similarly named personified abstractions in Peacock's novels, are meant to serve.[20] Byron's use of sparely rendered detail to evoke character proves doubly effective in the English cantos. Adding depth to the subordinate players would have been unnecessary for the ideal reader spoken of in the last essay, an insider who could have extrapolated one or several real people or rounded characters from the lines of each caricature. More important, such gratuitous detail at the edges of the episode would have distracted from its central interest—a matter at once real (in essence if not in fact) and ideal (in its rendering).

The story taking place against this elegantly evoked material and social backdrop is one entirely appropriate both to Don Juan as delineated in previous legendary, literary, and dramatic renderings and to Byron the literary lion of the West End. It is a tale of romantic entanglement—of unavoidable choice among women and the significance that such choice represents. Bernard Beatty's careful and enlightening argument presents this situation as culminating the poem's treatment of its four "great topics": Death, Thought, Sex, and Holiness. I share Beatty's sense of the importance inherent in the Adeline–Aurora–Fitz-Fulke episode and also his prevailing interest in considering literary means rather than conceptual ends—but focusing on different topics (England and the wider world, cosmopolitanism and insularity), I do not see the episode exactly as he does. Beatty considers Aurora—a predominantly spiritual being where Fitz-Fulke is sensual and Adeline social—as the English cantos' central presence, perhaps even the answer to the sustained inquiry that is Don Juan: "If, however, there is some single evolution in Don Juan then Aurora could reconcile both the satiric and romance thrusts of the poem and suggest the containment of comedy."21 For me, the unworldly Aurora and the unabashed Fitz-Fulke, along with the English cantos' host of lesser women, personify aspects and qualities of the class and gender Adeline represents completely. In my view Adeline combines, but never reconciles, impulses more simply presented in the other two—which is not to say that Aurora and Fitz-Fulke merely provide a cardboard chorus for Adeline, the flesh-and-spirit heroine designated by the narrator as the "fair most fatal Juan ever met" (DJ 13.12).

In coming into the sphere of Lady Adeline, Don Juan, grown-up, well traveled, and by now not exactly ignorant of English ways, shows signs of recapitulating the passionate progress he and Julia pursued some five years (in "narrative" time) before—a situation close to what had been enacted in real life eleven "actual" years earlier by Lady Caroline Lamb and Byron. Although Byron did not meet Lady Caroline through her husband (who never liked him) and never stayed at Brocket Hall, the Melbourne country house, the general lines of the triangular relationship coincide with the famous entanglement of 1812. The following early description of Lady Adeline and her relationship with Lord Henry neatly combines generally acknowledged characteristics of the Lambs with a

pair of attributes Byron often wished upon Caroline, discreet behavior and lack of present love for the man she had married:

    Sweet Adeline, amidst the gay world's hum,
Was the Queen-Bee, the glass of all that's fair;
    Whose charms made all men speak, and women dumb,
The last's a miracle, and such was reckoned,
And since that time there has not been a second.

14

Chaste was she, to detraction's desperation,
    And wedded unto one she had loved well;
A man known in the councils of the nation,
    Cool, and quite English; imperturbable,
Though apt to act with fire upon occasion;
    Proud of himself and her, the world could tell
Nought against either, and both seemed secure—
She in her virtue, he in his hauteur.   (DJ 13.13–14)

Interesting as it is to pursue the affinities and discrepancies between Adeline and Caroline, Henry and William, Juan and Byron, it
would be misguided to see Byron's very public private life as the
only key to the Norman Abbey episode. As McGann points out,
Don Juan had by the time of the English cantos replaced the Memoirs as Byron's vehicle for written recollection;[22] but even when
reminiscing Byron retains his interest in cultural contrast and his
fondness for parabasis. Now that he has brought Juan to England
the comparative effect cannot be achieved or the narrative illusion
shattered in the ways discussed in the last essay. Instead we encounter anachronisms that serve to highlight the difference between "England then" (whether 1790, 1816, or some time between) and "England now" (1823),[23] or moments of parabasis
inverting the device as employed in earlier cantos. Byron's favored
means of making the story of Juan and Lady Adeline resound with
richer tones than an unearthed Regency scandal could alone provide comes from the narrator's doing what the English cantos'
frequent classical quotations imply his capability of doing—stressing the eternal, or at least recurrent, nature of the situation by
emphasizing its mythic analogues.

    We are encouraged to think mythologically from the moment of
Adeline's entrance into the poem. A crucial line already quoted,

"The fair most fatal Juan ever met," takes on a specifically classical sense when qualified—"Although she was not evil, nor meant ill; / But Destiny and Passion spread the net"—and when the stanza's final line explicitly evokes Greek myth with references to Oedipus and the Sphinx (DJ 13.12). The "fatal" situation about to entangle Juan and Adeline is, one infers from this particular passage, that of Mars and Venus caught in flagrante by Vulcan's reticular trap. The mythic prototype is appropriate in some of its fictive particulars. Juan's warlike valor gives him a right to be Mars; Adeline's beauty makes her a Venus. Other details are significant inaccuracies. Lord Henry is far from being a deformed blacksmith and a jealous husband, though it is psychologically plausible for the cuckolder (Juan, the narrator, or Byron, depending on whose incipient or recollected adultery we take to be the cause of this inaccurate characterization) to minimize his guilt by seeing the wronged husband in a bad light. The allusion to Mars and Vulcan is also an interesting revision of actuality as Byron conceived of it in his days of love with Caroline. Making the lover godlike and the husband grotesque inverts Byron's previously quoted barding comparison between himself and William Lamb, a similitude reported by Caroline and transcribed into *Glenarvon*: "He is as superior to me as Hyperion to a satyr."

The Greek tale of adultery foiled, though it paves the way for our appreciation of the episode, is not the most important myth adding shape to the story. Two related stories seem yet more crucial. The first is brought directly into the poem as the narrator, having asserted Lord Henry's poise and potency at court and "in each circumstance of love or war" (DJ 14.70–71), nevertheless asserts that he lacks something women require. The effort to determine what this deficiency involves brings forward another mythic analogue:

> Still there was something wanting, as I've said—
>   That undefinable *"Je ne sçais quoi,"*
> Which, for what I know, may of yore have led
>   To Homer's Iliad, since it drew to Troy
> The Greek Eve, Helen, from the Spartan's bed;
>   Though on the whole, no doubt, the Dardan boy
> Was much inferior to King Menelaus;—
> But thus it is some women will betray us.   (DJ 14.72)

A related story of the Trojan cycle, one placing Juan in the same role but Adeline in a different part, is implicit in the configuration of three beauties presented for one young man's esteem. Obliged to choose, through his action or inaction, to acknowledge the preeminent claims of Aurora, Adeline, or Fitz-Fulke, the befuddled Juan reenacts the Judgment of Paris.

Other references to mythic situations and characters enrich the Norman Abbey episode. Medea and Nessus are briefly mentioned: the former in a facetious illustration of the single time business and passion were conjoined (DJ 14.76), the latter's robe as a hyperbolic simile for the sadness of dressing-gown dishabille after a festivity (DJ 16.11). Characters are given Olympian epithets. Aurora, of course, is named after the goddess of dawn. Juan is said to be "a full-grown Cupid" (DJ 14.41). Adeline, called the Venus she is elsewhere implied to be (DJ 14.55), is yet more significantly styled "My Dian of the Ephesians" (DJ 14.46).

If understanding the myths that serve as implicit glosses for the English situations alluded to above and grasping the appropriateness of the smaller details mentioned permits the intercultural comparison we have come to see as *Don Juan's* habitual mode of proceeding, the reference to "Dian of the Ephesians" concisely points out the range of qualities summed up in Adeline's person. The Ephesian Diana combined basically incompatible attributes, those of the Greco-Roman virgin huntress with those of an Asiatic fertility goddess. An embodiment of purity, Dian of the Ephesians was worshiped through rites of prostitution—a chaste being, her celibacy repressed fierce passions given vent in the chase. She presided over childbirth and shot arrows that could inflict sudden death on humans, beasts, and crops alike.

Set in a Regency context, the best of her class but very much of her class, Lady Adeline is partially understandable. The icebound intensity that makes her the poem's true epitome of the "moral north" is almost perfectly characterized by the justly acclaimed similitude in which she is compared to frozen champagne (DJ 13.37–38). Like the wine (fortified to brandy by its freezing) Lady Adeline is expensive, intoxicating, and cultivated—altered and imprisoned by artificial forces, the manners and social values that render her passions stronger and more volatile while holding them in check. But Adeline's catastrophic potential, her fatality, is missing from this urbane image—though present in the snow-covered volcano rejected as "a tired metaphor" in the previous stanza (DJ 13.36). The classical allusion to Dian of the Ephesians supplies what the realistic one to frozen champagne lacks, reminds us that this self-deceiving aristocrat "Fired with an abstract love of virtue" (DJ 14.46) is a being whose power is more than social, a woman (like Lady Caroline Lamb) whose explosions, when they occur, will entail more than the pop of a cork.

Once she trains that potentially explosive power on her quarry Juan, Adeline is again compared to Dian, though her weapon of choice is borrowed from the goddess's brother Apollo: "Graceful as Dian when she draws her bow, / She seized her harp" (DJ 16.38). In taking up the instrument to display three talents, "The voice, the words, the harper's skill" (DJ 16.39), Adeline resembles Lady Caroline, widely esteemed for her combination of poetic and musical gifts. Within the poem, Adeline aligns herself with Byron and the narrator, the best poets in Don Juan (Southey, Wordsworth, and Coleridge remain conspicuously lyreless among the poets and singers so equipped in Don Juan)—but yet more obviously with the composer and performer of Don Juan's only other inscribed lyric, the poet of "The isles of Greece."

Like the Greek poet, Adeline is an artistic cosmopolitan, proficient in the songs and styles of various nations—Italian " 'Mamma Mias!' " and " 'Amor Mio's!' " along with " 'Tu mi chamas's' " from "Portingale" (DJ 16.45), "Babylon's bravuras" as well as "Heart-ballads of Green Erin or Grey Highlands" (DJ 16.46). She too is a mobile improviser, the difference being that where the Greek gives his audiences what they want, Adeline (who need not sing for hire) makes her audience desire what she wishes to offer. Adeline's affected ease more appropriately connects her with Byron and his narrator. With a remarkably light touch akin to the narrator's deft juggling of readerly responses, Adeline gauges Don Juan's reactions and manipulates Lord Henry into pressing her to sing (DJ 16.37–39). Feigning unwillingness to press Juan on the matter of his experience with the Black Friar and reluctance to perform her composition as her husband suggests, Adeline conceals her two present purposes and after "some fascinating hesitation" sings with "much simplicity" (DJ 16.40), "as 'twere without display, / Yet with display in fact" (DJ 16.42). This nonchalance is a true sign, in her case, of the highest art, much as when the Byronic narrator, the metacontriver of the whole effect, claims that he "cannot say—at least this minute" what Adeline's purpose has been "in bringing this same lay / To bear on what appeared to her the subject / Of Juan's nervous feelings on that day" (DJ 16.51). Adeline, the narrator, and the composing poet with whom he has largely merged in these cantos share deep poetic and temperamental affinities represented in miniature by the fact that Adeline's lyric begins, as Byron's epic does, with a strategic mispronunciation. Her rhyming "Black Free-air" with "Beware" and "heir" suggests cultural contrast through time as Byron's "true one" / "new one" / "Don Joo-un" does through space.

The ballad Adeline sings is multiply appropriate for the poem. Considered on realistic grounds, it centers on the right order of cleric for Norman Abbey, Newstead having been a Dominican (Black Friars') foundation. On narrative grounds, it answers Henry's request and amplifies, for the interested audience around the breakfast table, the spectral tale precipitated by Juan's uncharacteristic pallor, negligence, and preoccupation. On psychological grounds, it delicately implies Adeline's disaffection from Henry and sympathy for Juan. The ballad describes how after Henry VIII's dissolution of the monasteries one friar stayed behind to perpetuate his order's claim and haunt the aristocratic incumbents by making his mournful or gloating presence felt at moments crucial to the endurance of the Amundeville line: marriages, births, and deaths. The song is descriptive rather than judgmental, its tone carefully neutral until the final lines, which are nicely calculated to reflect their speaker's benevolence and piety:

> "Then Grammercy! for the Black Friar;
> Heaven sain him! fair or foul,
> And whatsoe'er may be his prayer,
> Let ours be for his soul." (st. 6)

Although Adeline did not compose this ballad for the purposes to which she now puts it, her performance of "Beware! Beware! of the Black Friar" is brilliantly effective, not just at displaying her versatile genius but also at showing Juan that she can enter into his feelings and ally herself with his interests rather than her husband's. The lyric does not directly denounce the founding "Lord of the Hill, Amundeville"—such crudeness of effect would be bad art and bad manners alike—but by characterizing "Norman Church" as "his prey" it makes him a predator and his descendants secular interlopers. Though she was not privileged as the reader has been to see Canterbury Cathedral through Juan's eyes, Adeline seems to understand how Norman Abbey must look from his Spanish-Catholic perspective. Led to this insight by her temperamental mobility, she deploys the conscious, cultivated portion of her gift (and curse) to affect Juan, who is similarly susceptible to immediate impressions.

The sense that Adeline's character is more acceptable to the middle-aged and tolerant narrator than to the young and still exacting Juan becomes stronger after her second performance of the day, her "watching, witching, condescending / To the consumers of fish, fowl, and game" at Lord Henry's political "At Home" for voters in the borough (DJ 16.95). Here something quite uncommon for the English cantos occurs. We find a serious discrepancy between Juan's reading of things and the narrator's. Stranger still, Juan's is the harsher view.

> Though this was most expedient on the whole,
>   And usual—Juan, when he cast a glance
> On Adeline while playing her grand role,
>   Which she went through as though it were a dance,
> (Betraying only now and then her soul
>   By a look scarce perceptibly askance
> Of weariness or scorn) began to feel
> Some doubt how much of Adeline was real;   (DJ 16.96)

and without even ending his sentence the narrator goes on to present his alternate interpretation of this powerful woman's apparent hypocrisy:

> So well she acted, all and every part
>   By turns—with that vivacious versatility,
> Which many people take for want of heart.
>   They err—'tis merely what is called mobility,
> A thing of temperament and not of art,
>   Though seeming so, from its supposed facility,
> And false—though true; for surely they're sincerest,
> Who are strongly acted on by what is nearest.   (DJ 16.97)

The moment would seem exceedingly generous did we not realize that Byron is excusing in Adeline a quality he noticed in himself.

But even so, the stanza remarkably undercuts much of what has seemed true of the English Great World and its denizens. In Adeline's individual yet representative case, what seemed calculation is explicitly revealed as temperament—basic human nature modified by a sort of secondary instinct, deeply ingrained by social reinforcement—a slippery and complex attribute never fully understandable, hence always partly excusable, sometimes even admirable.[24]

This mobility, the narrator goes on to tell us, is the mental climate that produces actors, artists, romancers, speakers, bards, diplomatists, dancers—"Heroes sometimes, though seldom—sages never" (DJ 16.98). Juan, clearly no sage, fits intermittently into the categories of actor, romancer, diplomatist, dancer, and hero. He belongs to Adeline's class of being but is too young or too new to England to refrain from judging what he thinks he sees in her. With the rise of the moon and the return of the Black Friar in a new and yet more challenging form,[25] his own mobile heart, passions, and purposes change—but to what precise effect we can never fully know.

How might the Norman Abbey episode have concluded? And how might the poem have ended? Narrative clues and authorial statements of intent are plentiful enough; but predicting the closure of a remarkably errant poem by a man of radical mobility is bound to be highly speculative. Nonetheless, the shaky ground or thin ice or rough seas of conjecture have not kept Byron's best readers from sending forth their guesses. Jerome J. McGann points out that from canto 7 on, the narrative's sequence of time and event are precisely coincident with Byron's professed plan of ending Juan's adventures in France, on the guillotine—but he also acknowledges that Byron's intentions were so continually changing that the ultimate intention for Don Juan seems to have been keeping it "an epic with no plan." Andrew Rutherford believes that Byron had abandoned or indefinitely postponed Juan's death by guillotine and that he had plans for prolonging the poem almost indefinitely. Drawing on Byron's comments to Leigh Hunt, Lady Blessington, Parry, and others, Rutherford lays out such possible alternatives as making Juan turn Methodist or taking him to Greece as a revolutionary. Other readers would end the poem in England—whether by design or default. Cecil Y. Lang thinks that Juan would have married Aurora and that "they would have lived un-happily ever after—in the hell of an unhappy marriage." M. K. Joseph guesses that Byron intended to involve Juan and Adeline in a scandal culminating in the Amundevilles' divorce and precluding a union with Aurora but concedes that the poem's appropriate end is the narrator's demise, not the hero's. Echoing Joseph, Bernard Beatty points out that the poem is "inherently unfinished"—that its necessary conclusion will finish off Byron rather than Don Juan. Elizabeth Boyd also asserts that the narrative stops because it has to, though for a different reason. She believes that in bringing Juan to the point where he would be obliged to drift as before into disaster or to take a mature stand and oppose circumstances, Byron had carried the story as far as his skepticism and ambiva-lence would allow—that his principles and experience would have to change before the narrative could continue.[26]

My own sense is that definitive closure of any sort would act to betray the essence of *Don Juan*. Moving on to new things is natural to the poem, protagonist, narrator, and author alike. Pausing to rest and reconsider now and then, Byron might have spun out his quietly facetious opinions on "things existent" indefinitely—and the perpetual resurrection of Don Juan, dispatched to hell by one dramatist, poet, or novelist only to be retrieved by another, proves that no single literary death-stroke will suffice to end the adven-tures of so fascinating and resilient a protagonist. But even though the poem need not and probably should not end, it seems just as well to have it stop where it does. Presenting Don Juan's triple entanglement at Norman Abbey, Byron's tale has come to a point where it falls within the legendary tradition rather than standing outside it. Don Juan at last has achieved chronological maturity, though not the seniority generally associated with the legendary character. Because his exploits in love now involve balancing the mutually antagonistic claims of three women, he is called upon to demonstrate some of the romantic resourcefulness associated with his prototype.

Presenting that ambiguous revenant the Black Friar, Byron comes as close as he can, in the sort of realistic world his poem reflects, to enacting the traditional conclusion of the Don Juan story. Like Mozart's Giovanni and the others, Byron's hero will be dragged down into flames—but the figurative fires of passion, not a literal hell. The immediate agent will be a ghost of sorts—not a stone statue animated by the spirit of the man it represents but a voluptuous woman making use of her corporeal attributes to embody a specter. Byron's version of the legend being a modern and skeptical one, the ultimate cause will be not one deliberate being but the three women, weaving his fall as if they were Fates in unconscious collaboration. Juan's descent into hell will not simply indicate his succumbing to a sinful nature; it will exhibit his "high" qualities acting in concert with his "low" ones.

Time, place, and circumstances are right for a fall. All Byron's "machinery," "supernatural" and otherwise, is in readiness. But the completed part of the poem stops with the readiness rather than ending with a fall. For the moment Adeline, born and bred to be conscious of public responsibilities, has put aside her personal feelings for Juan. Disillusioned by Adeline's skill in playing her social role (or irritated at her ability to withstand her feelings for him?), Juan has been propelled out of his hostess's sphere of influence—though as we know he and she are both changeable creatures, and their powerful magnetism is likely to reassert itself. For now Aurora has renewed the higher sentiments Juan had lost some cantos back; and though in canto 16 the narrator withholds the details of the "tender moonlight situation" with the frolicsome Fitz-Fulke, from Don Juan's past history we can easily see that having waxed idealistic he is ripe for a tumble into sensuality, a conclusion borne out by the implications of the barely begun seventeenth canto as it begins to take shape.

Despite canto 17's tantalizing bits of continuation, I for one am content to leave Juan and his trio of Englishwomen here, caught in their different ways between soul and sense. The spiritual Aurora, thawed by the warm south of Juan's presence, is dawning into womanhood. The carnal Fitz-Fulke, also thanks to Juan's influence, is impersonating spirituality—and unlikely though conversion seems in her case, counterfeiting a quality can be the first step toward gaining it. The Schlegelian "hovering" is rather more complicated for Juan and Adeline. Each character is already in the mixed state toward which Aurora and the duchess seem to be moving. Each is "half dust half deity" (to borrow a phrase from *Manfred*), but their cultural differences, forces that in some measure override the human condition common to all and the mobility distinguishing both Juan and Adeline, limit them in different ways. In Dantean fashion, canto 16 leaves the two not-yet lovers in positions potentially retributive, conceivably rewarding, but in each case determined by their different qualities. Whether because of his Mediterranean origins or his true assimilation of the cosmopolitan spirit, Juan sinks and soars, reenacting the oceanic mobility that is at all levels, from verse to sense, the driving force of the poem. Adeline the quintessence of her class and its code, the perfect embodiment of English culture as Byron chose to represent it in the poem, is cosmopolitan only to the extent of appropriating things, words, fashions, and people from other cultures to serve in her own world. Mobility notwithstanding, she floats frozen, precluded from raptures of both kinds. To readers who have accompanied Juan on his lively, ever-varying travels, the Regency world whose spirit is summed up in Adeline may seem for all its sublime potential a ridiculously "tight little island." But we must not forget that beyond that island, yet encompassing it, is the higher cosmopolitanism of Byron—and

> In spite of all temptations
> To belong to other nations
> He remains an Englishman.

ABBREVIATIONS

NOTES

SELECT BIBLIOGRAPHY

Abbreviations

The following abbreviations appear in parenthetical references in the text:

CPW   Lord Byron, *Complete Poetical Works*, ed. Jerome J. McGann

DJ   Lord Byron, *Don Juan*, ed. Jerome J. McGann

G   Lady Caroline Lamb, *Glenarvon*, facsimile of the first edition, intro.
          James L. Ruff

LE   Robert Southey, *Letters from England*, ed. Jack Simmons

LJ   Lord Byron, *Byron's Letters and Journals*, ed. Leslie A. Marchand

NC   Lady Caroline Lamb, *A New Canto*

Notes

Introduction

1 Marilyn Butler, "Against Tradition: The Case for a Particularized Historical Method," in *Historical Studies and Literary Criticism*, ed. Jerome J. McGann (Madison: University of Wisconsin Press, 1985), 43.

2 Lord Byron, *Don Juan*, vol. 5 in *Complete Poetical Works*, ed. Jerome J. McGann (Oxford: Clarendon Press, 1986), canto 14, stanza 61. Subsequent citations will quote from this text, the standard one, and will parenthetically supply canto and stanza in the following abbreviated fashion: (DJ 14.61). References to prose passages within the volume—to Byron's Preface, for instance, or to the editor's notes—will cite page numbers in the form (DJ 743).

3 Lord Byron, *Complete Poetical Works*, ed. Jerome J. McGann, vol. 2 (Oxford: Clarendon, 1980), 3.

4 W. S. Gilbert, *Complete Plays of Gilbert and Sullivan* (New York: Modern Library, 1932), 131.

5 Peter J. Manning, "Don Juan and Byron's Imperceptiveness to the English Word," *Studies in Romanticism* 18, no. 2 (Summer 1979): 233.

6 In *English Romantic Irony* (Cambridge: Harvard University Press, 1980), Anne K. Mellor speaks of *Don Juan's* intellectual method of proceeding as the "associative arabesque," a phrase in which Schlegel attempts to capture the seemingly chaotic yet actually and intricately patterned intellectual phenomenon that is romantic irony (17–18, 57).

7 Hans Eichner, *Friedrich Schlegel* (New York: Twayne, 1970), 64.

I: Nothing So Difficult

1 Victor Brombert, "Opening Signals in Narrative," *New Literary History* 11 (1980): 489–502. Attending to opening signals generally proves rewarding, but especially so in *Don Juan*, which, as Michael G. Cooke and Peter J. Manning have separately but similarly concluded, proceeds by repeating and varying its initial pattern. See Cooke's "Byron's Don Juan: The Obsession and Self-Discipline of Spontaneity," *Studies in Romanticism* 14, no. 3 (Summer 1975): 290–300, Manning's *Byron and His Fictions* (Detroit: Wayne State University Press, 1978), 220–24.

2 Jerome J. McGann, *Fiery Dust* (Chicago: University of Chicago Press, 1968), 285–86.

3 The sense that *Don Juan* stops rather than concludes is widespread

among critics. For a range of discussion on causes and effects of this incompletion, see, among others, Elizabeth Boyd, *Byron's Don Juan* (New York: Humanities Press, 1968), 30–33; Jerome J. McGann, *Don Juan in Context* (Chicago: University of Chicago Press, 1976), 3–4; George M. Ridenour, *The Style of Don Juan* (Hamden: Archon, 1969, rpt.), 122; Andrew Rutherford, *Byron: A Critical Study* (Stanford, Calif.: Stanford University Press, 1967), 238–41; M. K. Joseph, *Byron the Poet* (London: Victor Gollancz, 1964), 303; Lilian R. Furst, *Fictions of Romantic Irony in European Narrative, 1760–1857* (London: Macmillan, 1980), 116–17; Anne K. Mellor, *English Romantic Irony* (Cambridge: Harvard University Press, 1980), 62; Bernard Beatty, *Byron's Don Juan* (Totowa: Barnes and Noble, 1985), 182; Peter J. Manning, *Byron and His Fictions*, 220–21. Michael Cooke, who sees "the unfinishable poem" as "a signal romantic contribution to the form and vital entelechy of poetry itself," is especially insightful on the rewards of incompletion ("Byron's Don Juan," 285–86).

4 McGann, *Don Juan in Context*, 69–70.

5 Horace, *Ars Poetica*, lines 286–87. Quoted in C. O. Brink, *Horace on Poetry: The "Ars Poetica"* (Cambridge: Cambridge University Press, 1971), 65.

6 See John Cam Hobhouse, *Byron's Bulldog: The Letters of John Cam Hobhouse to Lord Byron*, ed. Peter W. Graham (Columbus: Ohio State University Press, 1984), 257.

7 McGann, Commentary to *Don Juan*, 670.

8 See *The Works of Lord Byron, Letters and Journals*, ed. R. E. Prothero (New York: Octagon Books, 1966, rpt.), 6:381–83. As McGann points out in his editorial Commentary (*DJ* 666), the text reproduced is a corrupt one.

9 McGann, *Don Juan in Context*, 73.

10 Mellor, *English Romantic Irony*, 75–76.

11 William Wordsworth, *William Wordsworth: The Poems*, ed. John O. Hayden (New Haven: Yale University Press, 1981), 1:949.

12 See William A. Borst, *Lord Byron's First Pilgrimage* (Hamden, Conn.: Archon, 1969), 23–25; and John Cam Hobhouse, *Recollections of a Long Life*, ed. Lady Dorchester (London: John Murray, 1911), 1:10.

13 Wordsworth replaced these lines with "Though but of compass small, and bare / To thirsty suns and parching air" in the 1820 version of "The Thorn."

14 See Mary Jacobus, *Tradition and Experiment in Wordsworth's Lyrical Ballads (1798)* (Oxford: Clarendon Press, 1976), 247. Southey's remark appeared in the *Critical Review* 24:200.

15 The best introduction to the "brilliant, self-contained satire" of the Dedication and its relevance to the main body of *Don Juan* is "Honest Simple Verse," the first chapter of Ridenour's *The Style of Don Juan*.

16 Mellor, *English Romantic Irony*, 56.

17 McGann, *Don Juan in Context*, x, 3.

18 Hobhouse, *Byron's Bulldog*, 256–61. Short quotations in the paragraph that follows in text are also from this source.

19 On "tact" and income tax alike, see McGann's Commentary (*DJ* 680).

20 Writing to Hobhouse and Kinnaird on 19 January 1819, Byron enumerates his amours of the recent past in this epic list: "Which 'piece' does he [Lord Lauderdale, who had carried a tale home to England] mean?—since last year I have run the Gauntlet;—is it the Tarruscelli—the Da Mosti—the Spineda—the Lotti—the Rizzato—the Eleanora—the Carlotta—the Giulietta—the Alvisi—the Zambieri—The Eleanora da Bezzi—(who was the King of Naples' Gioaschino's mistress—at least one of them) the Theresina of Mazzurati— the Glettenheimer—& her Sister—the Luigia & her mother—the Fornaretta—the Santa—the Caligari—the Portiera [Vedova?]—the Bolognese figurante—the Tentora and her sister—cum multis aliis?—some of them are Countesses— & some of them Cobblers wives—some noble—some middling— some low—& all whores" (*LJ* 6:92). The tone and detail alike are reminiscent of "Madamina! il catalogo è questo," the aria in which Leporello catalogues, for a vengeful Donna Elvira, the international army of women seduced by Don Giovanni—640 Italians, 231 Germans, 100 French, 91 Turks, and 1003 Spaniards.

21 Lady Blessington, *Conversations of Lord Byron*, ed. Ernest J. Lovell, Jr. (Princeton: Princeton University Press, 1969), 47, 71.

II: Two Dons, a Lord, and a Laureate

1 Lord Byron, *Complete Poetical Works*, ed. Jerome J. McGann, vol. 3 (Oxford: Clarendon Press, 1981), 90–91.

2 Malcolm Kelsall, *Byron's Politics* (Brighton, Sussex: Harvester Press, 1987), 32–33.

3 Leslie A. Marchand offers a full and useful running account of the relations between Byron and Southey in his notes to his edition of Byron's letters and journals (see *LJ* 12:153 for the full list of citations); and Rowland E. Prothero devotes appendix I of volume 6 of *The Works of Lord Byron: Letters and Journals* (New York: Octagon Books, 1966, rpt.), 377–99, to the quarrel between the two poets.

4 Robert Southey, *New Letters of Robert Southey*, ed. Kenneth Curry (New York: Columbia University Press, 1965), 1:363.

5 One example among many might be the *Edinburgh Review*'s list of new travel books coming out around the time of *Letters from England*—10 (July 1807), 498: *Travels through the Canadas* by George Heriot, Esq.; *The Present State of Turkey* by Thomas Thornton, Esq.; *The Stranger in England, or, Travels in Great Britain* from the German of C. A. G. Goede; the anonymous *Observations on a Journey through Spain and Italy to Naples* . . . ; *A Tour through Holland* by Sir John Carr; *Journal of a Tour through Ireland* by Sir Richard Colt Hoare; *Travels in the Year 1806, from Italy to England* . . . by the Marquis De Salvo; and *The Travels of Bertrandon de la Brocquière* translated by Thomas

Johnes, Esq. *Letters from England* did not appear in the *Edinburgh* list until the next volume, 11 (October 1807), 236; and like a number of other travel narratives it can be found under "Miscellaneous."

6 Southey, *New Letters*, 1:307. In the period just preceding the composition of *Letters from England*, Southey was much and grudgingly involved in reviewing, a task that was always one of his principal sources of income. His letters of the time complain about the burden of the reviewer's pen and renounce it, only to resume it and renounce it again. See *Selections from the Letters of Robert Southey*, ed. John Wood Warter (New York: AMS Press, 1977; rpt.), 1:212–13, 238, 254, 321, 336–37, 364 (here Southey announces having "given up reviewing finally" to complete *Letters from England* and to undertake other projects), 383; and 2:14.

7 The literary advantages of this choice are delineated by Francis Jeffrey in the *Edinburgh Review* 11 (January 1808): 370–71. Jack Simmons discusses pragmatic reasons for anonymity in the introduction to his edition of *Letters from England* (London: Cresset Press, 1951), xviii–xix.

8 Southey, *Selections*, 2:23.

9 *Edinburgh Review* 11 (January 1808): 370–90, 285–89, 399–413.

10 *Edinburgh Review* 11 (January 1808): 372, 390.

11 Elizabeth Boyd, *Byron's Don Juan: A Critical Study* (New York: Humanities Press, 1958), 107.

12 Robert Southey, *Letters from England*, ed. Jack Simmons (London: Cresset Press, 1951), 13. Subsequent citations will refer to this modern text, which follows the first edition of 1807, and will appear parenthetically in this fashion: (LE 13).

13 Southey, *New Letters*, 1:306.

14 Besides the parallels discussed in some detail in the main body of the essay, a reader might notice the following resemblances between *Letters from England* and *Don Juan*: white cliffs of England (LE 17; DJ 2.12, 10.65, 12.67), entry through a custom house (LE 18; DJ 10.69–70), corrupt borough politics (LE 21; DJ 16.70 and following), the fire an English delight (LE 22; DJ 13.77), verdant fields (LE 30; DJ 10.76), approach to London on heath famous for robbers (LE 45; DJ, 11.10 and following), Spaniard mistaken for "Frenchman" (LE 48; DJ 11.13), monotony of metropolitan architecture (LE 70; DJ 11.21), English clothes dull compared to Spanish (LE 76; DJ 2.6–7), doors with knockers and significant knockings (LE 76; DJ 11.29, 12.67), international names and sources of fashionable foods (LE 89; DJ 15.63 and following), bilingual confusion of oaths (LE 110–11; DJ 1.14), fox hunting from Spanish perspective (LE 139–40; DJ 14.32–35), great alteration in society has made men more like one another (LE 140; DJ 13.110, 14.15–16, 15.26), marriage market and fashionable migrations (LE 164; DJ 11.49, 13.43 and following), scientific fads of the day (LE 297–99; DJ 1.129–32). Discussion of fashionable society, with its card leaving, fops, turf, boxing, agriculturists, philosophizing, "gentlemen in stays," and newspapers, fills letters 73 (LE 447–54), and *Don Juan's* English cantos, 11–16.

15 McGann concisely summarizes the importance of *Biographia Literaria* as a spur to *Don Juan*: see Notes to *Don Juan*, 668, and *Don Juan in Context* (Chicago: University of Chicago Press, 1976), 161–63.

16 One finds such cultural and climatological speculations throughout Madame de Staël's writings, but particularly in *De la littérature* (1800), *Corinne* (1807), and *De l'Allemagne* (1813). The possible influences of the first of these on *Letters from England* and of all three on *Don Juan* are topics well worth pursuing.

17 "And now we might add something concerning a certain most subtle spirit which pervades and lies hid in all gross bodies, by the force and action of which spirit the particles of bodies attract one another at near distances and cohere, if contiguous; and electric bodies operate to greater distances, as well repelling as attracting the neighboring corpuscles; and light is emitted, reflected, inflected, and heats bodies; and all sensation is excited, and the members of animal bodies move at the command of the will, namely, by the vibrations of this spirit, mutually propagated along the solid filaments of the nerves, from the outward organs of sense to the brain and from the brain into the muscles" (*Newton's Philosophy of Nature: Selections from His Writings*, ed. H. S. Thayer [New York: Hafner Publishing Company, 1953], 45–46).

18 Southey, *Selections*, 2:40.

19 Michael Foot, in *The Politics of Paradise: A Vindication of Byron* (London: Collins, 1988), offers the following resourceful explanation for the mutual admiration of the Tory poet and the Whig one: "Scott, Byron, and Ruskin are the three greatest dog-lovers of English literature. Hence their sympathy. For it is easier for a camel to go through the eye of a needle, than for one dog-lover to believe that another dog-lover could ever do anything very wrong" (395–96n).

20 Southey, *Selections*, 1:23.

III: All Things—But a Show?

1 Edward G. E. L. Bulwer-Lytton, *England and the English*, ed. Standish Meacham (Chicago: University of Chicago Press, 1970), 99.

2 Elizabeth French Boyd's *Byron's Don Juan: A Critical Study* (New York: Humanities Press, 1958; rpt.) is now over forty years old, but it remains indispensable for the student of Byron's literary sources. Chapters 6, 7, and 8, respectively titled "Byron's Library and His Reading," "The Literary Background of *Don Juan*: Incidents," and "The Literary Background of *Don Juan*: Ideas," are especially crucial. Among the finest of more recent studies adding to our knowledge of Byron's sources are Hermione de Almeida's *Byron and Joyce through Homer: Don Juan and Ulysses* (New York: Columbia University Press, 1981); Jerome J. McGann's *Don Juan in Context* (Chicago: University of Chicago Press, 1976); the *Don Juan* portion of M. K. Joseph's *Byron the Poet* (London: Victor Gollancz, 1964); Cecil Y. Lang's essay "Narcissus Jilted: Byron, *Don Juan*, and the Biograph-

ical Imperative," in *Historical Studies and Literary Criticism*, ed. Jerome J. McGann (Madison: University of Wisconsin Press, 1985), 143–79; and Peter Vassallo, *Byron: The Italian Literary Influence* (London: Macmillan, 1984).

3 Frederick L. Beaty, "Harlequin Don Juan," *Journal of English and Germanic Philology* 67, no. 3 (1968): 395–405. Beaty's piece not only indicates pantomime as a contemporary source for Byron's comic character Don Juan but also suggests, as I am doing, that the forms of pantomime and Don Juan are comparable.

4 Leo Weinstein, *The Metamorphoses of Don Juan* (Stanford, Calif.: Stanford University Press, 1959), 81. For other comparative surveys of the legendary figure, see George Gendarme de Bévotte, *La légende de Don Juan* (Paris: Librairie Hachette, 1911); John Austen, *The Story of Don Juan* (London: Martin Secker, 1939); and Oscar Mandel, *The Theatre of Don Juan: A Collection of Plays and Views, 1630–1963* (Lincoln: University of Nebraska Press, 1963).

5 Rather than produce an intricately annotated and slow-moving survey of pantomime and commedia conventions, I have tried to read widely, assimilate, and summarize. The account of spectacular theater that has resulted derives from the following works. David Mayer's *Harlequin in His Element: The English Pantomime, 1806–1836* (Cambridge: Harvard University Press, 1969) has because of its period focus and its critical intelligence been my single most important source. Most readers will find that the most effective and economical introduction to pantomime in Byron's day is Mayer's second chapter, "The Structures of Pantomime, 1806–1836" (19–74). I have also relied on M. Willson Disher, *Clowns and Pantomimes* (New York: Benjamin Blom, 1968); Pierre Louis Ducharte, *The Italian Comedy*, trans. Randolph T. Weaver (New York: Dover, 1966); Allardyce Nicoll, *The World of Harlequin* (Cambridge: Cambridge University Press, 1963) and *A History of English Drama, 1660–1900* (Cambridge: Cambridge University Press, 1952); and A. E. Wilson, *King Panto: The Story of Pantomime* (New York: Dutton, 1935). Throughout this chapter, I am indebted to Leigh Campbell Garrison, formerly my graduate research assistant, now a colleague in the VPI & SU English Department.

6 Mayer, *Harlequin in His Element*, 30–31.

7 Burletta and extravaganza are, like pantomime, forms of spectacular theater. Burletta was characterized by its champion George Colman the younger as "a DRAMA in RHYME, entirely musical—a short comick piece consisting of recitative and singing, wholly accompanied, more or less, by the orchestra" (Colman quoted in C. Hugh Holman, *A Handbook to Literature* [Indianapolis: Odyssey Press, 1972], 77). Extravaganza, as described by its creator J. R. Planché, consists of "whimsical treatment of a poetical subject as distinguished from the broad caricature of a tragedy or serious opera, which was correctly described as burlesque" (quoted in Holman, *Handbook*, 216).

8 Mayer, *Harlequin in His Element*, 7.

9 Sala quoted in Wilson, *King Panto*, 73.

10 Mayer, *Harlequin in His Element*, 44.

11 Quoted ibid., 47.

12 Disher, *Clowns and Pantomimes*, 291.

13 Mayer, *Harlequin in His Element*, 320–21.

14 Disher, *Clowns and Pantomimes*, 48.

15 Vandenhoff quoted in Wilson, *King Panto*, 135.

16 See Charles Dickens, *Memoirs of Joseph Grimaldi* (New York: Stein and Day, 1968), 214–16 and 226–27, and *Byron's Letters and Journals*, ed. Leslie A. Marchand (Cambridge: Harvard University Press, 1973) 1:152 and n, 3:9, and 4:153 and n.

17 Dickens, *Memoirs of Joseph Grimaldi*, 226–27.

18 Mandel, *Theatre of Don Juan*, 252; Weinstein, *Metamorphoses of Don Juan*, 51.

19 Boyd, *Byron's Don Juan*, 35, 165.

20 Anne Barton, "Don Juan Reconsidered: The Haidée Episode," *Byron Journal* 15 (1987): 16.

21 Quoted in Mayer, *Harlequin in His Element*, 77.

22 Leigh Hunt, *Leigh Hunt's Dramatic Criticism, 1808–1831*, ed. Lawrence Huston Houtchens and Carolyn Washburn Houtchens (New York: Octagon Books, 1977), 144.

23 Mayer, *Harlequin in His Element*, 6.

24 Ibid., 8.

25 Nicoll, *The World of Harlequin*, 22.

26 Beaty, "Harlequin Don Juan," 405.

27 Malcolm M. Kelsall, *Byron's Politics*, 8.

28 Readers interested in pursuing this subject will certainly want to see Susan J. Wolfson's " 'Their she condition': Cross-Dressing and the Politics of Gender in Don Juan," *English Literary History* 54, no. 3 (Fall 1987): 585–617. Her reading of the poem's "transgressions of gender," from linguistic cross-dressings to impersonations of the Juanna and Black Friar sort, is consistently insightful and solidly grounded. Her conclusion, that the poem "does not, finally, escape the roles fashioned and maintained by his [Byron's] culture, but it does explore the problems of living with and within those roles" (611), accurately characterizes one of *Don Juan*'s most important preoccupations. But it strikes me that the poem offers as much transcendence as is possible in its recognition that human roles are roles—fashioned and maintained by a culture but enacted by individuals whose freedom lies in recognizing play (or what they do) for what it is.

29 Wolfson, " 'Their she condition,' " 288.

IV: A Don, Two Lords, and a Lady

1 Throughout the essay, I shall refer to Lady Caroline Lamb as "Lady Caroline." Repetitive honorifics may sound stuffy to the twentieth-

century ear; but of all possible alternatives "Lady Caroline," the form of
address a stranger would properly use in speaking of or to the author of
Glenarvon, is the most appropriate on historical and social grounds.

2 Both of these mentions of *Glenarvon* are interesting enough to be quoted
in full and discussed in detail inappropriate to an introductory paragraph. The letter to Murray goes on to amplify on the "Motto—which
promises amiably 'For us & for our tragedy'—if such be the posy what
should the ring be? 'a name to all succeeding &c.'—the generous moment selected for the publication is probably its kindest accompani-
ment—and truth to say—the time was well chosen,—I have not even
a guess at the contents—except for the very vague accounts I have
heard—and I know but one thing which a woman can say to the
purpose on such occasions and that she might as well for her own sake
keep to herself—which by the way they very rarely can—that old
reproach against their admirers of 'kiss and tell' bad as it is—is surely
somewhat less than———and *publish*" (LJ 5:85). These words set the
tone for Byron's subsequent professions on *Glenarvon*. Facetious and
dismissive, he admits to some small irritation that the work exists (if
only because denying such annoyance might be interpreted as a sign of
serious concern) but to no curiosity about the particulars; and in a
misogynistic voice sometimes echoed and sometimes contradicted in
Don Juan, he characterizes the literary escapade as just what a woman
would do. The allusion to the motto, which was different for each
edition (LJ 5:85 n. 4), gives us a clue as to which version Byron is likely to
have read—an issue of some importance, given the scope of the revi-
sions that took place between first and second editions. The words
Byron quotes indicate that he was thinking of the first edition, which
had for its motto "He left a name to all succeeding times, / Link'd with
one virtue and a thousand crimes," a misquoted or strategically altered
couplet from his *Corsair*.

   The letter to Samuel Rogers is interesting partly because its recipient,
like Byron, had suffered Lady Caroline's slings and arrows: in *Glenarvon's*
first edition the cadaverous Rogers is trenchantly and unmistakably
depicted as "the *dead*, I mean the sick poet," fawning hyena to the
princess of Madagascar, in real life Lady Holland (G 1:249—for full
information on this abbreviation see below, note 15). But it is also
amusing that after quoting Pope against Lady Caroline, Byron goes on
to talk of another novel he has just perused, "Ben. Constant's *Adolphe*—
and his preface denying the real people—it is a work which leaves an
unpleasant impression—but very consistent with the consequences of
not being in love—which is perhaps as disagreeable as anything—
except being so—" (LJ 5:86–87). The juxtaposition of these two semi-
fictions, and during Byron's visit under the roof of Coppet at that, is
superbly ironic; for if the unseemly specifics of *Glenarvon* are clear
symptoms of Lady Caroline's continuing case of Byron fever, Constant's
Adolphe presents "with rather cruel detail (imperfectly camouflaged) his
cooling passion for Madame de Staël" (LJ 5:86 n. 9).

3 One must be cautious in attempting to interpret so paradoxical and complicated a nature as Lady Caroline Lamb's. Accordingly I have gathered a range of opinions prior to forming my own views on her life and character. The most useful sources have been Elizabeth Jenkins's *Lady Caroline Lamb* (London: Cardinal, 1974), and the chapter on Lady Caroline in Margot Strickland's *The Byron Women* (New York: St. Martin's, 1974), 40–66, both intelligent and sensitive appraisals; Byron's letters, less than objective but illuminating nonetheless; and John Clubbe's essay "*Glenarvon* Revised—and Revisited" (*Wordsworth Circle* 10 [1979]: 205–17), a model of how historical study can enhance critical insight. I have also consulted Henry Blyth's *Caro: The Fatal Passion* (London: Rupert Hart-Davis, 1972) and the entry on Lady Caroline in the *Dictionary of National Biography*. Biographies of those people close to Lady Caroline and firsthand accounts of the Regency period have also proven important, particularly Lady Airlie's *In Whig Society* (London: Hodder and Stoughton, 1921); Lord David Cecil's *Melbourne* (New York: Bobbs-Merrill, 1954); Leslie A. Marchand's *Byron: A Biography* (New York: Knopf, 1957); J. B. Priestley's *The Prince of Pleasure and His Regency* (New York: Harper and Row, 1969); Samuel Smiles's *A Publisher and His Friends: Memoir and Correspondence of the Late John Murray*, 2 vols. (London: John Murray, 1891); W. M. Torrens's *Memoirs of the Right Honourable William, Second Viscount Melbourne* (London: Macmillan, 1878); Harriette Wilson's *Memoirs* (London: The Navarre Society, 1924); and Philip Ziegler's *Melbourne* (New York: Knopf, 1976). I have also looked at Lady Caroline's albums and manuscripts at the archive of John Murray, London.

4 Cecil, *Melbourne*, 70.

5 Tillie Olsen, *Silences* (New York: Delacorte, 1978), 17.

6 Lady Caroline quoted in Cecil, *Melbourne*, 80.

7 Cecil, *Melbourne*, 135.

8 For the full circumstances of *Glenarvon*'s composition and the revision that took place between first and second editions, see John Clubbe, "*Glenarvon* Revised—and Revisited," 206, 209–13.

9 John Galt, *The Life of Lord Byron* (New York: A. L. Fowle, 1900), 181; Lady Caroline quoted in Cecil, *Melbourne*, 82.

10 Clark Olney, "*Glenarvon* Revisited," *University of Kansas City Review* 22 (1956): 275; Clubbe, "*Glenarvon*—Revised and Revisited," 205.

11 William Lamb and Samuel Rogers quoted in Jenkins, *Lady Caroline Lamb*, 153, 54.

12 Clubbe, "*Glenarvon* Revised—and Revisited," 206.

13 Hélène Cixous, "The Laugh of the Medusa," trans. Keith Cohen and Paula Cohen, *Signs* 1, no. 4 (1976): 888.

14 Ibid., 875.

15 This quotation comes, as subsequent ones will do, from the facsimile reproduction of *Glenarvon*'s first edition (1816), edited and introduced by James L. Ruff (Delmar, N.Y.: Scholars' Facsimiles and Reprints, 1972). Subsequent citations will be to this edition and will appear paren-

thetically in text in this form: (*G* 1:249). *Glenarvon* was first published in a three-volume edition by Henry Colburn in London on 9 May 1816; popular demand resulted in a second edition on 22 June.

16 Cixous, "Laugh of the Medusa," 888.

17 Clubbe, "*Glenarvon* Revised—and Revisited," 211.

18 Critical Fragment 34 in Friedrich Schlegel's *Lucinde and the Fragments*, trans. Peter Firchow (Minneapolis: University of Minnesota Press, 1971), 146.

19 Lady Caroline Lamb, *Glenarvon*, second edition (London: Colburn, 1816), 1:138.

20 Jenkins, *Lady Caroline Lamb*, 106.

21 Clubbe, "*Glenarvon* Revised—and Revisited," 210.

22 It seems worth mentioning that during 1812, the period of Byron's active involvement with Whig politics, William Lamb's views had diverged from the party line, and especially with respect to the frame-breakers, against whom he urged "ferocious penalties" (Ziegler, *Melbourne*, 67).

23 Malcolm Kelsall, in his essay "The Byronic Hero and Revolution in Ireland: The Politics of *Glenarvon*" (*Byron Journal* 9 [1981]: 4–19), discusses Lady Caroline's treatment of the Irish uprising of 1798, a struggle based on French Revolutionary principles and reflecting, mutatis mutandis, contemporary English political unrest. It is interesting to see that *Glenarvon*, like *Don Juan*, presents different times and cultures in dialogue.

24 Clubbe, "*Glenarvon* Revised—and Revisited," 207.

25 Susan J. Wolfson presents some good reasons for seeing Lady Caroline as a possible model for Don Juan, or at least for some of his attributes, in her essay "'Their she condition': Cross-Dressing and the Politics of Gender in *Don Juan*," *English Literary History* 54, no. 3 (Fall 1987): 592. If such is the case, then Lady Caroline as well as Byron is distributed throughout the poem, and *Don Juan* slyly offers something of a quid pro quo to the author of *Glenarvon*.

26 See especially the last two lines of *DJ* 13.94: "Society is smooth'd to that excess, / That manners hardly differ more than dress." Also *DJ* 14.16:

> A sort of varnish over every fault;
> A kind of common-place, even in their crimes:
> Factitious passions, wit without much salt,
> A want of that true nature which sublimes
> Whate'er it shows with truth; a smooth monotony
> Of character, in those at least who have got any.

27 Smiles, *A Publisher and His Friends*, I:405.

28 Lady Caroline Lamb, *Gordon: A Tale* (London: T. and J. Allman, 1821) canto 2, stanza 71.

29 Lady Caroline Lamb, *A New Canto*, quoted in Strickland, *The Byron Women*, 212–16. Quotations that follow in the text will refer parenthetically to this source, and by page number because neither the stanzas nor the

lines are numbered. Subsequent references will take this abbreviated form: (NC 212).

30 Strickland, The Byron Women, 11.

V: England in Don Juan

1 Peter Manning, "Don Juan and Byron's Imperceptiveness to the English Word," Studies in Romanticism 18, no. 2 (Summer 1979): 232.

2 Gilbert Norwood, Greek Comedy (London: Methuen, 1931), 11–12. For more on parabasis, see ibid., 59, 239; Princeton Encyclopedia of Poetry and Poetics, ed. Alex Preminger (Princeton: Princeton University Press, 1974), 597–98; Anne Mellor, English Romantic Irony (Cambridge: Harvard University Press, 1984), 17–18. G. M. Sifakis's monograph Parabasis and Animal Choruses (London: Athlone Press, 1971) deals with parabasis on pp. 7–70.

3 Mellor, English Romantic Irony, 17; Hans Eichner, Friedrich Schlegel (New York: Twayne, 1970), 62.

4 I have surveyed some two dozen readers on this matter.

5 See McGann's Notes to Don Juan, 692. Visiting Rome in 1817, Byron had found the perfect image of Lady Adelaide: "The Apollo Belvidere is the image of Lady Adelaide Forbes—I think I never saw such a likeness" (LJ 5:227). According to chronology, of course, the real Regency beauty would have to be the "image" of the classical sculpture.

6 Claptrap, a word whose earliest citation in the OED dates from 1727, refers to a device or expression employed to gain applause, as Byron saw Coleridge's German metaphysics, Wordsworth's Note to "The Thorn," The Excursion's "new system to perplex the sages," and the Lakers' mutual admiration attempting to do. Both the thing and the word claptrap come from spectacular theater—in fact, the OED's second cited usage of the word is in Dibdin's Musical Tour (lxiii. 461) (see The Oxford English Dictionary, 2d ed, prepared by J. A. Simpson and E. S. C. Weiner [Oxford: Clarendon Press, 1989]).

7 For a good example of Byron's delight in cultural contrast see LJ 5:129–32, Byron's letter of 17 November 1816, to Moore.

8 The idea of intentional, unresolvable doubleness of voice is explored in "Heteroglossia in the Novel," pages 301–31 of Bakhtin's long essay "Discourse in the Novel," which appears in M. M. Bakhtin, The Dialogic Imagination, ed. Michael Holquist and trans. Caryl Emerson and Michael Holquist (Austin: University of Texas Press, 1981), 259–422. Bakhtin sees such doubleness as an essential feature of prose (and especially the novel) rather than poetry—and its presence in Don Juan seems yet another indication that this "poem" embodies at all levels the cosmopolitan principle of mixed values.

9 Malcolm Kelsall, Byron's Politics (Brighton, Sussex: Harvester Press, 1987), 156–58.

10 Jerome McGann too sees Byron along with Southey in the "sad trimmer" of "The isles of Greece!": see "Byron, Mobility, and the Poetics of
Historical Ventriloquism," *Romanticism Past and Present* 9, no. 1 (1985): 74–
76.

11 Kelsall, *Byron's Politics*, 157.

12 McGann's impressive and concise gloss on these allusions is to be
found in *Don Juan*, 701–3.

13 See McGann, Notes to *Don Juan*, 694.

14 John Cam Hobhouse, *Byron's Bulldog: The Letters of John Cam Hobhouse to Lord
Byron*, ed. Peter W. Graham (Columbus: Ohio State University Press,
1984), 259.

15 See McGann, Notes to *Don Juan*, 702, and LJ 4:324–25.

16 Eight of *Don Juan's* eleven references to beef, that English indispensable,
occur in the shipwreck canto: see DJ 2.13, 47, 67, 153, 154, 155, 156
(twice). Tea is mentioned once in this canto (stanza 145) and at two key
points in canto 4. In stanza 52, "the Chinese nymph of tears, green tea"
seems to be controlling Don Juan's destiny by making the narrator, who
is drinking that beverage, "grow pathetic." Stanza 108 alludes to "Castalian tea," a matter discussed in the body of this essay.

17 See, for instance, LJ 6:237 (29 October 1819, to Hoppner) and 7:202 (12
October 1820, to Murray).

18 Cecil Y. Lang, "Narcissus Jilted: Byron, Don Juan, and the Biographical
Imperative," in *Historical Studies and Literary Criticism*, ed. Jerome J. McGann
(Madison: University of Wisconsin Press, 1985), 154.

19 Edward G. E. L. Bulwer-Lytton, *England and the English*, ed. Standish Meacham (Chicago: University of Chicago Press, 1970), 314–21.

21 Lilian R. Furst, *Fictions of Romantic Irony in European Narrative, 1760–1857*
(London: Macmillan, 1980), 109.

VI: Don Juan in England

1 John G. Lockhart, *John Bull's Letter to Lord Byron*, ed. A. L. Strout (Norman:
University of Oklahoma Press, 1947), 95–96.

2 See LJ 3:97, Byron's letter of 23 August 1813 to Lady Melbourne: "Would
that Luttrel had travelled—or that one could provide him with a mat-
tress stuffed with peachstones to teach him more philosophy in such
petty calamities—I remember my friend Hobhouse used to say in
Turkey that I had no notion of comfort because I could sleep where
none but a brute could—& certainly where brutes did for often have the
Cows turned out of their apartment butted at the door all night extremely
discomposed with the unaccountable ejectment.—Thus we lived—
one day in the palace of the Pacha & the next perhaps in the most
miserable hut of the Mountains—I confess I preferred the former but
never quarrelled with the latter—."

3 Lord Chesterfield, *Letters Written by Lord Chesterfield to His Son*, ed. Charles
Sayle (London: Walter Scott, n.d.), 68.

4 Anne K. Mellor, *English Romantic Irony* (Cambridge: Harvard University Press, 1980), 55.

5 M. M. Bakhtin, "The *Bildungsroman* . . . ," in *Speech Genres and Other Late Essays*, ed. Caryl Emerson and Michael Holquist, trans. Vern W. McGee (Austin: University of Texas Press, 1986), 40–42.

6 In his Introduction to the Oxford *Don Juan* (xxiii–xxiv), Jerome McGann distinguishes the "immediate context" (1818–24) from the time of Juan's story in the plot (1780s and 1790s) and from that of Byron's English recollections (1808–16). Peter Manning quotes the following passage on the triple complexities of time from Freud's essay "Creative Writers and Day-Dreaming" to illuminate Byron's fictive presentations, blending as they do current impressions, memories, and wish fulfillments: "We may say that [a phantasy] hovers, as it were, between three times—the three moments of time which our ideation involves" (*Byron and His Fictions* [Detroit: Wayne State University Press, 1978], 279 n. 3).

7 Bakhtin, "The *Bildungsroman* . . . ," 46.

8 Rees Gronow, *Reminiscences and Recollections of Captain Gronow* (London: John C. Nimmo, 1900), 2:82.

9 Anthony Paul Vital, "Lord Byron's Embarrassment: Poesy and the Feminine," *Bulletin of Research in the Humanities* 86, no. 3 (1983–85): 289.

10 E. D. H. Johnson suggests that having entered the "charmed circle" of the Whig aristocracy Byron had to a degree lost touch with the prevailing spirit of his time and thus failed to understand in what ways and to what extent *Don Juan* would offend public tastes. "*Don Juan* in England," *English Literary History* 11 (1944): 143, 152–53. As letters from Hobhouse indicate, Byron's extended residence abroad further isolated him from the wider reading public.

11 The catastrophic geologist seems to have stayed in Byron's mind as he was on the point of taking Juan to England, for his name appears again in canto 10 in an analogy speaking of Leila's character "As rare in living beings as a fossile / Man, 'midst thy mouldy Mammoths, 'grand Cuvier!' " (stanza 52).

12 McGann, Commentary to *Don Juan*, 742.

13 Peter Mathias, *The Brewing Industry in England 1700–1830* (Cambridge: Cambridge University Press, 1959), 112, 113, 524–25, 419–21.

14 Manning, *Byron and His Fictions*, 238.

15 Ibid., 217.

16 Jerome J. McGann, *The Romantic Ideology* (Chicago: University of Chicago Press, 1983), 145.

17 The narrator's quotations from and allusions to Greek and Latin are only a little less frequent (and a good deal more obtrusive) than are his lapses into fashionable French. See DJ 10.78, 11.21, 12.25, 12.70, 13.18, 13.35, 13.40, 13.81, 13.82, 14.50, 14.77, 15.16, 16.3, 16.5, 16.13, 16.109, 17.10, 17.11. Two classical passages are key to the meaning of these cantos and in fact the entire poem. They are DJ 14.21 (" 'Haud ignara loquor:' these are *Nugae*, 'quarum / Pars parva fui' "), which Cecil Y. Lang

explicates as "the richest lode in *Don Juan*," the place where Byron tells those who can understand it that he took part in the events related ("Narcissus Jilted," 168–69); and *DJ* 15.21 (" 'Omnia vult *belle* Matho dicere—dic aliquando / Et *bene*, dic *neutrum*, dic aliquando *male*' "), an epigram of Martial that neatly characterizes the importance of hetero-geneity, whether it be the hybrid utterance, the dialogue of styles, or the thematic importance of cosmopolitanism, in *Don Juan*.

18 Perhaps the best such speculator is Elizabeth Boyd, who in *Byron's* Don Juan (New York: Humanities Press, 1958), pronounces the English characters to be not portraits but distillations. She sees elements of Lady Caroline Lamb, Lady Frances Wedderburn Webster, Lady Oxford, Lady Jersey, and "who knows what other ladies besides" in Adeline (69) and perceives Lord Henry as a caricature of William Lamb with added features from Lord Holland and Sir James Wedderburn Webster (167 n. 7).

19 Malcolm M. Kelsall, *Byron's Politics* (Brighton: Harvester Press, 1987), 179; Frederick Beaty, *Byron the Satirist* (Dekalb: Northern Illinois University Press, 1985), 163; J. Michael Robertson, "Aristocratic Individualism in Don Juan," *Studies in English Literature* 17, no. 4 (Autumn 1977): 652; McGann, *The Romantic Ideology*, 144–45.

20 Boyd concisely treats the influential or coincidental affinities between Peacock's country-house symposia and the Norman Abbey episode in Byron's Don Juan, 155–57.

21 Bernard Beatty, *Byron's* Don Juan (Totowa: Barnes and Noble, 1985), 140–41.

22 McGann, Commentary to *Don Juan*, 742.

23 Two such anachronisms are the references to London's paved streets and gaslights, both improvements accomplished during the first de-cades of the nineteenth century—not in the 1790s, when Juan arrives.

24 For more on the interesting subject of mobility, see "Mobility and Improvisation," Appendix B of George M. Ridenour's *The Style of* Don Juan (Hamden: Archon, 1969; rpt.), 162–66; and Jerome J. McGann's "Byron, Mobility, and the Poetics of Historical Ventriloquism," *Romanti-cism Past and Present* 9, no. 1 (Winter 1985): 67–82.

25 I am convinced by Bernard Beatty's assertion (*Byron's* Don Juan, 87–92) that the first, and ultimately mysterious, appearance of the Black Friar is what suggests the erotic possibilities of impersonation to the second nocturnal visitant, the Duchess of Fitz-Fulke.

26 See McGann, Introduction to *Don Juan*, xxiii, and *Don Juan in Context* (Chicago: University of Chicago Press, 1976), 1–4; Andrew Rutherford, *Byron: A Critical Study* (Stanford, Calif.: Stanford University Press, 1967), 238–41; Lang, "Narcissus Jilted," 176; M. K. Joseph, *Byron the Poet* (Lon-don: Victor Gollancz, 1964), 186, 304; Beatty, *Byron's* Don Juan, 8; Boyd, *Byron's* Don Juan, 160–61.

Select Bibliography

Airlie, Mabell, countess of. *In Whig Society*. London: Hodder and Stoughton, 1921.

Austen, John. *The Story of Don Juan*. London: Martin Secker, 1939.

Bakhtin, M. M. *The Dialogic Imagination*. Edited by Michael Holquist. Translated by Caryl Emerson and Michael Holquist. Austin: University of Texas Press, 1981.

———. *Speech Genres and Other Late Essays*. Edited by Caryl Emerson and Michael Holquist. Translated by Vern W. McGee. Austin: University of Texas Press, 1986.

Barton, Anne. "Don Juan Reconsidered: The Haidée Episode." *Byron Journal* 15 (1987): 11–20.

Beatty, Bernard. *Byron's Don Juan*. Totowa: Barnes and Noble, 1985.

Beaty, Frederick L. *Byron the Satirist*. Dekalb: Northern Illinois University Press, 1985.

———. "Harlequin Don Juan." *Journal of English and Germanic Philology* 67, no. 3 (1968): 395–405.

Blessington, Marguerite, countess of. *Conversations of Lord Byron*. Edited by Ernest J. Lovell, Jr. Princeton: Princeton University Press, 1969.

Blyth, Henry. *Caro: The Fatal Passion*. London: Rupert Hart-Davis, 1972.

Borst, William A. *Lord Byron's First Pilgrimage*. Hamden, Conn.: Archon, 1969. Reprint.

Boyd, Elizabeth French. *Byron's Don Juan: A Critical Study*. New York: The Humanities Press, 1958.

Brink, C. O. *Horace on Poetry: The "Ars Poetica."* Cambridge: Cambridge University Press, 1971.

Brombert, Victor. "Opening Signals in Narrative." *New Literary History* 11 (1980): 489–502.

Bulwer-Lytton, Edward G. E. L. *England and the English*. Edited by Standish Meacham. Chicago: University of Chicago Press, 1970.

Butler, Marilyn. "Against Tradition: The Case for a Particularized Historical Method." In *Historical Studies and Literary Criticism*, edited by Jerome J. McGann, 25–47. Madison: University of Wisconsin Press, 1985.

Byron, George Gordon, Lord. *Byron's Letters and Journals*. Edited by Leslie A. Marchand. Cambridge: Harvard University Press, 1973–.

———. *Childe Harold*. Vol. 2 in *Complete Poetical Works*. Edited by Jerome J. McGann. Oxford: Clarendon Press, 1980.

———. *Complete Poetical Works*, vol. 3. Edited by Jerome J. McGann. Oxford: Clarendon Press, 1981.

————. *Don Juan*. Vol. 5 in *Complete Poetical Works*. Edited by Jerome J. McGann. Oxford: Clarendon Press, 1986.

————. *The Works of Lord Byron: Letters and Journals*, vol. 6. Edited by Rowland E. Prothero. New York: Octagon Books, 1966. Reprint.

Cecil, Lord David. *Melbourne*. New York: Bobbs-Merrill, 1954.

Chesterfield, Philip D. S., Lord. *Letters Written by Lord Chesterfield to His Son*. Edited by Charles Sayle. London: Walter Scott, n. d.

Cixous, Hélène. "The Laugh of the Medusa." Translated by Keith Cohen and Paula Cohen. *Signs* I, no. 4 (1976): 875–93.

Clubbe, John. "*Glenarvon* Revised—and Revisited." *Wordsworth Circle* 10 (1979):205–17.

Cooke, Michael G. "Byron's *Don Juan*: The Obsession and Self-Discipline of Spontaneity." *Studies in Romanticism* 14, no. 3 (Summer 1975): 285–302.

De Almeida, Hermione. *Byron and Joyce through Homer: Don Juan and Ulysses*. New York: Columbia University Press, 1981.

De Bevotte, George Gendarme. *La légende de Don Juan*. Paris: Librairie Hachette, 1911.

Dickens, Charles. *Memoirs of Joseph Grimaldi*. New York: Stein and Day, 1968.

Disher, M. Willson. *Clowns and Pantomimes*. New York: Benjamin Blom, 1968.

Ducharte, Pierre Louis. *The Italian Comedy*. Translated by Randolph T. Weaver. New York: Dover, 1966.

Eichner, Hans. *Friedrich Schlegel*. New York: Twayne, 1970.

Foot, Michael. *The Politics of Paradise: A Vindication of Byron*. London: Collins, 1988.

Furst, Lilian R. *Fictions of Romantic Irony in European Narrative, 1760–1857*. London: Macmillan, 1980.

Galt, John. *The Life of Lord Byron*. New York: A.L. Fowle, 1900.

Gilbert, W. S. *Complete Plays of Gilbert and Sullivan*. New York: Modern Library, 1932.

Gronow, Rees. *Reminiscences and Recollections of Captain Gronow*. London: John C. Nimmo, 1900.

Hobhouse, John Cam. *Byron's Bulldog: The Letters of John Cam Hobhouse to Lord Byron*. Edited by Peter W. Graham. Columbus: Ohio State University Press, 1984.

————. *Recollections of a Long Life*. Edited by Lady Dorchester. London: John Murray, 1911.

Holman, C. Hugh. *A Handbook to Literature*. Indianapolis: Odyssey Press, 1972.

Hunt, Leigh. *Leigh Hunt's Dramatic Criticism, 1808–1831*. Edited by Lawrence Huston Houtchens and Carolyn Washburn Houtchens. New York: Octagon Books, 1977.

Jacobus, Mary. *Tradition and Experiment in Wordsworth's Lyrical Ballads (1798)*. Oxford: Clarendon Press, 1976.

[Jeffrey, Francis.] Review of *Letters from England by Don Manuel Alvarez Espriella*. *Edinburgh Review* 11 (January 1808): 370–90.

Jenkins, Elizabeth. *Lady Caroline Lamb*. London: Cardinal, 1974.

Johnson, E. D. H. "Don Juan in England." *English Literary History* 11 (1944), 135–53.

Joseph, M. K. *Byron the Poet.* London: Victor Gollancz, 1964.

Kelsall, Malcolm. "The Byronic Hero and Revolution in Ireland: The Politics of *Glenarvon.*" *Byron Journal* 9 (1981): 4–19.

———. *Byron's Politics.* Brighton, Sussex: Harvester Press, 1987.

Lamb, Lady Caroline. *Glenarvon* (1816). A facsimile reproduction, with an introduction by James L. Ruff. Delmar: Scholars' Facsimiles & Reprints, 1972. Reprint of the first edition.

———. *Glenarvon.* London: Henry Colburn: 1816. Second edition.

———. *Gordon: A Tale.* London: T. and J. Allman, 1821.

———. *A New Canto.* In Margot Strickland, *The Byron Women,* 212–16. New York: St. Martin's, 1974.

Lang, Cecil Y. "Narcissus Jilted: Byron, Don Juan, and the Biographical Imperative." In *Historical Studies and Literary Criticism,* edited by Jerome J. McGann, 143–79. Madison: University of Wisconsin Press, 1985.

Lockhart, John G. *John Bull's Letter to Lord Byron.* Edited by A.L. Strout. Norman: University of Oklahoma Press, 1947.

McGann, Jerome J. "Byron, Mobility, and the Poetics of Historical Ventriloquism." *Romanticism Past and Present* 9, no. 1 (1985): 67–82.

———. *Don Juan in Context.* Chicago: University of Chicago Press, 1976.

———. *Fiery Dust: Byron's Poetic Development.* Chicago: University of Chicago Press, 1968.

———. *The Romantic Ideology.* Chicago: University of Chicago Press, 1983.

Mandel, Oscar. *The Theatre of Don Juan: A Collection of Plays and Views, 1630–1963.* Lincoln: University of Nebraska Press, 1963.

Manning, Peter J. *Byron and His Fictions.* Detroit: Wayne State University Press, 1978.

———. "Don Juan and Byron's Imperceptiveness to the English Word." *Studies in Romanticism* 18, no. 2 (Summer 1979): 207–33.

Marchand, Leslie A. *Byron: A Biography.* New York: Knopf, 1957.

Mathias, Peter. *The Brewing Industry in England, 1700–1830.* Cambridge: Cambridge University Press, 1959.

Mayer, David. *Harlequin in His Element: The English Pantomime, 1806–1836.* Cambridge: Harvard University Press, 1969.

Mellor, Anne K. *English Romantic Irony.* Cambridge: Harvard University Press, 1980.

Newton, Sir Isaac. *Newton's Philosophy of Nature: Selections from His Writings.* Edited by H.S. Thayer. New York: Hafner Publishing Company, 1953.

Nicoll, Allardyce. *A History of English Drama, 1660–1900.* Cambridge: Cambridge University Press, 1952.

———. *The World of Harlequin: A Critical Study of the Commedia dell'Arte.* Cambridge: Cambridge University Press, 1963.

Norwood, Gilbert. *Greek Comedy.* London: Methuen, 1931.

Olney, Clark. "*Glenarvon* Revisited." *University of Kansas City Review* 22 (1956): 271–76.

Olsen, Tillie. *Silences*. New York: Delacorte Press, 1978.

Priestley, J. B. *The Prince of Pleasure and His Regency*. New York: Harper and Row, 1969.

Princeton Encyclopedia of Poetry and Poetics. Edited by Alex Preminger. Princeton: Princeton University Press, 1974.

Ridenour, George M. *The Style of Don Juan*. Hamden, Conn.: Archon, 1969. Reprint.

Robertson, J. Michael. "Aristocratic Individualism in *Don Juan*." *Studies in English Literature* 17, no. 4 (Autumn 1977): 639–55.

———. "The Byron of *Don Juan* as Whig Aristocrat." *Texas Studies in Language and Literature* 17, no. 4 (Winter 1976): 709–24.

Rutherford, Andrew. *Byron: A Critical Study*. Stanford, Calif.: Stanford University Press, 1967.

Schlegel, Friedrich. *Friedrich Schlegel's Lucinde and the Fragments*. Translated by Peter Firchow. Minneapolis: University of Minnesota Press, 1971.

Sifakis, G. M. *Parabasis and Animal Choruses*. London: Athlone Press, 1971.

Smiles, Samuel. *A Publisher and His Friends: Memoir and Correspondence of the Late John Murray*. 2 vols. London: John Murray, 1891.

Southey, Robert. *Letters from England: By Don Manuel Alvarez Espriella, Translated from the Spanish*. Edited by Jack Simmons. London: Cresset Press, 1951.

———. *New Letters of Robert Southey*. Edited by Kenneth Curry. 2 vols. New York: Columbia University Press, 1965.

———. *Selections from the Letters of Robert Southey*. Edited by John Wood Warter. 4 vols. New York: AMS Press, 1977. Reprint.

Strickland, Margot. *The Byron Women*. New York: St. Martin's, 1974.

Torrens, W. M. *Memoirs of the Right Honourable William, Second Viscount Melbourne*. London: Macmillan, 1878.

Vassallo, Peter. *Byron: The Italian Literary Influence*. London: Macmillan, 1984.

Vital, Anthony Paul. "Lord Byron's Embarrassment: Poesy and the Feminine." *Bulletin of Research in the Humanities* 86, no. 3 (1983–85): 269–90.

Weinstein, Leo. *The Metamorphoses of Don Juan*. Stanford, Calif.: Stanford University Press, 1959.

Wilson, A. E. *King Panto: The Story of Pantomime*. New York: Dutton, 1935.

Wilson, Harriette. *Memoirs*. London: The Navarre Society, 1924.

Wolfson, Susan J. " 'Their she condition': Cross-Dressing and the Politics of Gender in *Don Juan*." *English Literary History* 54, no. 3 (Fall 1987): 585–617.

Wordsworth, William. *William Wordsworth: The Poems*, vol. 1. Edited by John O. Hayden. New Haven: Yale University Press, 1981.

Ziegler, Philip. *Melbourne*. New York: Knopf, 1976.

Index